Comments by

It was such a bad situation for everyone involved and I felt sorry for all the cast who were put out by these organizers!
—Rebecca Kirkland, representative for Bruce Hopkins

Amazing, pathologically intense degree of self-delusion wrapped in flim-flammery wrapped in self-delusion again — with the money aspect being just icing on the cake.
—David Salo, linguistic consultant for the *Lord of the Rings* film trilogy

Let this be lesson to all obsessive fans—this is NOT the proper way to stalk a celebrity.
—inDUHvidual, www.figwitlives.net

Bang on, but quite bizarre when you read the actual events that took place.
—Chaitan "Kit" Shah, representing his uncle, stuntman Kiran Shah

It's so good to know there's someone following up with everything to ensure those two women don't get away with it.
—Matt McLeod, manager, The Black Seeds

WHEN A FAN HITS THE SHIT

the rise and fall of a phony charity

Jeanine Renne

HEISENBERG PRESS

Glendale, California

HEISENBERG PRESS
Post Office Box 1178
Glendale, California

Cover design by John Malkinson
        Email: thejohn@plotwhatplot.com

Book design & production by DIMI PRESS
        Email: dickbook@earthlink.net

ACKNOWLEDGEMENTS

Many people have helped make this book possible. Folks who fell prey to the deceptions came forward to explain what really happened. Friends from the rogues' past offered links and emails that established motives and timelines. Strangers from the Internet sent information and pictures to help keep track of the scoundrels. Others simply sent well-wishes, assistance, advice, or comic relief—random acts of kindness that helped me keep fighting another day. To all of you, too numerous (and anonymous) to list here, thank you.

Maureen Clifford, my publicist, eliminated the terror factor by breaking down the monumental tasks into bite-sized pieces.

Rebecca Kirkland at Oracle Productions, **Ellen Nicholson** at Sandra Marsh, **Kevin Rau** of the Marion County Sheriff's Office, the Oregon Department of Justice, **Matt McLeod, John Howe, Kit Shah, Jed Brophy,** and **Paul Randall** provided information and photographs.

"Sagralisse" rose unbidden to my defense with one of the finest smackdowns in the history of internet wank.

Ken Gullekson taught me about metaphysics and the Platinum Principles, which I can rely on to determine Right from Wrong.

Susan Astle was the Sam to my Frodo, helping me with research, spreading the word, and fixing dinner for my family so I could write. More importantly, she wouldn't let me stop fighting at the times I felt defeated while we were *living* this story.

David Salo served as a linguistic consultant, although his objective in this tome was not quite as lofty as in the LOTR films.

My most darling boys patiently entertained themselves and each other while Mommy obsessed over the computer. Special thanks to the Teletubbies for their help with that.

Finally, my love and gratitude to my long-suffering husband, for his unruffled forbearance of my breakneck enthusiasm for projects that don't always turn out to be a good idea.

FOREWORD

I've been an observer of The Lord of the Rings and online fandom for nearly six years, and I think few things have appalled me as much as the Tentmoot scam. We're used to thinking of Lord of the Rings fans as good people. I think almost everyone that's run a Lord of the Rings website would, like me, have dozens of stories about overwhelming generosity and honesty they've seen among their constituency. That's why the sheer greed and duplicity that brought down Tentmoot are so shocking. The repercussions will continue to be felt in the world of fandom, with wariness and disenchantment that affects both fans and event organizers.

Maybe we should have been more cautious. In recent months I've talked to people involved in charity work and from what they've said, it seems that charities and goodwill projects are EXACTLY the kind of thing that attracts a certain kind of fraudster or pathological personality type. Other people running charities or non-profit organizations had fearful horror stories, and the chilling thing was that they might have been talking about Amy and Abbey. Details were different, but the essence was the same. I guess that abusers always have a sixth sense for detecting the perfect victim. The most common example is the way some people only seem to attract violent partners, time after time, while the same secret chemistry reverses itself to ensure that other people never have that kind of violence so much as cross their path. Violence attracts victims, and it seems that in the same way, goodwill attracts sociopaths. Pathological liars recognize organizations where an atmosphere of trust and enthusiasm will protect them from being found out.

Jeanine's story is a revelation of the depths some people will go to fulfil their fantasies. She and her friends witnessed an incredible construction of lies, deception and fantasy, and then they had to watch it all come tumbling down - unraveling their lives in the process. They were lucky to escape as lightly as they did, because it seems that Amy and Abbey would stop at nothing to keep their castle of lies airborne.

The strangest thing of all, as Jeanine says at the end, is that it was all for nothing, or for nothing that any normal person would covet. At most, the pitiful reflected glory of having stood next to the stars they idolized, spoken to them, and been forgotten by them as soon as they were out of sight.

—"Tehanu," Co-Founder, TheOneRing.net

INTRODUCTION

Readers must suspend their disbelief in order to enjoy a fictional novel. They have to overlook that the characters were never real, live people; the events didn't actually happen, and even the places and "facts" may be figments of the author's imagination. In general, readers don't mind doing this at all. They accept the course of action within the book's little realm, without reacting to the story by indignantly shouting things like, "Hey! People can't really go to Mars!"

In the case of non-fiction, the opposite is true. The facts must agree with historic records and the locations must appear on maps. The reader expects a non-fiction story to conform—at least somewhat—to the reality of daily experience.

The account you are about to read is 100% true. However, it probably will *not* conform in the slightest to your daily reality. This is a tale of con artistry and manipulation that succeeded in shaking down not only ordinary Joe Shmoes and mom-and-pop businesses, but also celebrities from the cast and crew of New Line Cinema's blockbuster *Lord of the Rings* film trilogy. People who read this story compare it to watching a burning building, just to see who gets out alive.

Nonetheless, the events described herein really took place. Documentation is available on credible websites of the Internet, the public records of the Oregon Department of Justice, the testimony of the people involved, and in two overstuffed file folders in the black cabinet by my desk. The emails quoted are in my computer and the Tentmoot mailbox at

Yahoo.com. Most names have been changed to protect the innocent, but to preserve the credibility of the story, names of public figures and celebrities have not.

Buckle up, dear reader, because you're about to take a *wild* ride . . .

PART I:

GOING THERE

OCTOBER 10, 2003

After weeks of waffling, the decision finally came down from the upper echelon: Pikachu. Spiderman, Batman, and the vaguely described monsterbeast thing would have to wait for another Halloween. It was time to go to the fabric store for some goldenrod fleece and brown felt. As I loaded the baby into the van, he squawked in ire at being stuffed into his carseat. He must have known he was doomed to wear Big Brudder's hand-me-down "Gentleman Bug" costume. It was a perfectly ordinary fall day in the Pacific Northwest, crisp and cool with a hint of smoke in the air—until we got home and discovered the business card wedged into the screen door.

From a detective.

With "Please Call Me" scrawled on it in black pen.

I instantly knew this was about Jordan.

I wasn't so much angry as amused. Having never really interacted with The Law before, other than the occasional speeding ticket, this was like being on an episode of "CSI." I couldn't wait to see what this was all about.

I called this Detective Myers and got his machine. Unacceptable. This was far too interesting to wait around for a return call—I needed scoopage right then! Jordan still hadn't found a new apartment in Los Angeles, so there was no way to reach him directly. I finally got through to Jordan on his roommate's cell phone. I said only, "Jordan, WHY is there a detective leaving his business card on my door," and waited for what promised to be a whopper of an answer.

MARCH, 2003

I met Jordan Wood and his girlfriend Abigail Stone through the Internet. In my customary daily perusal of TheOneRing.net (TORn), a popular Tolkien fan website, I came across this interesting tidbit:

2/26/03 Sean Astin News. Tehanu @ 2:10 pm

In Portland, Oregon the gardening/literacy project BitofEarth.net is delighted to announce they have received official confirmation that Sean Astin will be making every effort to attend Project Elanor on April 6, 2003. Previously, Mr. Astin had generously offered his name and support and indicated his interest in attending, but we can now confirm that, barring any last-minute changes of plan, he will be present for the building and dedication of the children's reading garden he inspired with his own dedication to community service.

TORn frequently announces LOTR-related events from around the globe. When they report a celebrity appearance, it's safe to bet that it is no mere rumor. What an exciting surprise to see that Sean Astin was coming right here to Oregon! This Project Elanor business was definitely worth a closer look.

Bit of Earth (BoE) was run by Abbey "Orangeblossom Brambleburr" Stone, the self-proclaimed "chief cook and bottle washer," and Jordan Wood, aka "Mr. Frodo, Storyteller and Master of Bag End." Their website was eloquent and charming, with beautiful illustrations. Its message board was full of other *Lord of the Rings* devotees and was friendly and welcoming. Many of the posting members had a wry sense of humor like my own. In short, I found a little slice of Geek Nirvana. The TORn blurb linked to this page from BoE.net:

Project Elanor

BitofEarth.net, in partnership with **Sean Astin** and **Reading is Fundamental**, is proud to announce Project Elanor, a community service outreach to create a children's reading garden in Portland, Oregon as part of the United Day of Service.

Mr. Astin has long been a vocal supporter of literacy programs for children, and we are delighted that he has chosen to lend his support to our endeavor. His portrayal of Samwise Gamgee in Peter Jackson's Academy Award-winning movie *The Lord of the Rings: The Fellowship of the Ring* has led millions of new readers to the complex and exciting world of Middle Earth as vividly portrayed in J.R.R. Tolkien's original masterpiece.

Reading is Fundamental has been serving the cause of children's literacy nationwide since 1966, and through a national grassroots network of more than 400,000 community volunteers, RIF programs provided 15 million new, free books and other essential literacy resources to nearly 5 million children. A special action committee has been formed in the Portland area to facilitate the partnership with BitofEarth for Project Elanor, and we are honored to be associated with such a compelling leader in the cause of children's literacy.

We feel that the creation of a children's reading garden is in accordance with both the theme of literacy and Sam's own love of all things green and growing. With his roles a gardener, the loving father of a rather large family, and the keeper of the Red Book of Westmarch, we can think of few things that would be more appropriate for BitofEarth to undertake.

Currently, the specific site remains unchosen, but we intend to fully landscape it with child-friendly plants and an abundance of pathways and benches to form little nooks and crannies to read in as well as birdhouses and feeders to encourage wildlife. The centerpiece of the garden will be a plaque embossed with a gilded nut - Sam's precious mallorn seed - and this inscription from Return of the King, taken from Frodo's final words to Sam: *"...Your hands and your wits will be needed everywhere. You will be the Mayor, of course, as long as you want to be, and the most famous gardener in history; and you will read things out of the Red Book, and keep alive the memory of the age that is gone, so that people will remember the Great Danger and so love their beloved land all the more."* It will be dedicated *"From those over the Sea and those who labour in their spirit, that the Age of Men shall have been left in good hands. In love and Fellowship, the members of Bitof Earth and their Company."*

Volunteering for charity, meeting Sean Astin, building a garden for RIF...what hyperactive LOTR fangirl could pass that up? Certainly not this one! I wrote to Orangeblossom (OB) and offered to make pottery for the garden—planters, pots, or garden stakes. OB was very gracious in her responses, saying she would keep the offer in mind and get back to me as the plans firmed up—the garden was still in the early stages of design and so on.

A few days later, it occurred to me that perhaps I could make the dedication plaque that OB described. I pictured a stoneware book laying open on the deck, with the inscription glazed onto the "pages." A permanent book for a Children's Reading Garden—beautiful! I wrote to OB again and asked if they would be interested in such a thing and got an enthusiastic "Yes!" Off I raced to the ceramic center to make this happen.

It was a damn good thing I heard about Project Elanor well in advance, because I hadn't realized it takes a slab of clay 4 inches thick about a month to dry. And actually, it takes a little more time than that. That book was quite possibly the nicest piece I'd ever made. It looked like I'd taken a real book and just dipped it in slip. In my eagerness to finish it in time for Sean Astin and the volunteer crew to see it, I put it in the kiln too early and it exploded. Dampness is the bane of the ceramic artist, particularly when it's buried in a thick slab of clay.

I emailed OB in tears, explaining that my book blew up and wouldn't be ready for Project Elanor. Her response: "Hugs, Hugs, and More Hugs! I know exactly how you feel, I worked for months on a glass project for my mom and then just before I gave it to her I dropped it and broke it. I ended up giving her the broken shards in a box."

I felt such guilt about letting everyone down and I expected OB to pitch a full-scale *fit* over the centerpiece of "her" garden not being ready on time. Instead, she responded with empathy and encouragement. How sweet! How patient! I liked this young lady right off the bat.

The good impressions kept right on coming. By late March, 2003, TORn and BoE were abuzz with news that OB interviewed Sean Astin.

Orangeblossom (OB): I'm talking to Sean Astin, the actor and director who played Sam Gamgee in Lord of the Rings. Sean has offered to talk to us tonight about Project Elanor and thank you very much for talking to us tonight.

Sean Astin (SA): My pleasure.

OB: How long have you been involved in children's literacy?

SA: How long have I been involved in children's literacy? Well, since I was a child... I'm just now finalizing my relationship with a major telecommunications company to be a literacy champion for them, and we're partnering up with the National Center for Family Literacy. I was recently appointed to the President's Council on Service and Civic Participation...

OB: That's actually my next question.

SA: The mission of the Council is to promote volunteerism in America. I just had a conversation with Gerald Green, who's the chairman of our Council. I was just telling him that literacy is what I want to focus my energy on, and he was totally fired up about it. I'm starting to figure out how to use my mind and acumen here, and understanding the way that bureaucracy and politics work, to really try and have a positive and broad impact on the importance of reading and education and literacy.

OB: Cool!

SA: Yeah! So when I was approached in Washington about coming to do the Bit of Earth thing, I instantly got what symbolically was trying to be achieved with the garden. I understood the connection of the character I played, and it just seemed and felt like exactly the right thing for me to do.

The man who brought Sam Gamgee to life on the Big Screen was all fired up to do the BoE thing. That fired up everyone involved, including me. I emailed Jordan to ask if I could be of any more help prior to the project, since The Book was no longer on my immediate agenda.

Jordan called a few days later, saying there was "one little project" with which he needed help. "The woman in charge of arranging the lumber for the Garden Deck, well, she just decided one day that she was tired of helping and wasn't going to do any more volunteering for us. She started working things out with a lumber mill, but then she just stopped answering their calls and stuff. They got pretty mad and now they won't have anything more to do with us. I have so many things going on right now, if you could take over that for me, and get lumber donated for a 30 x 30 cedar deck, that would really help a lot."

Boy, it just stinks when you have to depend on volunteers and they flake out on you! I've had first-hand experience with that. I once worked on a barrier island off the South Carolina coast, where we rescued sea turtle eggs by moving new nests every night to a safe hatchery. The university employed three of us to work out there, but sea turtles lay 150 eggs at a time. When turtle love was in the air (or the sea, to be exact) we counted on local volunteers to help haul those sacks of eggs. The cabin got booked up months in advance with nature lovers eager to commune with the modern dinosaur known as the loggerhead turtle. But when the time came, only about half of them actually showed up. We staffers were left to trudge along the beach for miles, loaded down with 60 pounds of precious, leathery, dimpled ping pong balls. It wasn't bad enough to let *Caretta caretta* just go extinct, but my back and I will never forget that being stood up by volunteers can make for a rough time.

Besides, how hard could it be to get a few pieces of wood donated here in Logging Country? Much to my surprise, I learned that I was asking for around $3000 worth of wood—and for immediate delivery! Three days of constant long-distance phone calls later, I finally found a Portland company, Parr Lumber, that was willing to help out. Parr couldn't donate it outright, but they sold it to BoE at cost ($1800), and they agreed to accept payment in 3 weeks, after the project's donations were tallied. Jordan piled on the kudos, making me feel like an important cog in a really cool machine.

OCTOBER 10, 2003

Jordan didn't miss a beat.

"Oh, not again," he groaned. "I know *exactly* what this is about. I have this ex-girlfriend, Lauren. She's nuts. She thinks I look like a girl named Amy Player who was a friend of Abbey's. Lauren started this huge rumor that Amy and I were the same person. She even 'maniped' a picture of my head onto a woman's body to prove I was Amy. Back in February, she hacked into the BoE site and diverted it to the picture, to try to ruin my reputation in BoE. She even sent a copy of that to Amy's parents and they actually fell for it!"

The frustration, that once again this girl was making trouble in his life, came through in his voice. "Please, just explain this to the officer, that I'm a guy, that this has come up before because of this lunatic girl who just won't let go. Please."

Detective Myers came by my house to chat soon after, with a stack of photos that seemed to fit the story Jordan told me.

Amy Player (parents' photograph ca. 2002);
Jordan Wood (DMV record, 2003).

21

I admitted that I noticed a resemblance. And yet, what couldn't be explained by a vicious ex with too much free time and access to Adobe Photoshop? Frankly, I thought it looked like a little *too much* resemblance. Almost as though the "boy" picture has been flipped 180° and touched up with a little mop-top hair and a few white pixels for teeth. The head was tilted at the same angle in both pictures and the ear looked disproportionately large. Having heard Jordan's explanation, it sure looked like this detective was walking around with a piece of manufactured "evidence".

On top of that, Myers was a poster boy for the classic stereotyped cop. The off-the-rack suit, the abrupt mannerisms, the tone alternating between condescension, entreaty and belligerence. Not the cops you've seen on "The Shield" or "Hill Street Blues," or even "Barney Miller." Think "Cop Rock" trite.

He started off with a sob story: Amy Player's parents received a suicide note from their little girl, dateline Newport, Oregon, and were desperately looking for her. Wouldn't I help them find their daughter? I told him I couldn't help, because I didn't know their daughter. Myers explained that he was rock solid positive that Jordan was this girl—but he wouldn't say why. I had two choices: trust a stranger (without a trace of proof) whom I didn't know from Adam-12, or trust my friend, who impressed me for six months as an upright, civic-minded citizen. I told Myers I thought he had the wrong guy.

Then Myers started up with edgier stuff. He wasn't *just* looking for Amy Player because of this missing person report. He said Amy committed crimes of property, ripping off money and goods

22

from people she lived with. After that detail proved not particularly convincing, he dropped some hints of narcotics charges.

Hello? This loser is supposed to be the same Jordan that puts together community service projects like the Elanor Garden?

The volunteers of Project Elanor, April 6, 2003.

APRIL 6, 2003

Sean Astin walked out of the Riggs Institute in Beaverton, Oregon at 9:30 AM to a crowd of 60 volunteers munching on bagels and fruit and waiting to get started. He was greeted by the obligatory group squeal, to which he responded, "OK, you guys, we need to get past the celebrity thing first." He wore a tie-dyed T-shirt, a red cap (backwards), jeans, and brand new white leather Nike sneakers. During his pep talk, he made a joke that if he were running for politics, he would run over and kiss "that baby." That baby happened to belong to me, and I had a good laugh, because Sean's offer to smooch came right as my little hedgehog had an *extremely* runny nose. Sean introduced Myrna McCulloch, the director of the Riggs Institute, who came out and spoke, and spoke, and spoke . . .

Sean Astin,Bob, and Abbey. Note the white nikes.

The Riggs Institute lot had been prepped the day before by a crew of intrepid volunteers—including my hubby and older boy. They removed the weed-choked lawn with a cantankerous sod-rolling machine, exposing the sturdy Oregon clay soil, smack in the middle of rainy season. As Myrna talked about the Institute, Sean noticed he and his beautiful new sneakers were sinking into that clay soil. He went behind to the Bit of Earth van to change into some knee-high rubber boots.

That alarmed me, because my ceramic books were in the back of the van. The shrapnel of the exploded book could hardly get any worse, but I also brought its replacement, which was still in the very fragile "greenware" stage. And here was the handsome, tan Sean Astin pulling at his long rubber boot, steadying himself against my greenware book in its wrapping. There is only one thing a serious artist can do under those circumstances.

"Sean, I love you, but that bag you're leaning on has a ceramic in it, and if you break it, I'll have to kill you. And I REALLY don't want to have to do that."

All that training for the LOTR movies apparently gave Sean catlike reflexes. In an instant, he assumed the "Hand Check" position, the boot dangling from his upraised foot to make him look like the Karate Kid gone fly fishing. He yelped "Oh, no! I'm sorry!"

"MissTree," who was busy making friends with my runny-nosed tot, noted, "It would be a terrible thing if Project Elanor ended in tragedy when the guest of honor was murdered by an irate sculptor."

Sean eventually tossed his shoes in the van and headed out to grab a shovel. Now, in general, a ceramicist can be fairly blasé about getting greenware grubby, as most substances will simply evaporate

26

when the piece is kiln fired. However, clay soil is a different story—clay is dirt, after all, and the last thing my pristine pages needed was a muddy footprint, even if it was Sean Astin's. Besides, the cheapskate in me couldn't bear to see those nice shoes ruined. I decided to clean them off. How many fangirls can say they've had their hand inside Sean Astin's shoe, still warm and moist from those infamous Hobbit Feet discussed at such length on the Extended Edition DVD? Well, this one can.

Many hands made light the work on the garden project. Soil was loosened, paths were marked out with spray paint, gravel was hauled, plants were set out, holes were dug, and after a few hours the chaos began to transform into a semblance of a garden. Sean's older daughter even came out and planted some flowers.

Sean busting up some Oregon dirt.

Somehow the plans for the deck got left back at BoE headquarters. "Diamond," one of the core staff, drove 45 minutes each way to fetch them, but discovered she had grabbed the wrong box. After all my effort to procure the lumber, I was not about to let the deck founder, so my little one and I raced off to Home Depot and bought a handyman book with deck plans inside. Soon the deck crew was busily sawing wood and laying out joists on the gravel bed.

Sean spent a lot of time in the beginning giving hugs and chatting with people; I cynically wondered if he would turn out to be a "paper tiger." But soon he was shoveling, hauling, raking and pick-axing with everyone. He continued to stop for hugs, which definitely had an energizing effect on the rest of the crew. It was pretty cool to look up and see him raking dirt, or leaning on a shovel, or hugging someone.

OB made it clear in advance that the volunteers were there to *work*, not to fawn over The Movie Star. Cameras were a no-no; a professional photographer volunteered to come and take pictures all day and there was also a video crew. They would supply us all with mementos from the occasion later. OB did let each volunteer bring one thing for Sean to sign during brief autograph sessions throughout the workday. The plan was for groups of five to break off from their tasks and take a few minutes to get their autograph.

During the first autograph group, the inevitable Oregon rain came. By the bucket, cold and windy— and no shelter but the small porch of the Riggs building and a canopy tent full of T-shirts, papers, and people's memorabilia for autographing. And of course, that was also when lunch arrived—fish and chips from a place called "The Gaffer's." A little rain could never get between a hungry Oregonian and a tasty lunch, especially after a morning of hard work, but unlike Gollum, most of us preferred our fish hot off the grill over cold and wet.

Thankfully the sun returned after 20 minutes or so, but by then Sean offered to speak about the garden and Riggs at the Beaverton Public Library across the street—which would involve going *indoors*. Wimpy Californian. One can only imagine what the patrons felt when the solemn stillness of the library was broken by the PA system: "In Meeting Room A, we have a special appearance by Sean Astin, star of *Lord of the Rings,* starting in five minutes." Sean spoke for half an hour to 20 stunned bookworms, speaking of volunteering, LOTR, and his current film project (*50 First Kisses* was its name at that time).

Sean came back from the library and set to work on the deck. In the same way he organized the flight plans of helicopters on location in New Zealand, he got "On System" and whipped the Deck Crew into high gear. The Planting Crew was sorry to lose him, but what guy can pass up a chance to hammer on something? Besides, after the snafu with the plans, they needed all hands on deck to make up for the late start.

Sean finally announced that his agent insisted he come home early. He planned to work until evening and then christen the new garden by reading aloud a chapter from *The Hobbit* to all of us on the new deck. Unfortunately, he was filming the next day in LA and his handlers decided to rein him in. He posed for group photos and for a special portrait with the day's raffle winner; he signed his tie-dyed shirt as a memento for the Riggs Institute; he auctioned off his Project Elanor name badge in the name of charity for $100. We volunteers collectively realized that our day hanging out with Sean was coming to an end. The clock struck midnight and the carriage turned back into a pumpkin; suddenly he was once again a celebrity, and we the adoring anonymous masses.

He swore in a few of us as Honorary Goonies and gave out a few last autographs. He tried one last time to buddy up to my seven-month-old, but despite Mommy's urgings to "do something cute for the Movie Star," my shy rascal would only show Sean the back of his fuzzy head. Baby and I got the last hug from Sean, just before he hopped into the van. Top of the line hug, strong squeeze, not rushed, good contact as opposed to the A-frame type, I'd score it 9.5/10 all around.

Amazingly enough, soon after Sean and his family zipped off to the airport, about a third of the volunteer gardeners mysteriously disappeared. That left a lot of work unfinished that day, but the diehard locals came back for several weekends to remove all the sod and get the deck fully built.

A muddy, empty lot transformed into a charming garden filled with beautiful plants, a winding path, and a roomy deck wrapped around a birch tree. What a mitzvah for kids and adults alike; a place to read, eat a quiet lunch, play, or just enjoy a little serenity in the middle of the city.

Detective Myers spent more than an hour at my house. "So these kids moved to LA but they haven't got an apartment yet, and you're absolutely certain that Amy is alive and with them."

"*Jordan* is definitely with them, yes."

Myers smiled. "Well, since I know that Jordan is Amy, I'm going to take that as a good sign. But I need to get ahold of them."

There was no way I was going to drag Jordan's roommate into this by giving the detective his private cellphone number. I said, "Well, they've been checking in with me every couple of days. They're just staying at motels and so forth, I don't even know which ones. They need me to help them by cosigning their lease, so I've been getting faxes from apartments."

I showed Myers the faxes I had received that day from Abbey, for apartments in Chinatown and San Dimas, CA. Sent and received through Kinko's stores on each end, the faxes had no specific contact information. Myers frowned—these were from Abbey, not Jordan.

"Is there anyone else down there in LA that can confirm that Amy is with them?" he asked.

I rolled my eyes. "There are all kinds of people that know Jordan is down there. They've probably checked in with Sean Astin, for Pete's sake."

"Sean Astin…"

"The movie star...? Been in Bit of Earth from the beginning? He came up to Portland to build the garden?"

I wondered just how much investigating this guy had done—it's not like Sean's participation was a members-only, hidden Easter Egg buried in obscurity on the BoE website. Neither was the kids' contact information, for that matter. Their address and phone number were prominently displayed on the "Contact" page of the website, both when they were living in Portland and during their brief stay in Salem. Interestingly, their Salem apartment shared a wall with the Iberis Street Substation of the Marion County Sheriff, the very entity that was now hunting for them—and which seemed blissfully unaware of all these facts about their quarry. Images of the Keystone Cops began to pop into my mind.

"When they left, the kids told me they had an appointment the next week, which is this week now, to meet with Sean Astin and give him some pictures from the garden. I don't know when they were going to do that but maybe he can confirm that Jordan is alive and well."

Detective Myers peered at me, trying to decide if I could possibly be serious about a celebrity like Sean Astin having anything to do with a couple of oddballs like Abbey and Jordan.

JULY 26, 2003

Screen captures from video at Hall of Fire (3Dorks Productions) and Gen Con ("LunaHobbit").

Sean's involvement with BoE was not limited to Project Elanor. He really seemed connected to these kids. The following phone conversation took place between Abbey Stone and Sean Astin. Both were on stage, being videotaped at the time.

AS: Hi, Sean!
SA: Hello, Abbey, how are you?
AS: I'm all right.
SA: <technical difficulties spoiled the record of Sean's comments here. He starts discussing a proposal for a documentary that Abbey sent him. He seems to say he doesn't have time to help her with this project>
AS: Well, I understand you're a little busy right now...

SA: Eh, I've been a little busy. Also, I was thinking about it, I thought was the kind of thing that you should do on your own. I thought that if I did it, it would kinda corrupt the...the process. I mean, I sort of...but I appreciate your asking me to do it. I just, there's no way I can focus my... the energy of myself or the company at the moment on that kind of project. But I really do believe it's something that should be done, and you're probably the perfect person to do it, so don't be dissuaded by my lack of involvement with it—you should just attack and get it done.

AS: Well thank you!

SA: Ok, well, I'm actually calling today for someone else. Someone there loves you very much. He's a little shy so he wanted me to ask this question. You don't have to say yes if you don't want to, but Jordan wants to know if you'll marry him. (Background behind Sean Astin: Squeeeeeee!)

Jordan: Well?

AS: (gasp!) Of course! (laughing) Of course!

SA: She said Yes! All right, congratulations Abbey, both of you, and best of luck in the future.

AS: But...I'm sorry Sean, I'm going to have to set the phone aside for just a moment.

After Abbey and Jordan smooched onstage, Jordan took the phone and thanked Sean. Jordan later said he originally asked Elijah Wood to do the proposal, but Elijah's cell phone connection went bad, so Jordan asked Sean to fill in. Sean agreed to do it on one condition: that the Fellowship had to be invited to the wedding.

OCTOBER 10, 2003

I was really surprised Jordan never called me back that evening. If someone called *me* and said "Gee, there's a detective looking for you, I gotta go speak with him now," I would be very curious about that conversation! I resolved not to call him, as I was suspicious and angry and felt I deserved an explanation. But around 8:00 PM, I caved and tried Bob's cell phone again. Jordan answered and said he would call me back immediately from a pay phone.

Amidst the traffic noises, Jordan's voice was calm and assured. "Yep, that sounds like the picture Lauren made. Dammit! Did you explain all this to the cop?"

"Jordan, I told him I thought you were a guy and he didn't believe a word of it. He is absolutely certain you are this Amy Player girl. He also says she's nothing but trouble—exactly who the hell is she, anyway?" I asked.

There was a slight pause and a sigh. "OK. I don't usually talk about this. Amy was Abbey's girlfriend." He paused again. "Abbey really doesn't want all that to become known. She broke up with Amy after just a few weeks, it was just something she did during her divorce, you know? An experiment, sort of; really, it was more of Amy's idea anyway. But yes, they were together a while, then I came into the picture. And several people noticed that she really did look a lot like me—"

"I'll say. There was a *strong* resemblance there, Jordan."

"What can I say? Abbey has a certain type that she likes. She was attracted to both of us for the same reasons."

I shrugged. "OK, fine, but this cop was going on more than the picture alone. He said Amy had received mail at you guys' address, even here in Salem. Is she still hanging around with you?"

Another sigh. "You know, this is a tough subject. I really think you better talk to Abbey about it."

There were sounds of shuffling as the phone changed hands and Abbey got on the line.

"Abbey, what the hell is going on?" I asked.

"Goddammit, Jeanine, I'm so sorry, this stupid bitch, I never should've, I've really screwed everything up...BAW!" She was in hysterics, sobbing into the phone and making no sense whatsoever.

It took ten minutes of "it's all right; this is just me, your friend, talking to you; nothing bad's happened; just calm down and tell me the truth and we'll get this straightened out," before I could quiet Abbey down to mere whimpering. She finally got to a point where there was at least a modicum of air going in, between sobs, and she haltingly told her story.

"I kept in touch with her. I'm just a big stupid softie, I couldn't just cut her off, even though Jordan and everyone else told me to. She'd moved here from Virginia to be with me, and she really didn't have anybody else, no place to go . . . I let her use my address to get her mail, and she came by every couple of weeks to pick it up and stuff, use the phone, talk a minute . . .

"On the day we left for LA, she told me she had one last favor to ask me, and then she'd stay out of my life forever. Stupid, stupid, stupid! I said 'OK, what?' She said she just wanted me to give her a ride out to the coast, she'd met a guy there over the Internet and she wanted to move in with him. Jordan told me to just tell her to take the bus. I thought maybe this time, if I did it, she really would leave me alone. So I said I'd take her out there."

Now we were getting somewhere. If Amy called from a public place, maybe we could track down some witnesses to confirm this story. I asked Abbey, "Where was she?"

"I don't know. We met her at a bus stop downtown."

"In Salem? Which one?"

"I don't know, it was just down by where all the buses go."

"OK, the transit mall. What happened next?"

"I picked her up. The van was all full of our stuff, so she had to sit up front with me and Jordan. She sat in the middle with her box on her lap."

"Really," I said dryly. "That must have been quite a drive."

Abbey cleared her throat. "Yeah, it was pretty intense. Nobody really said much. It took us two hours to get to Newport. The traffic in Lincoln City was really bad. Jordan was just sitting there glaring the whole time."

"OK, so where did you take her on the coast?"

"She wanted to go to Newport, but first she had to mail a package. So we stopped at the post office, but it was a little after five by then, so the post office had just closed. We asked around a little, if anyone knew any other places to mail packages and some guy told us that the Thriftway had a mail station." Abbey's sobs renewed with vigor. "So we drove to the Thriftway, the one down by the highway to Corvallis, right on the corner. Amy got out with her package and that was it."

This sounded even more promising for potential witnesses. It would be easy to track down the people working at Thriftway when Amy mailed her package. "That was the last time you saw her? Did you drive away before she came out?"

"Yeah. I went in the store for a minute because I wanted a drink, but they didn't have Rock Star, so I didn't buy anything. I just came out, and by then I guess Amy was in the back at the mail place. Jordan was pissed that we were there in the first place, so we just went over to Mom's house. We stayed there a little while to say goodbye, and then we started for California."

"Did you tell your mom that Amy had been with you?" Perhaps Abbey's mom could also corroborate some of this story for Detective Myers.

"No, oh, God, no; my mom would have a fit if she knew I was still . . ." More sobbing.

"All right, all right. Let's think a minute, here. Was there anyone in the store that might have talked to Amy?" I asked.

"Um, I guess so."

"OK, that's good. Maybe someone will remember her. What was she wearing?"

"She had on, lemme see, a red tank top...denim shorts...Do you really think they'd remember her?"

"She's a pretty girl, Abbey. It's possible."

We went over the details again, trying to pin down the precise time Amy went in the store. Maybe the mail clerk noticed her when she paid for her package. Maybe she bought a snack afterwards and the checkout clerk would remember her. All it would take was one eyewitness to get the detective back on the right track for his missing girl. When I finished grilling Abbey, Jordan returned to the phone.

"OK, Jordan, you sat next to this girl in the car for two hours. You had to have said *something*."

"Not really. I mean, we did, but just small talk. She mentioned meeting the guy on the Internet, and that she was gonna do some sailing. I really . . . I was so disgusted that she was even *there*, I really didn't want to listen to her bullshit, you know? It was bad enough just having her in the car."

"What about this package she had? Did you look at the address on it?"

"Hmm…No, not really." Jordan paused. "I think it was addressed back East though."

"All right. What else did she have? Did she have a suitcase?"

Jordan sounded a bit puzzled. "No, you know what? She didn't. I didn't really think about it at the time because she had her box, and I assumed that was her stuff, but that was the box she was going to mail…That *is* weird, that she was moving but didn't have any luggage."

"Well, who knows, maybe she had to sell her things or something."

Jordan grunted as though he were pleased with that idea. "Yeah, could be."

"And you don't remember anything else about this guy she was going to meet, his name, anything?"

"No, I mean, she said his name was Larry, but that was just his screen name. That doesn't mean anything. All she said about him was that they met in a chatroom and they were going to do some sailing."

Abbey's voice chirped up from the background. "He must not be in Newport, then, because no one sails out of Newport. It's too rocky."

Jordan gasped. "Oh, my God! She said she was sailing *into the west*. Into the *WEST*."

Any Ringer worth their salt would recognize that reference: the West is the way to Elvenhome, Valinor, the Blessed Realm. Heaven. At that moment, Abbey and Jordan realized Amy was dropping hints all the way to the coast about killing herself. She brought no luggage despite the fact she was "moving" there—nothing but a package to mail to her parents, which must have contained her suicide letter.

Abbey went into Crying Overdrive at that point. Once again I had to chant a litany to calm her down, talking about adults making decisions for reasons we don't understand and have no control over, and similar existentialist crap. When she got back down to a simmer, I told her I would talk to Myers and let him know where he needed to look for his missing girl. Then we said goodnight.

I left a message for Myers that briefly detailed my concern that there seemed to be a suicidal young lady wandering around on the Oregon coast (if she hadn't already washed up on it). At the same time, though, I wasn't sure I believed it myself. I had no proof of Abbey and Jordan's story—just as I had no proof of the detective's. The mystery all hinged on whether Jordan was male or female, which is not the type of decision one has to make every day about one's friends. To get to the bottom of this, I needed to find some irrefutable facts, some actual proof of either story.

I started with a third party, "Zinnia," an acquaintance from the BoE message board community, "The Prancing Pony." Zin was a moderator of the message board and seemed like a mature, reasonable person. She handled some administrative duties at Project Elanor, including arranging the Astins' travel and coordinating the fundraising for those yummy

40

lunches. She joined BoE long before I had, so hopefully she had more information. I reached her answering machine once and found out she held a very responsible job. In short, I could count on reliable information from Zinnia.

Zin confirmed that the BoE site was hacked just as Jordan described. "The Pony message board was redirected to some bizarre journal page with these weird pictures of Jordan, and said he was a girl. We never found out who did it. They didn't even give any sort of explanation of *why* they did that to us. It didn't make any sense."

Jordan 1, detective 0.

I got in touch with "Helen" and "Klyta," twin sisters so charming and affable they were nicknamed "the Ambassadors of Twinny Goodness." I met them at Project Elanor, where Kly took over the unenviable job of figuring out the garden blueprints and turning them into an actual garden. They went on, as I did, to become friends of Abbey, Jordan, and the other "Hobbit Kids," even driving down from Seattle several times to visit before The Kids moved to LA. Helen and Kly each made several insightful comments about the detective's story.

- If [Abbey and Jordan] didn't want to be traced, why would they leave their phone number to be contacted? Why would they tell people where they were going? Why would they be involved in a highly visible charity involving celebrities? Why would they leave a long paper trail and an address they've been at for a while?

- In terms of verifying Jordan's masculinity, I know that Little Sam has seen 'stuff' quite by accident when he was 'pantsed' in front of her.

.

- My older sister once had her identity stolen by a black woman. It's been three years now and she's still having to prove she really is herself because the woman has never been caught and keeps trying to get away with more fraud. If 'Amy' looked like Jordan, then it would be pretty easy to try and assume his identity.

- They have indulged in 'herbal relaxation' once since I've known them, but they in no way are drug runners. I know their financial situation reflects that.

- I just keep thinking of the people I've come to know and love and I can't imagine they'd intentionally break the law. They do enjoy stirring up controversy, but they don't like stirring up trouble with the law. I mean, they lived next door to the sheriff's substation, they've been inside the Portland police station for permits, and they're trying so hard to keep BoE's reputation intact. They've worked too hard to make BoE what it is to endanger it.

- Saw a guy on tv tonight that both Klyta and I thought, 'Hmmm, if you put a wig on him, he'd look remarkably like a girl named Amy.' Years from now, we'll look back on this and laugh, right?

Jordan 2, detective 0. Well, technically, Jordan 3 (the twins can't stand being lumped together as one).

I called the Kids' new phone down in San Dimas and asked to speak to Diamond. I told her, "This is going to sound like a crazy question, but I want you to just answer it. Di, are you absolutely sure that Jordan is a man?"

She sputtered a little, much as I had when Myers first brought this up to me. "Well, yeah! He's a guy!"

"How do you *know* this, Di? I mean, have you seen him with his shirt off, or what? I need to know what you're basing this on."

"Yes, I've seen him without his shirt, back when he broke his ribs. He had bandages on, but you could still tell...He's a guy!" Di was adamant.

Jordan 4, detective 0.

Things just weren't adding up. Detective Myers stopped returning my calls and emails. I thought, "This guy comes in my house and tells me that Jordan is a complete fraud and I am likely to be his/her next victim. He asks me to be a bleeping Stool Pigeon and wheedle Jordan's address out of him without telling him why I want it, so that he can send storm troopers from the FBI to kick in Jordan's door and arrest him. He scares and upsets my son, who is just old enough to understand that something is wrong about his friends the Hobbit Kids. Then he cuts me off. Nice."

I didn't know if Myers was pursuing the real Amy and keeping mum about it, or if he was an incompetent boob who decided that Jordan was the one he wanted to catch, regardless of the truth. My inclination to help Myers was *rapidly* dwindling. It sure seemed like Barney Fife was alive and well in the Marion County Sheriff's office. I wanted my taxes back, if they were being spent on this.

In comparison, Jordan was given a Faramiresque opportunity to show his true mettle. I utterly tipped him off that the police were looking for him. He was already on the move and miles ahead of the cops. If he really were a bad guy (or girl!), he could easily rip off his roomies, drive the two hours to Mexico, and put everything behind him. Instead, he and the rest of the gang signed a lease for an apartment in

San Dimas, California, a quick freeway trip from downtown LA and Hollywood. Criminal on the run, or victim of malicious ex-girlfriend?

By that point, I wouldn't even dignify that question by consulting the Magic 8-Ball.

FEBRUARY 20, 2003

The Prancing Pony message board had around 200 members who posted under a range of topics from analysis of *The Silmarillion* to whether Pippin or Merry was the bigger hottie. "Pony Pals" shared pictures, chatted about real-life topics, arranged to meet one another at conventions or movies, and generally made new friends all over the world. But when they tried to log in on February 20, 2003, they found the Pony had disappeared, replaced with this page from an Internet diary (aka LiveJournal or LJ).

This image was caught just before OB deleted it from the Bit Of Earth server when she was confronted with the question of Mr. Frodo's identity.

In other words, beyond a shadow of a doubt, Mr. Frodo is Victoria Bitter, Victoria Bitter is not dead, and Victoria Bitter is living with Orangeblossom B. the very woman who says she's an ex-parrot.

Honestly, I wouldn't believe a single word out of either of them ever again. They're blatant liars and throw around wild accusations when confronted with the truth. Faking your death online does not make you a sympathetic character, nor lying about it to cover your antics. Give it up.

There was no explanation for this hack job on the Pony. Hundreds of posts were gone. Peoples' mementos, address lists, private messages and photos were lost. The Pony Pals were enraged—not the least bit inclined to favor the hacker or the website they were sent to. Even Lauren, the owner of the LJ, disapproved of this tactic:

> **Time out!** Okay, whoever hacked the BoE message board to link to one of my entries on the VB fiasco? While I appreciate the gesture in getting the information out on the OB-VB fun, games, and manipulative lying... hacking the site is **not** the way to do it.

Zinnia agreed, in a comment on the LJ.

> The fact that anyone would hack a site well loved by so many LOTR fans reflects horribly on the person who would do such a thing. Whoever has done this has deeply hurt many people. Personally I feel violated and sickened by what has

occurred. It is one of the sickest, most immature actions I have ever witnessed. Please know that whoever has done this has hurt many people. It is inexcusable.

At the same time, OB vehemently denied the accusation that Victoria Bitter and Jordan were the same person.

It seems some people have a bad case of Ex-Girlfriend. Well, I find that *highly* amusing, considering *you are not talking about who you think you're talking about.* I know this because VB (a) was also my girlfriend at one point, (b) is *dead* and therefore not on livejournal, and (c) I just got out of bed where a very *not* female Jordan was rubbing a very unmistakable *cock* against me...well, I'm *fairly* certain he's not her. VB did move out here. That doesn't mean she's *still* here. As a matter of fact, she died this fall. And I have tried to keep this offline, because frankly, it's *nobody's fucking business.* I *am* aware of the fact that people "fake" deaths and have new handles to cover it. And there was no obituary, she was new to the town and committed suicide. I didn't see any reason to send an obit to the paper, and I don't exactly keep track of the East Coast to see if one was published.

Lauren's journal, and its links upon links and more links, told a story about a young lady, Victoria Bitter or VB, that was too stunning to absorb in one sitting. The tale began with a bored teen in a podunk backwater town in Virginia, with greater ambitions and imagination than small-town life could contain. Born July 26, 1983, VB was as intelligent as she was pretty, graduating high school at age 16 and enrolling at Christopher Newport University. She had a job drawing caricatures at a nearby theme park. In 2001, VB became involved in "Star Trek: Voyager" and "Horatio Hornblower" fan clubs on the Internet. They served as outlets for her to express her creativity and to portray her life as much more dramatic and interesting than it really was.

When *Fellowship of the Ring* hit theaters in December, 2001, VB shifted genres. She rapidly became popular in the online community of *Lord of the Rings* fans, for her fan fiction stories and digitally manipulated or "maniped" photographs.

Real life became less important as VB developed a fantasy personality on the Internet. Smart but lazy, VB did poorly in college in the spring of 2002, even failing to show up for her final performance in a drama class (an act of dramatic irony in itself). She started meeting online friends in Real Life, finally showing up in April, 2002, to a fan fiction (fanfic) convention called Connexions (sporting a fake British accent, no less). There she met Lauren and things took a new turn: she could no longer deny her homosexuality.

She started off by breaking this to her fiancé, Adrian, "my best friend and the love of my life the moment I met him, though it took me a week's denial to accept that I'd fallen helplessly in love with something that had a penis." He seemed OK with this at the beginning, even encouraged her to explore this aspect of her sexuality. Her parents, however, were another story.

I tried coming out to my parents, but my mother was of the opinion that just because I talked a lot about Tom Paris and Benton Fraser when I was twelve and thirteen, I must be straight, because that means I've Had Crushes On Guys. After all, homosexuality was a Lifestyle Choice made by strange people who were either sick, traumatized, rebellious, or just plain sinful.

Lauren lived several states away, so that relationship was mainly confined to the abstract, verbal realm of the Internet. VB wrote in her LiveJournal of being torn between Lauren and Adrian, distressed that she loved Adrian as a human being but her sexual attraction was all for Lauren. Was she bi, was she lesbian, was she just plain screwed up?

Finally, it was Adrian who decided matters. He pointed out that there was nothing that I was enjoying in our relationship that had to do with sex, and when you remove sex, then we're not really left in a romance any more...We're now agreeing to be the dearest of friends forever.

Apparently that cozy summary didn't fully reflect the situation. Adrian led Victoria's parents to her LJ, where she kept her collection of homoerotic fanfic stories and her personal memoirs about her sexual orientation. VB noted, "I've lost my best real life friend . . . There is talk of mental institutions." She told acquaintances that her parents were limiting her Internet time, so she could reflect on "the error of her ways about being gay." To her closest friends, she bewailed that her father was inviting male friends over to the house and forcing her to have sex with them, in order to "change her mind about being gay."

Later in April, 2002, things went from bad to worse. VB wrote in her LJ:

> I am trying unsuccessfully to deal with the sudden dump of over 100 years of crystal-clear memories from the sort of life that would keep a shrink happy for millenia. I no longer think in English, and no one else currently living speaks the language I do think in now.

This language would be Westron, the tongue spoken in Tolkien's Middle Earth by the races of Men and Hobbits.

Tolkien may have thought he was composing fiction in his tales of Elves, Dragons, Dwarves and Hobbits, but VB understood that he actually recorded a real history. The tales of Glaurung and Turin, Beren and Luthien, and Frodo Baggins and the Ring of Power really happened, only to be forgotten when the Eldar left Middle Earth and took with them all remnants of magic from the world of Men. Somehow Tolkien became attuned to the spiritual emanations of the elves in Valinor and was receiving their memories. Tolkien attributed their tales to his imagination, but VB discovered the true secret—and now she, too, was receiving messages from Kalimac Brandagamba, whose name was Anglicised by Tolkien as Meriadoc Brandybuck.

Many of the Westron words VB learned from Merry Brandybuck were different from Tolkien's Westron[1]. But even if her on line friends were unaware of that inconsistency, most of them assumed she had gone stark raving loony, hold the straight-jacket.

"Hearing voices" certainly qualifies as a bona fide psychotic symptom. And yet when she wrote,

---

[1] See Appendix A

she maintained a logical, sensible style that didn't resemble the loose, disorganized speech of the delusional person.

I am...suddenly old. I have all of his memories. All of them. From toddler to the day he died. Over a hundred years of memories, every day, every moment crystal-clear in full sensory detail. He's five times my age in life-years. I don't know what to do with this. It's overwhelming me by sheer mass of memory. I know things now, understand things that I'm just too young to, and I don't know what to do with it. I don't even think in the same language any more. My own cradle-tongue is now something as if learned, something I have to translate INTO for speech and text. My thoughts come in the words of his youth… And I'm so very, very tired already. Indeed, I am exhausted. No, exhausted doesn't begin to cover it. I am exanimate. But I'm already way past my curl-up-and-hide limit at school. Way overdue on a lot of projects. It's the last two weeks of the semester. And I have work atop that. So no rest for the weary...I know too much... Namenast. Namenast, mi amma.

In late April, someone apparently tried to intervene. VB wrote that she was

blinded. Fucking blinded because like a good little girl I took my pills and now I think in English and the memories are a dull whisper instead of a clear voice and yet the edges of my soul are itching and I know something is about to happen...and I have a motherfucking drug-induced psychic blindfold on!!!! Made myself chunder. Bye-bye little pills.

However strangely her Internet persona might behave, her Real Life seemed to stay in some semblance of order. She broke up with Lauren, saying she was "far too fucked up to sustain anything approaching a fair relationship." She was aware of her poor grades and hoped she would improve, or maybe go to a different college. She continued working at the amusement park and her boss complimented that she was such an effective money maker she was "wasted on a small market."

VB started a Yahoo message board called "Bit of Earth" in January, 2002, as a Sam Gamgee fan club and a showcase of LOTR fanfiction (mainly her own). An Oregon woman named Abbey Rice joined the board within the first week, because she was a big fan of VB's stories. Within days, Abbey made herself at home on the new Yahoo board, making regular posts to compliment VB on her latest fanfic.

One of her posts described the results she received from a "hobbit name generator" website: "My Hobbit name is Orangeblossom Brambleburr of Bindbale Wood."

Abbey had, in her own words, "jumped in with both feet, of course, and insisted on becoming one of the primary members of the community." She began planning an independent website, BitofEarth.net, for the Yahoo board to call its own.

When VB was hospitalized in February, 2002, Abbey wrote a poem for her and posted it.[2] When VB acknowledged the gesture, Abbey was delighted this "famous writer" had finally taken note of her and soon she was obsessed with her newfound friend. When the Hobbit Channeling started, Abbey willingly joined in. She and a few other Internet

---

[2] See Appendix B

friends asked VB to teach them Westron, which VB was delighted to do.

Although VB simply told others she was channeling Merry, she gave an extra special explanation for her new admirer, "Orangeblossom Brambleburr:"

> My Master says that the surge of interest in Tolkien's Middle Earth has created a huge explosion of creational energy, which is a powerful force, not only through the fans, but through the thousands of deeply devoted people in the production itself. That energy has been directed so strongly towards the ideas of Elves and Ents and such that the *real* star-spirits and tree-spirits are reacting to it, reaching out in return. But like any spirit or God or divine, they come through a form we can comprehend. This is why the Gods of any culture resemble the bodies and customs of that culture. In our case, they reach to us through the most closely identified aspects...hobbits.

Abbey began distancing herself from her friends and husband, captivated by VB's fascinating stories. VB, who had just dumped Lauren saying she couldn't handle a relationship, immediately leaped into one with Abbey.

On June 2, 2002, VB went to Oregon and met Abbey at last. They had a delightful time chatting with the channeled Merry and Pippin, much to the dismay of bystanders (except for the proprietor of a pagan shop, who could actually see Merry and took it upon himself to cast a protective spell over Abbey). Abbey even brought her "cousin" to the office where she worked, to "job shadow" her for a week. They went with friends on a road trip to Astoria, Oregon, where *The Goonies* was filmed—Bit of Earth was, after all, a Sean Astin/Sam Gamgee website. OB and VB spent much of the two-hour drive to the coast chatting in Westron. "Pippin" even insisted they stop for a Slurpee, having become fond of them while inhabiting the body of Billy Boyd during the filming of the LOTR movies.

Later that summer, an even bigger surprise came regarding the True Hobbits and the film actors. Abbey noted:

> Merry had quickly uncovered my unholy passion for juicy gossip. He'd been supplying me with tales of the Fellowship actors for days, but on this day he was unable to access Dom, so he thought he'd try dipping into Elijah's memories. When he came back he had a lot of Elijah's mannerisms, including a fierce desire for a cigarette. I gave him two, but neither he nor VB could handle the smoke. As I refused to give him more cigarettes, he tried to duck back to Elijah to get a buzz. He somehow managed to fall in, and in the process Elijah was knocked into VB.

Over the next few months, VB's capacity for channeling extended to the entire Fellowship and others from Middle Earth, as well as continued contact with Elijah Wood.

Abbey was released from her duties by her employer on August 22, 2002. Free to pursue her interests in hobbits full time, Abbey took a trip to Virginia to visit Victoria. Abbey returned to Oregon speaking of having to choose between VB and her husband someday. A former friend lamented, "I think Abbey got sucked in because she liked the attention and the power. She's always been all about what works for her, screw everyone else. And VB knew how to feed off of peoples' ambitions and dreams. Abbey wanted to be a writer, and VB was going to let Abbey interview all the main people from LOTR, who would of course be channeled by VB."

On September 11, 2002, Sean Astin hosted a Community Service promotion during the 9/11 memorial services in Washington, DC. Victoria Bitter waited in the crowd that day to meet Sean and asked him if he would be interested in participating in an event she had proposed the day before on the BoE Yahoo board, namely the building of a children's reading garden. Having just given a speech on the merits of community service, Sean could hardly say no. Abbey began contacting Sean and his PR people to set up the details for the garden project.

Abbey and VB noticed from publicity photos that Elijah Wood appeared to be losing weight. She and VB grew concerned for his health and casually mentioned it to Sean Astin one day. Sean replied that he was also concerned, because Elijah was depressed and not eating well. Sean asked Abbey if it would be all right for him to give her phone number to Elijah. He thought Elijah might feel better if he had a friend like her to talk to. Abbey was willing to give it a shot.

Elijah called Abbey and they became great friends. He even flew her up to Washington at his expense to have dinner with him. "I can't tell anyone, because they wouldn't believe me!" Abbey wrote to a friend. "I'm an Abbey-Sue!" She told her closest friends how Elijah was in love with Dominic Monaghan and felt confused about his sexual orientation, but eventually he realized he loved Dom as a soul-mate.

Abbey encouraged Elijah to vent some of his stressors in the form of an anonymous LJ, so he set up a journal called "PadawanS." He maintained this for a few months, keeping his identity secret, but kept dropping accidental hints (such as music preferences,) and was absent on dates which coincided with his public appearances.

The problem with the whole Elijah story was that no one bought it. Abbey's LJ entries about her friendship with Elijah and PadawanS's true identity were restricted from the general public, but word of her boastful claims spread anyway. People quickly got tired of this obvious farce and started shunning Abbey and VB. Regulars of the Yahoo board stopped posting, and didn't register at the fledgeling BitofEarth.net website. The only people who moved to the new BoE were from the outermost circles: those who had no access to restricted LJ pages, and didn't network with the people who did.

Abbey finally confessed to her closest friends that she *had* fibbed about the phone calls to Sean. In reality VB was simply channeling Elijah, and authored the PadawanS journal while under the influence of his astral projection. That explanation didn't go over any better than the "phone calls" version.

Finally Abbey and VB decided this wasn't getting them the kind of attention they wanted and suddenly the PadawanS journal was gone. A few weeks later, VB suddenly made this post on all of her journals and message boards:

Date: Sun Nov 3, 2002 6:50 pm
Subject: Sailing••••Sailing•••
I regret that for a variety of reasons, I am leaving online fandom. This has been unofficial for a long

time now, but I want to make it right by giving Orangeblossom the credit she richly deserves. Since the very beginning, she has been the proverbial power behind the throne, and since April, she has truly been the *real* Head Gardener who has kept BoE green and growing. I give her the title now, gladly and with gratitude for all she has done.

I'll miss you all.

BoE.net continued on with no more word from VB. Plans were made for Project Elanor and BoE was moved completely from Yahoo Groups to BitofEarth.net. Abbey broke off contact with any online friends that did not appreciate the PadawanS/ Elijah stories. Abbey's Real Life friends also found themselves getting the brush-off, or worse; one friend endured a furious, foul-mouthed confrontation in the middle of a toy store, while dumbfounded shoppers watched. Abbey divorced her husband, claiming he stole money from her and was "not the man she had married."

In December 2002, BoE threw a Line Party at the Lloyd Center 10 Cinema in Portland, OR, for the premiere screening of *LOTR: The Two Towers*. All ten theaters were sold out for the premiere, so roughly 5,000 people waited in line outside the cinema. There was no sign of VB at the party, but Abbey was there, and with her was a young man named Jordan Wood. The two of them organized quite a festival in the parking lot, with trivia, movies, karaoke, and a raffle—which was described as a fundraiser for Reading is Fundamental.

Between the publicity at the line party and the news about Sean Astin's plan to participate in Project Elanor, the membership of BitofEarth.net expanded in early 2003. Jordan took on a managerial role at

BoE and kept a fairly low profile, but in February, 2003, he made some inflammatory remarks on an Internet journal . . . which belonged to none other than Lauren, VB's ex-girlfriend. Lauren's friends took offense to Jordan's comments and in the ensuing kerfluffle, several people took a look at BoE.net and noticed a strong resemblance between VB and Jordan, and pointed it out to Lauren . . .

OCTOBER 21, 2003

I found this letter CC'ed to my email box from
Jordan.

Dear Mr. and Mrs. Player –

I am writing to inform you of an unfortunate development with our staff. "Bob," our former Head
of Security, has been fired tonight for attempted
blackmail. He is an extremely untrustworthy individual who was trying to make a second chance
through BitofEarth. He has threatened to contact
you with allegations, the precise nature of which
we do not know, but which concern the disap-
pearance of your daughter, Amy. He may imply
anything ranging from us harboring her to mur-
dering her, and we know that this is a very emotional and difficult time for you and do not wish
you to suffer more at the hands of this man's ven-
detta.

Our Director of Celebrity Relations, Jordan Wood,
is the young man who was involved in Amy's identity theft, as well as the main target of Bob's attack. There have been threats of telling you that
Jordan and your missing daughter are the same
person, and this is not only untrue, but directly
intended to place Jordan in danger.

Jordan is fleeing an extremely dangerous and
abusive home situation, and to have him exposed
to the police prematurely (he is preparing testimony) would put him at extreme risk from those
associated with his family (they were involved in
criminal activities in which he refused to participate). We would ask that you please do not allow

this man to use your grief to endanger an innocent youth.

We know that with your daughter's history of falsehood, it may be difficult to trust people, and we
are not asking you to do so blindly. Bob does have
the sympathy of Susan Astle, one of our staff
members who is not yet aware of his less savory
side - he can be quite charming and professional
when he wants to be, and she may support his
claims for the time being. However, we are willing to provide, if necessary, notarized statements
from myself, Cherie Deuvall, and Dr. Jeanine
Renne (M.D.PhD) supporting Jordan's identity.
Sympathies

Abigail Stone and the Staff of BitofEarth

Aside from being very displeased at being used
as a character reference without my permission, I
didn't know what to make of this news. Bob had
been their roommate since the 2002 line party and
participated in many BoE events; he certainly
seemed OK to me.

JULY 26, 2003

Bob, whose heart of gold cannot be captured on film.

At Project Elanor, Bob was in charge of the Security Detail for the Astins. We referred to him as Bob the Bison, as he looks stout enough to stop a truck with one hand. With his long hair and beard, he could easily pass for a dwarf if he were to find himself in Middle Earth, although he would be tall enough to play on their NBA team.

Bob took on many responsibilities of BoE's second fundraising event, the "Hall of Fire Summer Music Festival," held in Portland's Holladay Park. Bob had friends in the Portland music scene and staked his reputation on the festival to entice several bands to play. BoE planned to host a twenty-band jam session in the park for two days, and there were hints Elijah Wood might be the emcee.

Unfortunately Elijah was in New Zealand filming ROTK at that time, but HoF still looked viable for the Portland scene. Even without a movie star, a weekend of tunage in the park would surely draw a paying crowd. Bob helped arrange an impressive list of bands from Seattle and California, in addition to local groups. He and another volunteer, Susan Astle, called in some favors and outfitted the festival with high-quality sound gear for no charge.

On Friday, July 25, 2003, BoE volunteers arrived early at Holladay Park to help set up for the festival. Huge speakers were unloaded from a van, a video crew was setting up, a few disheveled band members were trickling into the parking lot, and a rather irritable-looking park ranger was rapidly approaching. There was no sign, however, of Jordan or Abbey, the people in charge.

The ranger told everyone to pack things up because there was no permit for a festival in the park that day. Frantic phone calls to BoE headquarters went unanswered, but finally Jordan was spotted—napping in a sunny patch of grass in the park.

Jordan was stunned by the ranger's news. "MissTree was supposed to take care of the permits! They aren't ready?"

The ranger reiterated he had no permits on file. He told Jordan how to procure the necessary papers and said the festival could continue the next day if these were obtained. Jordan quickly established Plan B—to distribute fliers announcing the date change, to beg the Equipment Dude to return the next day, and to round up the necessary permits.

By that point, several bands had arrived and were less than thrilled to find the event postponed and possibly cancelled. Jordan grabbed the BoE checkbook and raced across town to gather the permits. The remaining volunteers were left in an awkward limbo, with no explanations for the bands, onlookers, or even each other. They sheepishly bought CDs from the bands, hoping to assuage their irritation. This didn't work particularly well; one band that drove four hours from Seattle regarded the situation as "a giant cluster fuck." Most of the musicians were actually fairly good sports about things, but their girlfriends and groupies gave the volunteers The Hairy Eyeball as they huddled together smoking clove cigarettes and wishing they knew what to say.

Finally Jordan returned, having taken care of the necessary paperwork, announcing things *would* go off the next day as scheduled. Everyone tucked their tails between their legs and headed home, hoping the next day would make up for the dismal failure of Day 1. Abbey rushed a message to TheOneRing.net in a last ditch effort to advertise.

7/25/03 Portland Tentmoot Happens Today!
Demosthenes @ 9:08 pm
BitofEarth.net, the people behind Project Elanor, have advised that technical difficulties has forced last-minute major rescheduling to their Hall of Fire Summer Music Festival. Held at Holiday Park, on the Trimet Max line across from Lloyd Center Mall from 12:00-9:00, this event will feature a wide variety of the Northwest's best independent local artists.

With all body parts crossed, BoE returned to the park the next day. The situation went from Red Alert to Full-On Biblical Cataclysm. Two DJs came to perform, but instead of attracting crowds, they mainly succeeded at annoying a family reunion party going on nearby. Only one scheduled musician, Ariel Rose, showed up, and although she played spectacular music, there were simply no audience to listen. John Malkinson, the unfortunate soul stuck emceeing this nightmare recalls "watching person after person basically ignore our show. Jordan supposedly fainted." The marriage proposal from Sean Astin was exciting and fun, but it didn't draw any donations. BoE finally resorted to begging a nearby street musician come up on stage and play the blues, just to give their 5-foot speakers something to do.

On July 28, 2003, OB posted this message on the Prancing Pony.

Good News

We got through Hall of Fire and really found out what staff members will work their butts off in a pinch, and we are more confident than ever that we can pull off miracles when the occasion call for it.

Bad News

Yesterday was not a good day for showing up. Only one of our bands showed up (Ariel Rose...we love you forever and would gladly kiss your sparkly Elven toes!), and despite our begging, pleading, posting, and massive distribution of fliers we had **ABSOLUTELY NO ONE** come. We know that this is mostly due to Elijah not being able to come but we are still more than a little disappointed, especially as the band thing was directly related to the bad behavior of the bands....whom did I mention **did not show up?**

Good News
During this whole thing we managed to get some wonderful donations and make some wonderful contacts that will let us hold several more fantastic fundraisers for TentMoot with no overhead whatsoever

Bad News
There *was* overhead for this one...a considerable amount of it for the park and equipment, and because of that, BoE is seriously in the financial hole. If we don't have $2,500 by tomorrow, the site is going to go under and there will *be* no TentMoot...or anything else. We didn't think we were being irresponsible with the overhead, because we *did* have an event that would have been pretty damned big at the point that we paid out all this money

Good News
Between the staff that were there that day, we have managed to scrape up $1,550 from a combination of savings accounts, friends, mothers, cashing in college classes, etc.

Bad News
We still need another $950

Good News
We know that Geeks is good people and won't let us go down.

Bad News
While everyone will be paid back, it definitely won't be until the 22nd, maybe not until the end of September and Lost Palantir.

So the fate of ~~the world~~ BoE is in your hands.

Several "Pony Pals" were willing to donate to BoE under these terms and Zinnia offered to set up a Paypal account to make this easier. Zin accumulated roughly $500 and sent it off to Abbey. Other people sent money via Western Union. On July 31, 2003, Jordan thanked the Prancing Pony profusely and posted more information.

> BoE is in the clear thanks to your wonderful generosity - you've all been amazing...We have definitely learned our lesson. Given the massive attendance at Sean's event and the interest in Elijah, it seemed safe to shell out the big dinero...we will never again put out one more penny up-front than we can easily afford to lose without putting ourselves or the site in jeopardy.

Not everything was just peachy at that point: on August 1, 2003, some of Those Evil Bands responded on the Prancing Pony:

- On July 1, I received an email saying "how 'bout 5:00?". I responded with some questions regarding PA//gear availability. No response. Finally a note telling me to re-direct questions to someone else. I did. No response. Finally one week before the gig, I sent another email asking if the gig was still on, and where the venue was, what do we need, etc. No response.

- It seemed to me (from the band side of things) that communication was very lacking but also that the event itself was rushed. It has been in my experience that most venues have schedules set and bands booked within months of the actual gig.

66

MissTree the Permit Person also had a few things to say:

> I handed a bunch of demos to Frodo with contact information. Frodo - you said you'd lost them(?!) but I see that three of the bands I suggested were scheduled to appear. I have talked to all three bands at this point and NONE of them had been contacted by BoE or knew they were on the schedule.

Jordan bellowed in indignation. The first band had been completely unreasonable in their requests and hounded him with emails until he finally gave up trying to meet their demands. He couldn't believe *they* had the nerve to accuse *him* of being unprofessional. He never really addressed MissTree's complaint, but he continued to blame the permit issue on MissTree, and her posts on the Pony became far less frequent. Zinnia finally spoke the voice of reason.

> I think our wonderful leaders did learn a lot from this experience. And I want to thank you for posting your point of view on the event. I think anything anyone can do to help us all learn to do a better job is helpful. It would be best if folks who have concerns speak directly to Orangeblossom or Mr. Frodo. From my pov. it doesn't serve anyone to place blame - either BOE blaming bands or bands blaming BOE or anything in between. Blame rarely helps anything. What matters is learning from the past and moving into the future.

OCTOBER 23, 2003

Jordan called to say he and Bob reconciled their differences and Bob was back in both the apartment and BoE. While I was not pleased with Jordan's harsh and hasty condemnation of Bob, it seemed if they could work things out, then I should move on, too. I did give Jordan a dressing-down about that character reference.

> Jordan, I don't know your identity. I know the stories you've told me, and what contradictory and confirmatory "evidence" I've gathered from what people have told me, and from my observations. I think I'm pretty good at distinguishing between fact and opinion, and right now I am absolutely sure that I DON'T know any facts regarding who you are, or even whether you're male or female. I know you don't seem like a typical con artist, but then again, I also know you are capable of playing fast and loose with the truth at will. In short, if Amy's parents had contacted me, I would have had to tell them I wasn't sure if you were their daughter or not. And for you to claim that I would fully support your story was presumptuous and incorrect, and a bit manipulative as well.

What else could I do but keep a wary eye on Jordan and see what happened next?

When Abbey brought up the Hall of Fire in the letter about Bob, it reminded several of us about an important point: money was raised for BoE after HoF flopped. If Jordan was some sort of con artist, then he probably stole all that money. Fortunately Zinnia had reassuring news.

Zin received a copy of the cancelled check to the Portland Parks Department, written by Jordan Wood on July 25, 2003, for $1835. Zin also had a receipt for $600 from an insurance agency on the same date. We were both relieved to know Jordan raised and spent money on legitimate BoE expenses for the Hall of Fire Music Festival.

Early in the summer, Abbey sent out an email to several of the more "established adults" from Project Elanor, asking for help. Her ex-husband let their house go into foreclosure and now she had to move out by the end of July. The core staff of BoE, including Abbey, Jordan, Bob, and Cherie "Diamond" Deuvall, were losing their home and headquarters, which they had shared for eight months. They dearly wanted to stick together, as each of them came from difficult backgrounds and they found strength in one another. They couldn't bear to part ways and move back home—or back on the street. Furthermore, if they had to split up their home, they doubted they could work out the details for either Hall of Fire or the following BoE event, The Lost Palantir Film Festival, so both events would have to be cancelled.

Abbey asked if anyone would let the small band of Hobbit Kids borrow some space until they could get on their feet. Did anyone have a basement, a guest house, a room over the garage? They promised babysitting, housework help, cooking and entertainment in return, as well as a Quiet Moment with celebrities at Lost Palantir and Tentmoot 2003.

I felt sorry for the kids. I've seen several girlfriends get financially wiped out by vindictive exes in very similar ways. I asked some good friends about empty basements or rental properties, but no one wanted to take on four smokers rent-free for two months. We couldn't take them—with our new baby, we barely fit in our place as it was. But Hubby knew how fond I had gown of the Hobbit Kids, so he suggested we help them get an apartment. I'd earned a little extra money that summer and we had the bills covered pretty well for a change—we could afford to spring for a place.

The kids found a small, cheap unit in a rough neighborhood. I paid two months' rent and deposits up front, plus a few utility hookups, totaling $1,635. The Kids were planning to move to Los Angeles after Lost Palantir, so this would take care of them until they were ready to head south.

They followed through on their promise of service. Diamond and Abbey babysat for me several times while I worked on ceramics. My exploding book was finally rebuilt and painstakingly lettered with the BoE inscription. I made a second commemorative book with all the volunteers' names, which took even longer to write with my glaze pen. Both had broken up the spine during the final firing, probably because the thin center cooled and contracted at a different rate from the heavy wings. Ceramics is a tedious art, but fortunately one that corrects well with Bondo. While I sat in the garage cementing book halves together and covering the evidence with a porcelain bookmark, Abbey and Di played with my two precious children. Abbey even helped my big boy program the secret code into his new light saber.

I tried to give the Hobbit Kids their space, but I did visit a few times. Jordan and I chatted during the evenings on the patio. Some of these chats got very personal and heart-to-heart, although heart-to-ear would be more accurate. He divulged many fascinating secrets and I sat glued to my chair.

Jordan explained his family was not just abusive, it was involved in organized crime—the Irish Republican Army, to be exact. Jordan refused to join the "family business" when he came of age. He was forced to live in exile because he knew too much about prominent IRA figures. Even though his family understood he was only acting out of conscience, they could do nothing to stop the IRA from putting a contract on his life.

Jordan was hoping to get into the Witness Protection Program, to testify and put some bad guys away, but that was a long and tedious process. Until things came to trial, his best bet was to simply hide in unlikely places like Milwaukie, Oregon.

I could sort of accept this story. My niece married a fellow whose father was testifying in some sort of murder. Though I only met him once, I still wrinkle my nose in memory of the fleabag motel he stayed in while a "protected witness."

I pinned Jordan down about the gender business. From the moment I shook his hand at Project Elanor, I believed he was female—the bones in the hand and wrist were simply not those of an adult male. Furthermore, I had to show him how to effectively drive nails when he was working on the Elanor deck. I figured Abbey and Jordan had good reasons to put on the appearance of a boy-girl couple. There are bashers even in cool cities like Portland, and when you're trying to operate a charity, the last thing you need is an idiotic controversy over the directors' sexual orientation. If they wanted to be closeted, that was OK with me.

Jordan assured me he really was a male—he had a rare testosterone resistance disorder, which feminized his features. He explained he had enough testosterone; it was a genetic defect in the testosterone receptors causing the effects. His explanation was very sophisticated, and when I looked it up that night in my *Harrison's Textbook of Internal Medicine*, sure enough, the symptoms of this extremely rare disease were just as Jordan described.

There was one detail that didn't match Jordan's story. The diseases described in my book were X-linked genetic illnesses, passed down from mother to son. Jordan explained his cousin also had this disease and their fathers were brothers—yet the defective genes would have come from their moms. That discrepancy didn't bother me too much, though, because *Harrison's* only had a few paragraphs about this class of disorders and I assumed Jordan must have some variant that was autosomal in nature—that is, passed down from either parent. I would have to drive an hour to Portland, find a parking spot at the medical school library, and consult a neuroendocrine textbook if I wanted to pin that detail down for sure. Very few things are worth seeking a parking spot on Pill Hill; I decided to take Jordan's word for it. Besides, I was too busy trying to wrap my head around Jordan's comments about his cousin—that is, his cousin Elijah Wood.

Jordan explained that Elijah is short and slight and has little facial hair for the same reason as Jordan. Obviously Jordan's disease was worse, but I vaguely recalled factors like variable penetrance and random proliferation of the gene defect, which can produce that sort of effect. Genetics was not a favorite subject of mine back in medical school.

I asked Jordan if he expected me to believe the cousin business. He looked me in the eye, shrugged, and said. "Hey, I don't tell people about this because I know how it sounds. Even worse, if they *do* believe me, they could blow my cover. But you've been a good friend for a long time, got me this apartment, I figure I can trust you with the truth."

Jordan told me how Elijah helped him get a job in New Zealand as a set assistant for the LOTR movies. Jordan worked and hung out with everyone in the cast, including Sean Astin. They became acquainted to the point that many of them gave Jordan their contact information and told him to keep in touch.

"But wait a minute. If Elijah is in the family," I wondered, "why isn't he in *The Family Business*?"

Jordan explained, "You remember those stories a while ago, in the tabloids, about how just after FOTR, Elijah's dad tried to 'get back into his life?' And Elijah turned him down flat?"

Of course I remembered! I read those blurbs on TORn like any good fangirl. I thought at the time it was awfully convenient that long-divorced Daddy how up just after $onny Boy appear$ in a megahit movie. But according to Jordan, this wasn't simply a case of a father trying to mend fences with his e$tranged $on. It was an obligatory attempt to indoctrinate Elijah into the IRA when he "became a man" at age 21.

Fortunately, Elijah's mom, Aunt Debbie, never told her son about the whole IRA aspect of the family, so he didn't represent a threat to anyone. He had no knowledge worth killing over, unlike cousin Jordan who grew up in the midst of it all.

I wasn't sure what to believe, but as a good scientist, I was willing to consider all possibilities until they were proven false. I didn't expect to find an IRA website to look up their hit list to see whether Jordan was on it. The testosterone story checked out pretty well. I checked the credits on my FOTR DVD and didn't see Jordan Wood's name, but who knew if lowest-level set assistants merited a spot in the credits? Jordan certainly resembled Elijah Wood, about as much as I look like my cousin Ronnie. A family connection would explain how a couple of unemployed oddballs who dressed funny came to have Sean Astin's number programmed into their cell phones. It all made sense in a tweaked sort of way.

Besides, it was an entertaining story that even MIGHT be true—what difference would it make if I humored him a little?

When Zinnia and I discussed Jordan's situation, her immediate reaction was, "Well, shoot, all he has to do is turn himself in. The police will figure out right away that he can't be Amy Player." That had certainly crossed my mind, too, but nothing was ever quite so simple with Jordan.

"He says if he goes to the police, they will automatically run his Social Security Number through the computer for a background check. The IRA monitors that system and will figure out his location, and he'll end up a little soggy spot on some remote terrain," I explained.

From the other side of the country, I could sense Zin's eyes crossing during this explanation. Of course it was crazy, unlikely, and outrageous, but this is precisely why we have clichés like "Truth is stranger than fiction." People really do get into messed up situations.

If Jordan was telling the truth, then turning himself in would get him killed. If Jordan was telling the truth and Myers busted him, then Myers would get him killed. If Jordan was telling the truth and I helped lead Myers to him, then I could get him killed. Of course, if Jordan was lying, then I was helping a criminal avoid The Law—and not just any criminal, a criminal that still owed me $1400! I had no way to tell one way or the other and the wrong guess could result in either the death of my friend or the loss of my money. I was trying to drive a penny nail with a sledgehammer.

Zin was flabbergasted as well. She told her husband the sordid tale, fully expecting his eyes to cross as well, and to her surprise, he wasn't particularly taken aback by the mob story. "He seems to think that kind of thing is more usual than we might suspect. In fact, he reminded me we have a friend who originally became a pastor to escape the Jewish mafia in New York." Sometimes the voice of reason is rendered speechless too.

My life was starting to resemble a William Gibson novel. All I needed was a sentient computer and some Japanese bodyguards.

Jordan and I brainstormed for a solution to this problem and finally came up with a concept. What if Jordan were to go to a doctor down in San Dimas, one the detective could choose (at random from the yellow pages if necessary), and be examined? We could fax down Jordan's photo so the doctor could assure Myers he was examining the right person. If such a physician were to confirm Jordan was male, surely Myers would accept that Jordan couldn't possibly be Amy Player? This seemed like a way for Jordan to prove his innocence without having to involve the police or their background checks. Jordan enthusiastically agreed to speak to Myers about this solution.

SEPTEMBER 20, 2003

Before BoE moved to San Dimas, the Kids threw one more event, the Lost Palantir Film Festival, at Lloyd Center 10 Cinema in Portland. "LP" was to be a showcase for amateur filmmakers from all over the country, in homage to Tolkien and the LOTR films. The kids booked a 700-seat theater, the same one in which Sean Astin hosted The Two Towers in April, 2003. Admittedly, it did seem a bit of a stretch to summon up 700 people interested in student films or worse—but not if everything went according to plan and Billy Boyd hosted the event.

An orphan, Billy struggled up from the dregs of poverty to make a career in acting. He was gaining a reputation as a patron of acting schools and small independent films, making him a perfect choice to emcee a grassroots film festival. BoE certainly came through with Sean Astin, so LP sounded like a promising event. Billy was listed on the LP web page only as a "possible guest appearance," but Jordan assured us Billy was interested and would attend.

On August 26, 2003, Jordan asked a BoE member, "HeadDesk," to raise funds for Billy's airfare. HeadDesk posted the exciting news that Billy was confirmed for LP on "The Forum," the message board at Billy's official website, www.BillyBoyd.net. She asked anyone who planned to attend the festival to please make a donation to BoE toward Billy's airfare. Within a day, her post produced four small donations for Billy's ticket—and attracted the attention of Stewart Steel, Billy's webmaster.

Stewart deleted HeadDesk's post. When she asked him for an explanation, Stewart told her although Billy was planning to attend LP, he would *not* be confirmed until *after* he had a plane ticket in his hand.

Jordan responded that Stewart was just lashing out at HeadDesk because he didn't like learning about Billy's future events from his own message board. Billy had two PR agents representing him: Aude in London and Daphne in Los Angeles. Jordan arranged everything through Daphne, so Aude had not been involved. But Stewart, being in Scotland, naturally contacted Aude when he saw this claim about Billy's schedule and Aude knew nothing about LP. Stewart leapt to the conclusion this was a scam and then refused to lose face by admitting he had been mistaken.

Jordan spent weeks trying to work things out with Stewart, Daphne, and Aude. Daphne sent an email stating Billy was no longer interested in appearing at LP because of this controversy. Stewart wouldn't even answer Jordan's emails. Finally, three weeks before LP, Abbey and Jordan called in the cavalry. Abbey punched the Sacred Sean Astin Speedial and explained the situation to Sean. Sean spoke to Billy, cleared up the confusion, and assured Billy that BoE was legitimate. Because of Sean's recommendation, Billy decided to appear at LP after all! Another BoE miracle was in the making.

By that point, Billy's people had booked up his schedule, so it would take some rearranging in order for him to make it to LP. That proved too tricky. Billy tried to squeeze LP in, but he was slated to appear on the Conan O'Brian show on the night of LP and Conan was a notorious diva who just wouldn't reschedule his guests. The Lost Palantir lost Billy to Conan's prima donnitude.

Not wanting another Hall of Fire debacle, Jordan got in touch with Sean Astin, Viggo Mortensen, and Dominic Monaghan, hoping one of them would be interested in coming instead. And amazingly, all three agreed—things were slow in LA, it was a short plane ride to Portland, so they decided to do it together just for fun.

Furthermore, Sean had just been approached by the E! Entertainment Network because they were developing a short series about celebrities and volunteering. This was a perfect opportunity for a crew to tour the Elanor garden with Sean and meet some of the BoE volunteers.

Days later, New Line Cinema released the movie *Secondhand Lions*, which featured the first theatrical preview of ROTK. People went to the movie just to get a look at the trailer and New Line wasn't going to let a promotional opportunity go to waste. Suddenly schedules that were wide open the day before were booked solid with interviews, sound bites, and whatever else movie stars do to publicize their films. Once again, whimsy robbed LP of its celebrity hosts. Even Sean had to postpone, although E! was still sending up a team to tour the garden.

Well, if you can't have a celebrity attend, what's the next best thing? Jordan sent Sue Astle to Los Angeles on the evening of September 18, 2003, armed with a video camera and the blank Winner's Certificates for the film festival. Sue was to visit with Dom, Viggo, and Sean, to tape their personal video greetings for LP. She would also get their autographs on the certificates. It wasn't optimal, but not a bad substitute either!

Sue flew to LA and, after a snafu with her rental car, took a cab to her motel. She was supposed to meet Sean Astin, pick up the tape Sean already made for LP, and have him sign the certificates. Jordan called in to let Sue know that, unfortunately, Sean was in such a hurry, he just left his tape with Gibson, his PR representative.

The next morning Sue went straight to Sean's PR office. Gibson handed her a tape and apologized that Sean had missed her; he had to leave town suddenly.

Sue called Jordan and was told Viggo Mortensen would be next. Viggo was doing voiceovers in a studio up the street and he wanted her to stay put for the moment. Jordan would call her back as soon as Viggo was ready to meet her.

Ahem.

Read a few stale magazines.

Cross legs.

Examine fingernails.

Uncross legs.

Look out window.

Get the Hairy Eyeball from the receptionist.

Repeat from "Ahem."

Actually, it wasn't really that bad. Gibson and her staff were friendly and they even helped Sue figure out how to operate the camcorder that had been thrust in her hands just before her flight to LA. Sue spent two hours there, but she finally sought refuge downstairs at Nibbler's, the lobby restaurant. The prices were somewhat different from typical Oregon fare. Sue nibbled free mints from the bowl by cash register and ordered one tea bag and a lake of hot water. She begged forgiveness from the wait staff for being such an utter cheapskate, but they didn't mind her a bit—they even kept her supplied with bread and crackers. Six hours later, Jordan finally called in. Viggo had just finished his work, and although he was too tired to talk now, he wanted to meet her right there tomorrow at 11:00 AM.

The next morning, Sue ate her meager breakfast of crackers smuggled from Nibbler's and went back to the PR firm to wait for Viggo. It was Saturday and the restaurant was closed, so there weren't even any free mints. She was reduced to pacing on the sidewalk.

No Viggo.

No explanation from Jordan.

An hour went by.

Viggo must have stood her up. She had to leave to make her next appointment, which was with Dominic Monaghan at his home.

Sue called yet another cab at her own expense and headed toward the address Jordan supplied. Traffic was terrible. It came to a point where Sue had to choose between getting to Dom's house and making it to her flight. This was Saturday, September 20, 2003, the day of the LP Festival, and Sue was *holding the video from Sean Astin in her hand*. Missing her flight would mean missing the festival and Sean's lovely gesture would end up a waste of his time. The cabbie pulled an illegal U-turn and raced Sue to the airport; they pulled up with 11 minutes to get to her gate. She ran through LAX as though the very whips of Saruman were behind her. The jetway was already starting to retract when she charged up, breathless, but she made it to her seat just in time to spy one of Air New Zealand's LOTR jets roll by, painted with the rolling hills of the Shire and the faces of Frodo and Sam.[3]

_____

[3] Unfortunately Sue was so out of breath from her sprint through the airport that she could only gasp and point at the window. Her fellow passengers, already not disposed toward this latecomer, nervously assumed she was trying to say, "There's a man on the wing!"

So Sue made it, the tape made it, the audience made it, and an odd but fun time was had by all. Sean's video alone was worth the $10 ticket. He shot it in his own garden, making all sorts of supportive comments about amateur films and BoE, and generally being the sweet, upbeat goofball that everyone remembered from Project Elanor.

The biggest disappointment was finding out the E! crew decided not to film after all. Kly had organized a special work party to weed the garden so it would look nice for the tour. I rushed to install the finished ceramic plaques for the benefit of the E! cameras, too. Jordan indicated the E! crew wanted to interview some of us about our contributions to the garden. We were thrilled at the prospect of being able to show off our good work.

The reporters came to LP, but they decided not to tour the garden. Jordan said they wanted to wait until Sean was available. Kly was crushed, as she bought $250 in new plants just for the video crew, but what could be done? I asked Jordan if he could persuade them to at least conduct their interviews, since volunteers from out-of-state were in Portland to attend LP; this was a rare opportunity to have so many of us in one place. Jordan said he'd already tried. The E! folks wanted to get Sean on tape first, then bounce his comments off the volunteers, instead of the other way around. The garden looked great, so our hard work wasn't wasted, but it was still disappointing to see the E! crew in the LP audience, knowing they had ignored our efforts.

During the week after LP, the kids packed up all their things and moved out of the apartment I rented for them. They were constantly running all over town doing errands, with only one car between the four of them. Diamond asked if I would mind driving her over to Wells Fargo Bank, so she could take out a personal loan for the trip.

Di had just turned 21 and had no prior credit. She lived with her parents until she moved into BoE headquarters in early 2003. She thought, as a current Wells Fargo customer, she was eligible to take out a personal loan. But when we got to the bank, they explained they were sorry, but based on her credit rating, they simply had to say "no."

Di was on the brink of tears. All the Hobbit Kids were counting on that loan money to finance their apartment in Los Angeles. Each of them cashed out all their savings and sold most of their stuff to afford this move, but they knew it wasn't enough. Apartments in LA are not cheap; during the seven years I lived there, I was too poor to pay attention.

I asked the Wells Fargo agent if Di could get the loan with a cosigner. I had no problem trusting Di. She was bright and worked hard. She helped support the BoE household on her paychecks for eight months. She simply hadn't been out of her parents' home long enough to establish a credit rating. Wells Fargo was more than happy to lend the money (at an APR of 21%) with my 20 years of immaculate credit on the second dotted line. Di and I sat together and listened to the loan officer explain the repayment terms, which were roughly $110 a month. Di would be working full time, splitting the rent with five other people. She had no car payment and no other debt. I felt confident Di would be able to make a monthly payment of that size. And heck, if I absolutely *had* to help her out, I could afford an occasional $110 a month, too.

The kids spent their last night in town sleeping on my floor. Jordan handed me $200 in cash the next morning, saying it was the returned deposit from their Salem apartment. I tried to get him to take it for the trip—what if they needed gas or food or had car trouble? Jordan assured me they had all they needed.

At around 2:30 PM on October 2, 2003, Abbey and Jordan piled into their overstuffed old van and headed to the coast to say goodbye to Abbey's mom. Sue, Bob, and Diamond were sardined in Sue's car, with The Great Luke Ski's "Stealin' Like a Hobbit" cued up on the tape deck. As they drove away, I had a taste of what it might feel like when my own little sproggies leave the nest—a wistful mix of hope, loneliness, even a little jealousy that my days of grand adventures were behind me. I was going to *miss* those damn Hobbit Kids!

OCTOBER 29, 2003

Zinnia attended a conference called Generations United in Virginia. Sean Astin was a guest speaker at this family policy conference and he made a public comment about BoE.

> The Bit of Earth folks decided to turn that parking lot into a garden. I was approached on Sept 11 2002; to ask me if I wanted to be a part of this thing. I was a little nervous about the level of intensity of their fandom, but I recognized in them a kind of leadership capacity. I wanted to support and nurture in a small, limited way because there was a lot of emotional dysfunction in their group. I didn't want to deny the energy that was being directed towards me. I wanted to help shape their imaginations for a moment—to hopefully inspire them to use that passion in service.

Zin talked to Sean after the closing ceremonies. When she mentioned she was with Bit of Earth, Sean said he had spoken to Detective Myers about Abbey and Jordan.

"Sean asked me if I had any insight on the situation," Zin wrote. "He said he is quite concerned for Jordan and is convinced that Jordan is indeed Amy. He wants to help them be who he knows they can be. He has been holding up BoE as an example to his fellow cast members of what can happen if they interact directly with fans, and now he is getting notices from law enforcement ... ."

Zin and I each wished we could crawl into a deep, deep hole. I would give *anything* to find out why Sean believed Detective Myers' side of the story. Sean obviously thought Jordan was a man back in July, when he proposed to Abbey on Jordan's behalf. What the heck had changed his mind? Whatever it was, I wanted some, because I was sick of being in in doubt about this issue.

Jordan called a few days later to tell me he spoke at last to the detective, cleared things up, and had been exonerated. I absolutely *had* to check that story out myself.

Myers confirmed he was no longer looking for Jordan, because Jordan confessed to everything, including being Amy and committing the crimes ascribed to her. Myers found his missing person, so he was closing his interest in the case—but he would forward his findings to the District Attorney. He didn't think the crimes were significant enough for the DA to extradite them from California, so if Amy stayed out of trouble and continued doing good deeds for charity, then in all likelihood, this escapade would end here. On top of it all, Myers thought so highly of Sean (from their telephone calls), he finally decided to read *Lord of the Rings*.

Jordan had a little bit of 'splaining to do. Fed up with long distance calls over this insane business, I sent him an email.

> While I would not exactly call this an exoneration, I think it's true that Detective Myers, and probably the rest of The Law, are finished pursuing you.
> Of course, the detective still maintains that the two pictures of Jordan and Amy are separate shots taken months apart, which I believe is not true. So either you hacked into the DMV record and gave yourself a new picture, or Amy Player's parents (or whoever is behind all this investigation) deliberately handed the detective a fake

photo, or the detective is trying to pull one over on me. Either way, I'm finding this whole business less fascinating and more irritating. I still feel I have no idea what the Truth is, despite having gathered all this information—the more I learn, the less I understand—it's like a giant David Lynch movie.

I have this little fantasy, Jordan, that at the core you are a genuinely good person, but you were brought up in some kind of hellish environment in which you had to become an expert at deception to survive. Having escaped that situation, even though you no longer need to deceive, and probably don't even particularly WANT to, it just comes naturally to you. But the problem is, you've decided to hang around with gentle, loving people. Those old habits can really bite you on the ass, because kindhearted people don't see them as a game, or a defense mechanism, or just a bad habit, but as a destroyer of trust and of relationships.

As I waited to hear what Jordan had to say for him/her/itself, I got a call from Sue down in LA. Sue was sure Jordan was in fact Amy Player, and faked her own suicide in order to start a new life. Detective Myers had told her why he let Jordan off the hook: Myers thought BoE was a worthwhile project and he'd just as soon see Jordan free and doing good works, rather than behind bars at the expense of the state for minor crimes committed as Amy Player.

Zin was relieved by this latest development. "I'm glad things are now clear. I am, however, still very angry at the amount of lies involved in this whole mess, and especially the number of lies which were told to you. I hope you are not too quick to let them off the hook for this."

I replied:

I haven't quite figured out how to react. On the one hand, I'm trying to remember I don't know the whole situation, I don't know why Jordan wanted so badly to split with his family of origin. It may have been truly terrible, in which case the lies may have been an act of pure desperation. Of course, it also might not have been so bad, and this may be a very egotistical and selfish person manipulating at will to get what he/she wants. I don't know what the motives are, so it's hard to figure out how mad I should be. On the other hand, those guys owe me a LOT of money, and if I cloud up and rain on them because of the deceit, I may never see any of it again. I may never get paid back no matter what I do, but opening up a can of whoopass will probably ensure my money and I will never meet again.

Zinnia felt "the only acceptable solution is for them to come clean to those they have been dishonest with. In my mind, they are on 'probation' from any further help or trust from me until they do that."

We agreed to prod Jordan with increasing intensity to make an announcement to the entire BoE community, as it seemed far more appropriate for "him" to do it than for us to just "out" the news.

We stuck to this plan contentedly for all of two days, until I got a phone call from Jordan.

Jordan said Myers forced the confession out of him, as in "I don't want to hear a word out of you, you either say you're Amy Player or I'll have you arrested right there by the San Dimas Police."

89

Jordan couldn't risk having the police haul him in because the IRA would find him for sure, so he had no choice but to confess. Jordan also said when the detective put him on the phone to Amy Player's parents, they admitted his voice didn't sound like Amy's.

I *had* to share this with Zinnia.

> I gotta give Jordan credit, if this is all a story, he's sticking to it INCREDIBLY well. He says Sue and Bob are siding with the detective, and at this point they are content to believe Jordan is Amy and has confessed all, so the charges have been dropped. Jordan says he didn't see any other option but to make this fake confession, as he needs to stay below the law's radar. I guess the one salient point is that EVERYONE says the detective is no longer pursuing Jordan and there are no charges pending that could embarrass BoE.

Zinnia's response was quite concise. "What the fuck. That is completely insane. I've so had it with this. I don't even know what to think any more."

Tell me about it , Zin.

BoE had been great fun at first. The next planned festival, Tentmoot 2003, looked very promising. But it was going to have to be a *damn fine* party to make up for all of this!

It was also pretty clear I was long overdue to establish some boundaries with Jordan. I emailed him on November 7, 2003.

> If the detective really has cleared the name of Amy Player, then it would seem reasonable, if you were Amy, to just accept your identity back. Of course, there are a lot of unhealthy/manipulative

possibilities for sticking to a story that is not true. Perhaps Abbey is dead set against being identified as a lesbian. Maybe as Amy Player, you did some more major crimes that *would* get you thrown in jail if Detective Myers kept this case open longer and discovered them. Or you could just be saving face—refusing to let yourself be caught in a lie. Or maybe you really are a girl—but not Amy Player. Or a guy—but not really EJW's cousin and/or not really being pursued by the IRA, and you don't want to admit those stories are phony. It boggles the mind as to how many possibilities there are here.

I'll just tell you, Jordan, I really don't care who you are, whether you're a dyke, whether your parents are really OK people and you just wanted to get away from them, or what. If you have been pulling my leg, NOW is the time to tell me. Actually, a while ago was the optimal time to tell me, but this has come to a point of no return. I don't like to give ultimata, but in this case I'm going to make an exception: if you stick to this story after this email, and I determine it is a lie, that will be an end to my friendship with you and Abbey. If my friendship is important to you, then the next email you send me had better be 100% honest.

PART II:

TENT MOOT CRASH

THE (BIT OF) EARTH SHATTERING KABOOM

When BoE started delegating Tentmoot tasks to volunteers, I felt I had more than served my time. I was promised Mithril Passes to the festival for getting the kids a place to live, and after The October From Hell, I was looking forward to just kicking back and enjoying the festival—and not just as a spectator, but a VIP!

Besides, by all appearances, things were coming together beautifully! The guest list for Tentmoot was huge and impressive. The prestigious Oregon Convention Center was booked as the venue, with its steepled glass roof creating a "tent with a view." There were going to be games, panels, art and fiction galleries, tournaments, music, and to wrap it up, a wedding! John and Talisha decided to get married in LOTR costumes at the close of the festival, with the entire Washington/Oregon fan community joining the reception at the Gala Ball. We would dance the night away—until it was time to line up for the premiere of *Return of the King*. Some of the guests of honor were interested in attending the premiere in Portland. There was the potential to share an armrest with Howard Shore, Ngila Dickson, John Howe, Lawrence Makaore, or even Figwit! Of course, that also presented a risk of sitting behind all seven feet of "Tall" Paul Randall—but the odds were the same for ending up behind four-foot Kiran Shah.

On October 19, 2003, Jordan publicly announced that BoE had Celebrities, Hotels for Celebrities, Food for Celebrities, Food for TentMoot, Donors for TentMoot, Contest Prizes, and other necessities. He claimed BoE and the Lloyd Center Cinema arranged More Tickets Released for [Trilogy Tuesday]. Jordan also mentioned the Airline Tickets for the Celebrities were nearly arranged. Other encouraging announcements followed:

•**Oct 29**: We're getting things ready with some of the video appearances for TentMoot, and this is where you guys come in! The appearances will be a taped greeting, followed by a taped Q&A...but we need questions! Send them to tentmoot@bitofearth.net, or post them on the Prancing Pony under the topic 'Ask A Celebrity.'

•**Oct 30**: Who Comes From A Land Down Under? BoE is seeking Australian or Kiwi Ringers who own/can get their hands on a camcorder and would be willing to meet with Miranda Otto and David Wenham to tape video appearances.

•**Nov 5**: High priority on the Andy Serkis questions! Looks like we might be getting his interview this week, and we need the list of questions to send to his agent TOMORROW!

•**Nov 18**: We're looking for people to volunteer as judges for the costume contest at Tentmoot. Applicants must be willing to argue costuming details with Ngila Dickson.

•**Nov 26**: Tickets are going fast and WILL get more expensive as the date grows nearer, finally reaching between $10-45 higher at the door. The first increase will be occuring on December 1st, so hurry and grab them while they're cheap.

•**Nov 28**: The Convention Center is giving us $60,000 worth of A/V equipment rental, security, medical, insurance, concessions, and all the smaller rooms fully equipped for no additional charge. Tickets have been selling pretty well, but to get all these nice shiny benefits, we need to sell another 25 standard weeklong passes (or the equivalent) by Monday.

Sue and Bob came back to Portland in November and were bustling all over town setting things up. I hadn't noticed a lot of advertising for Tentmoot, but I listen to the '80's radio station and NPR and pick up an alternative zine once in a blue moon. Fossils like myself aren't exactly the audience BoE was trying to reach. The Tentmoot banner was flashing up on the Convention Center's billboard and the Doubletree Hotel gave me the Tentmoot Discount Rate when I booked a room. Tentmoot appeared to be a smashing success.

On December 2, 2003, the phone rang. It was Jordan, asking if I could help him brainstorm about a problem.

"We'd gotten everything arranged months ago with Air New Zealand for free airline tickets. They have this program where they give 20 free tickets away each month to charity. They first give them to people who need to fly for organ transplants, and if there are any left over, they pass those out first come, first serve. They had 14 tickets left over for December so they gave them to us.

"Well, after the world premiere of ROTK in Wellington, tourism to New Zealand has skyrocketed, so someone high up decided that they weren't going to give out so many free tickets when business was going so good. So they cut it in half, to ten tickets. But nobody told US about that, and when I called them up to make the final arrangements, suddenly they tell me we can't have the tickets!"

I said, "What the hell? They waited till NOW to let you know?"

"Someone was supposed to call me three weeks ago, but apparently they never got around to it. I just found out about it today."

"Oh, for God's sake. What about the last four tickets?"

"They said they would rather give the four away to a group that only needed that many. Since they couldn't give us what we fully needed anymore, they'd rather save them for someone where they could fully meet their need."

"So they'd rather screw you completely than only partially...Well, I suppose from a PR standpoint it's a lot nicer to say, 'So-and-so needed four tickets and we supplied them.' But surely they recognized they left you in a bad situation. Didn't they at least offer you a discount so you could purchase flights?"

"No, I asked, but they're just washing their hands of the whole thing. They don't want to admit that they went back on their promise or something."

Harrumph. Nothing quite like the soulless mentality of big business. Well, shoot, after 20 years of volunteering for all sorts of different groups, I had a few connections and resources. I was up for the challenge to get those flightless Kiwis here for Tentmoot.

I called up my friend "Helga," a beautiful blond Norwegian Lutheran, who is also a professional mercenary. She is in the business of pulling dignitaries off the roofs of burning embassies and she had just spent Thanksgiving dinner chasing my sons under the dining room table. I was hoping maybe she could just fire up one of her big Russian helicopters and fetch the celebs directly.

Her boss wouldn't go for that, however—you never know when an embassy will go up in smoke. Still, she did have an idea. "Let me talk to my travel agent. Cost isn't usually an issue when I travel for a client, but I've used her for personal trips too, and she always comes up with great deals."

Sounded good to me! In the meantime, I did some looking into private jet charters, saw some prices, and quickly looked away again.

Helga's travel agency, PTP, thought they might be able to help. PTP used an airline ticket wholesaler in Chicago that might be able to snag 14 tickets, possibly for as little as $1000 each. Jordan told me around 800 tickets to Tentmoot had been sold so far, and BoE could afford up to $1500 per flight. The wholesaler sounded like it would work. On December 5, 2003, PTP sent all the names and travel dates to the wholesaler. But when they got back to us the following Monday, the news was grim: it was too close to the date of departure for them to run the tickets. We were back at square one, and Tentmoot started in three days.

Jordan told me at that point, cost was no object. "We won't have much left over for RIF, but we won't have anything if we don't get those Kiwis over here."

I called PTP and asked Donna, the owner, if she could just book some tickets the old fashioned way. By 3:00 PM, she had 14 tickets totaling $70,000 reserved—and that was for international travel to LAX only! There were no seats remaining on any direct flights to Portland, so BoE would have to buy *additional* domestic tickets to get the celebrities from LA to Portland. That was when Jordan informed me BoE couldn't actually pay for airfares just then.

"All our money is tied up! The tickets to Tentmoot have been sold through this internet agency, Ticketweb, and they won't release any money until after the event! Can PTP credit us for the tickets now, and let us pay her back after Tentmoot?" he pled.

Donna said the airlines typically take a week or so to actually collect payment for ticket purchases, so she was willing to wait for payment until Tentmoot closed on December 16, 2003. Hooray!

Ticketweb announced that "after the event" was not intended to mean "*immediately* after the event." The soonest they could possibly release the money was the 20th, or ten days after the purchases. Boo!

PTP couldn't wait that long for repayment; they simply didn't have $70,000 in spare cash to pay Air NZ when they came to collect on the 17th. But Donna was willing to accept multiple credit cards to pay for the airfares. BoE could call on the volunteer league to put airfares on their cards just until Ticketweb could reimburse them on the 20th. Hooray!

Abbey said, "No problem! We have at least 35 people we can ask to do this, and we'll have them paid back so fast their cards won't even go through a monthly billing cycle."

The next morning, December 9, 2003, the plan changed. The Black Seeds, a New Zealand band featuring Bret "Figwit" McKenzie were cancelled. That eliminated nine airfares. Furthermore according to Jordan, "Sala Baker is flying to LA for family reasons on his own nickel, so we don't have to bring him from NZ after all. We only need a ticket for Sala from LAX to Portland." So the list of travelers was down to Lawrence Makaore (who played Saruman's pet *uruk-hai*, Lurtz), Jed Brophy (the badass orc that tossed Aragorn over the cliff), Brian Sergent (hobbit Ted Sandyman) and Paul Randall (size double—Extra Tall).

I emailed Jordan that this was all fine and good, but I still needed credit card numbers to give to Donna. Jordan called back to say they were still working on credit card information. He asked me to get the ball rolling by putting $10,000 worth of tickets onto my own cards. I gulped and said I would think about it. I checked with Ticketweb, who confirmed they would be mailing out checks on the 20th, and with Abbey's permission, they could send one straight to me. I reluctantly decided that if other folks in BoE would finance the rest, I could do my part, too.

Donna re-priced the new travel package, which came out to $19,000. But she said we needed to make a decision about the international tickets *now*, because they couldn't be purchased at all if we waited too much longer—it was getting too close to departure time. Holy Smoke, it was already December 10, 2003 in New Zealand! The Kiwis had to leave *that night* in order to be in Portland when Tentmoot opened on the 11th. I knew Jordan didn't have any other credit cards yet. It all came down to me: if I didn't pay *right then*, there would be no celebrities and no Tentmoot.

I asked myself, "What's the use of having two Platinum MasterCards if you never use them?"

$15,000 later, I realized a number of things:

1. I just brought the celebs to Los Angeles, not Portland;

2. Neither Jordan nor Abbey provided me with more cards to take care of the domestic air fare;

3. I couldn't purchase the remaining travel without some additional cards;

4. No one in BoE—except Jordan—knew I had done this; and

5. It was time to send an email to all the BoE staff I knew.

OK, I just put $15,000 on my two cards to pay for all the international travel. We still have to buy all the domestic travel, and that includes Lawrence's trip to Hawaii. My cards are now maxxed out. And I mean not one penny more.

I've really truly 100% put my ass on the line, Jordan. And I'm not a happy camper either. I need the rest of the credit numbers ASAP (along with full name, billing address and exp. date on each card) to get the domestic stuff arranged.

Ten minutes later, I received a reply from Zinnia: "I'm appalled about this. How did you end up putting this on your own credit card?"

I sent Zin a quick rundown of what happened. By the time I sent it, she'd already seen it for herself:

I just got a call from Abbey asking for my help with the 'travel emergency.' She needed my help to get credit card numbers to pay $5000, plus the airfare for Kiran because they can't reach his donor. Could I help them by giving them the names and phone numbers for Pony Pals...I know it is difficult letting people fail, but I frankly believe that is the only way they are going to learn. Don't you see the pattern here? Every single event, some last minute crisis happens which threatens the event, and they have to run to you or me or others to bail them out.

If it were me, I would cancel that credit card transaction immediately and demand a written contract with BoE ensuring that you will be paid back every last penny. Let them deal with the mess they have made.

Zin was correct on all counts, but even as I read her answer, things were looking up a bit. Donna had, by switching travel dates and sacrificing a few goats, brought the total cost of travel down to $18,000, an amount I could put on my cards. There was no need to get any additional donors to bring the celebs up from LA, and no rush to actually pay for the domestic travel (yet).

I told Abbey what I learned from Ticketweb. She assured me she would set things up right away so I would directly receive a check on Dec. 20, 2003. Then while Abbey was gushing, Zin sent another email. "I just wanted you to know, I just sent an email to Air New Zealand to see if they would confirm Abbey and Jordan's story. I think it is very important to find out."

For a brief Zen moment, there was nothing I needed to do. I had all the airfares covered. Ticketweb was getting set to reimburse me. The Kiwis would be getting on their plane in a few hours. Zin was checking out Jordan's story for me *just in case*. I decided to let this roll until Zin checked in again—I could always cancel the tickets if she had bad news.

The solitude shattered at 1:10 PM, when I got this message from Zin.

I just spoke on the phone with Jenny Simpson, the director of sponsorships at Air New Zealand. They have never heard of Tentmoot or Bitofearth.net. They directed me to speak with Rebecca Weaver, who is in their LA office and is handling LOTR related events. She also has never heard of the convention or BoE, and finds it highly unlikely that they would have agreed to such a thing because she has people calling and begging for tickets all the time.

Magic 8-Ball was leaning heavily toward canceling the tickets. However, I wasn't completely convinced yet. What if Jenny Simpson or Rebecca Weaver were mistaken? Sure, the two of them obviously handled official New Line/LOTR events, but maybe someone else handled the Organ Donor program. Jordan told me long before that the bad news came from "someone named Sharon or Sherry," and neither of those names came up in Zin's letter. If neither Jenny nor Rebecca had anything to do with the Organ Donor program, then naturally they would not be aware of the situation with BoE. If I cancelled the flights and it turned out Jordan was telling the truth, that would be a one-way ticket to Sucksville.

Fortunately, there was still time to check out the full story. I dashed off a detailed version of events to Zin and she forwarded them to Rebecca Weaver. Rebecca said she would check the Organ Donor story out. At 3:15 PM, Zin reported the following:

I have some very bad news. Rebecca just called me back, and she said that Abbey and Jordan's story is completely false. She has checked with the staff in NZ, and they have record of a written

104

request from BoE of 25 tickets which they did not grant. They have no such program as the one which Jordan described where they give away a certain quota to charity each month. They said this sounds to them to be an elaborate scam.

Based on this single email, my entire perception of BoE and Jordan, extending all the way back to Project Elanor, exploded. My insides felt like a building being demolished by a professional pyrotechnician; one kaboom and the whole thing just slowly topples into itself.

I had told Jordan, "No more lies." He turned around and made up a story in elaborate detail— the same kind of elaborate detail as the stories of the IRA, Cousin Elijah, and the Ex-Girlfriend from Hell. All the time I had helped Jordan, shared my home, fed him, defended him to the Sheriff, he had been pulling the wool, nay, the entire flock of sheep, several border collies, and the pasture over my eyes. It didn't seem possible! How could the last eight months have been one gigantic lie?

It was time to make some phone calls to Air NZ myself. I got through to Rebecca's cell phone at 3:40 PM on December 9, 2003. I had to make absolutely sure she truly checked into the organ donor story. Naturally, her phone cut out before she had a chance to answer me. I tried her cell phone, her office phone, her cell again…no answer. I was reciting a litany of every four-letter word I ever knew.

At 3:50 PM, I decided to go straight to the source. I dialed Jordan's number.

"Bit of Earth." That unmistakable voice.

"I told you NO MORE LIES."

"Wha…what are you talking about? Jeanine?"

"Yes, it's me. I just talked to Air NZ. They said they don't even HAVE an organ donor charity program. They said the only time they'd ever heard of BoE was last week, when you sent them a request for 25 free tickets."

"Why, why, why, why would I do that? I never needed 25 tickets. That doesn't make any sense! Why would I ask for 25 tickets?"

"That's what they tell me. Now exactly who am I supposed to believe?"

"It doesn't make sense! I never asked for that! She doesn't know what she's talking about, she's mixing me up with someone else!" Jordan protested.

I wasn't having any arguments. "Jordan, I told you no more lies. Tell me the name of the person that promised you the free tickets. I need to hear it straight from them."

"I don't remember the name! That was months ago!" he cried.

"All right, then tell me the person that told you the tickets were off. That was just last week. You *must* be able to remember *that*."

"I don't know offhand!" Jordan implored. "I told you, it was Sharon or Sherri or something. I've got the letter on my computer. But it's all packed up in the van! We were just about to leave for Portland."

That was a plausible explanation; Abbey had posted a note on the Pony just 20 minutes earlier, saying they would be leaving within an hour, with all their gear in tow.

"Go out and get your computer and hook it up," I said.

"That'll take half an hour! We've gotta get on the road!"

"You're going to start out a little late. I'll give you half an hour to find that name. Otherwise there won't be any point in driving up."

"Okay. Okay! I'll go get it. Just, please, don't do anything until I get a chance to prove this to you. Please. This is crazy." Jordan's voice was frantic.

"Call me in half an hour," I said evenly, and hung up.

Now I had half an hour to kill, but it felt more like it would kill me. Rebecca still wasn't answering. I got Jenny Simpson's number from Zinnia. I tried to check in on Jordan, but the phone was answered by a teenager, who informed me all hell was breaking loose in the apartment and Jordan was locked in the bathroom, puking nonstop. "OK," I thought, "Jenny Simpson it is."

I made my very first international phone call, only to be transferred from office to office at Air NZ, where apparently everyone was taking a long lunch. I finally got through to a lady low enough on the totem pole to actually be *working* during the day. She told me she had never heard of the Organ Donor program, and she worked in the office that handled just that sort of thing. And no, there wasn't anyone named Sharon or Sherri in that department; the closest they had was a Sue, who was a receptionist and not in any position to make decisions about free tickets.

For no particular reason, I called BoE one more time—no answer.

By now it was 5:15 PM. The four celebrities coming from New Zealand were scheduled to take off at 7:20 PM. I called Donna at PTP and hoped like hell she hadn't already gone home for the day. She hadn't.

"Donna, oh my God, we've been conned. It was all a lie. I have to cancel those tickets!" I blurted.

"You're kidding me!" she exclaimed. "Oh, no! All right, let me get to my computer."

I blathered snippets of the story as she clicked and clacked away.

"OK, we're really cutting it close," she said. "It's possible they have already checked in. I better call Reservations and make sure we can really go through with the cancellation."

She put me on hold for a few minutes while she talked to Air NZ, then came back with good news. "As far as they could tell, no one has checked in. I put in the cancellation in, and she said it came through on her computer."

It was 5:30 PM. Donna and I did all we could. Jordan kept *all* contact information for celebrities to himself. There was no way we could reach the actors to let them know what happened. They were in for an unpleasant surprise when they went to check in and found there were no tickets for them.

At 8:00 PM, Abbey called me from a hospital payphone, to let me know Jordan was being held under mandatory 48-hour observation after an apparent attempt to commit suicide.

THE MORNING AFTER

Wednesday, December 10, 2003, started out with a cheery message from Rebecca Weaver, forwarded to me from Zinnia.

> I am so glad to hear that this has been straightened out. Thank you SO much for your persistence and your special efforts. It is good to know that there are still people in this world who go that extra mile to help undo a wrong. I am also very glad that Jeanine was able to avoid losing a very significant amount of money. I spoke with her late yesterday afternoon, then we got cut off, and I was unable to call her back due to getting pulled into meetings non-stop for the rest of the day. On behalf of all Air New Zealand, thanks again for stepping up to the plate on this issue.

Unfortunately, things all went into the proverbial handbasket from there. Air NZ Reservations still couldn't tell me anything about the celebrities. They informed me they don't keep track of who actually boards the flights, but their computer still indicated that the Kiwi's tickets had been cancelled.[1] Abbey checked in; she hadn't heard anything from the actors, but she emailed them to explain what happened. In a sad but steady voice, she told me she didn't understand exactly what had gone on, but she and Jordan were taking full responsibility for everything.

Abbey's next call was not quite so upbeat. She had just spoken to an angry celebrity who was

---

[1] I've always wondered what the Homeland Security Department would say about the "not keeping track of who gets on the plane" part.

stranded at LAX, but had run out of coins at the payphone before she could even find out which one he was. We had no way to reach him, and for all we knew, he wasn't alone. This was a job for a travel agent.

"This is Donna, how may I help you?"

"Hi, it's Jeanine. We gotta problem. At least one of those guys made the flight last night," I said hurriedly.

"Oh, boy. Let's see." Clickity-clack. "The plane landed, so now I can see a passenger manifest. Paul Randall, Jed Brophy, and Brian Sergent. There's no Lawrence Makaore. Well, that's good news, at least."

Clickity-clack. "They tried to make their connection to Portland on United Airlines. They were denied," Donna continued.

Clickity-clack. "Looks like they tried to check in at Alaska too."

Ugh. The Kiwis were wandering through the airport, trying to make their connection, with no idea there was none to be made.

Time for one more round with Air NZ Reservations. I pitied the poor lady, Kirsten, who answered my call. It took half an hour to explain the situation and let her verify it with Rebecca Weaver. She finally got back to me and said Rebecca would alert the Air NZ staff at LAX to intercept the travelers.

I called Abbey and suggested we might as well go through with Tentmoot, since the actors were here after all. She said that was impossible. Bob had been furious when he heard the news, and had cancelled all the bands and volunteers. We now had celebrities, but nothing else.

Between Donna, Rebecca, and Abbey, the phone never had a chance to cool down all day. We finally gathered that the Kiwis had checked into a hotel and Rebecca and Kirsten would try to arrange a return trip that wasn't on my nickel. It looked like I would have to pay for their flights to the States, but Rebecca was optimistic either Air NZ or New Line would help to bring them home.

I expected to hear something from Rebecca or Kirsten the next day—which was December 11, 2003, the opening day for Tentmoot. I didn't hear a peep all day, but I thought they deserved some slack; it was going to take time to sort out a flub of this magnitude. Abbey called that morning with good news: the Kiwis were in better spirits. She took them sightseeing in Hollywood and they were trying to enjoy themselves a bit. Furthermore, a friend in San Dimas offered them a vacant condo to stay in until they flew home. The Kiwis hadn't brought much spending money, since they expected to be wined and dined as guests of honor at Tentmoot. Brian was bunking with a relative, and now Jed and Paul had a free place to sleep, too.

Over on BoE.net, seven people (including Zinnia) posted resignations from BoE on the Prancing Pony. Oddly, though, there weren't very many indignant comments about the cancellation of Tentmoot. At some point on the 10th, Abbey posted a very inadequate message on the Tentmoot page, simply stating that Tentmoot was off, explanations would have to wait, and tickets could be returned for a full refund at Ticketweb. I expected the Pony to be aflame with angry complaints and demands for more information, but the message boards were quiet as a church basement on Bingo night between calls. Even the Tentmoot mailing list was calm.

When I hadn't heard anything from Air NZ by Friday morning, December 12, 2003, I thought it was time to get a little more proactive. I ended up talking to a fellow named Eddie at something called "The Prepaid Desk." Eddie explained Air NZ didn't do electronic ticketing, so what I actually bought through Donna were four paper tickets. The celebs picked these up when they checked in, and they were actually vouchers good for travel at any time in the next calendar year. The intent was to apply the vouchers specifically to the reservations I had made—and it was only those *reservations* that were cancelled on the computer. The paper tickets were still good, which is why they were honored when the travelers came up to the gate.

Well, what about Lawrence Makaore? Eddie said Lawrence had not checked in when the reservation was cancelled, so Air NZ never gave him his paper ticket. The full cost of that ticket would be refunded to me (minus a $75 fee); in fact, he was working on that right when I called.

I started scratching my pointy head. If those paper tickets were a done deal, and were good for travel at any time, why didn't Air NZ just give Lawrence his paper ticket when he came to the airport? Eddie told me Lawrence could use his paper ticket for any flight—so why did the check-in clerk tell Lawrence his travel was cancelled? Obviously the clerk must have understood that the entire *ticket* had been revoked, not just the particular *flight reservation*. But if the airport staff recognized that Lawrence wasn't supposed to fly *at all*, why didn't they also stop the other guys who were traveling with him? Lawrence (who was cast as an *Uruk-hai* for a *reason*) made it known LOUD AND CLEAR at the check-in desk that his friends were probably already back at the gate. There was more than a mere whiff of fish in the air.

Rebecca must have smelled it too, because she was no longer acting like one of those "people in this world who go that extra mile to help undo a wrong." She now maintained this was pretty much all my problem. I reminded her Donna cancelled the tickets because she spoke directly to Air NZ and was told the travelers hadn't checked in. It can hardly be my fault (and my expense!) that Air NZ couldn't tell whether or not their customers had checked in. If it was too late to cancel the tickets, then Air NZ had no business offering Donna the option!

Rebecca reacted by going into Hostile Corporate Defense mode, interrupting me when I got too close to making a point, and trying to divert me with irrelevant questions. I countered with Doctor Renne mode, which I used to use on belligerent patients in the Emergency Room[2]. I finally forced her to admit Air NZ just *may* be responsible for part of the mess, since they failed to notify Donna it was too late to cancel the tickets. Rebecca said this was beyond her authority and she would have to "forward the whole thing to the main office" to get this resolved. She refused to provide me with contact information for those folks, or a time frame in which I could expect an answer to this issue, and ended the conversation abruptly, saying she had to go to a meeting.

Well, well, well. It was pretty clear Air NZ thought they could bully a housewife from Oregon into shouldering those airfares. I wondered if Kiwis,

---

[2] Of course, this mode was even more effective when I had a rhinoceros needle in my hand and the patient was strapped to a gurney.

beloved national celebrities from the movie that put New Zealand on the map, could extract a different answer out of Air NZ.

Abbey answered my phone call with news that Kiwis were not so cheery today. The condo deal fell through—the friend's ex-wife had emptied it since he'd last checked it—so Jed and Paul spent the night at the BoE apartment. Jed slept on Sue's flimsy little camping bedroll on the floor. *ON THE FLOOR.* I asked if I could talk to Jed or Paul, and although Abbey icily refused to let me speak privately, she did put me through on Speakerphone. I explained the situation to them as best I could—that their paper tickets were good for travel, but if they used them, I would have to pay for it all. I was honest about not getting much help so far from Air NZ but told them I would keep working on it if they could wait a little longer. The connection was bad, I could barely hear anyone, but apparently they could hear me; Abbey said they would discuss things and get back to me with a decision.

About an hour later, I finally got a call from someone I could trust: Sue. And boy, did she have a story for me! Tentmoot had been collapsing on all fronts.

There were *only* 28 tickets sold in advance—not "800 on the will call list" like Jordan had told me.[3]

---

[3] Amy also stated this in writing to the Oregon Convention Center, when they learned from Bob and Sue that 28 tickets had been sold to Tentmoot as of December 5, 2003. Amy said Bob and Sue had misunderstood the readout from Ticketweb, because this readout "does not include holds in calculation." Amy explained to the OCC that this meant Ticketweb only reported "shipped" tickets, not tickets that were being "held," i.e. tickets that were purchased but would be picked up at the will-call desk. In fact, the Ticketweb statement simply referrred to which tickets it used to calculate the percentage sold. Thus

That certainly explained the lack of rioting on the website! There weren't any disappointed ticketholders to complain about the cancellation! The Convention Center was going to cost $4,500 a day, not "a percentage of the door." They also weren't supplying any free AV equipment—Jordan accepted their rental bid for $9,200! Sue pounded the pavement to set up a "merch room" for Tentmoot, but most of the vendors that expressed interest changed their minds when they saw the ticket sales. Another volunteer, Brit, spent hours on the phone asking shops to donate goodies for prizes at Tentmoot, but had only three takers—who were not happy to learn that BoE's non-profit ID number "wouldn't be available until January."

Della really arranged for a few TV and radio stations to come to Tentmoot and do promotions, despite receiving the press releases at the eleventh hour. Lawrence, Jed, and Kiran cooked up a wonderful plan to perform a mock fight and then teach a workshop about doing the stunts from their demonstration. Bob really set up bands to play. But that was *it*. There was no shopping, no workshops, no panels, and *no customers*. Tentmoot had been doomed long before, and Sue had been begging Abbey and Amy for weeks to cancel it. She found out about the cancellation when she happened to glanced at BoE.net and discovered Abbey's post. Then she got my "goddammit" letter and learned for the first time about the travel fiasco . . .

Which wrapped up at 9:00 PM, December 12th, when Abbey sent me an email saying the Kiwis just caught a flight home on Air NZ.

---

she incorporated an element of truth in her lie, making it apppear more credible.

THE BIRTH OF A KLINGON

I knew I would get no more help from Abbey or Rebecca, so I filed a complaint on Monday, December 15, 2003 at the Air NZ website, to dispute the ticket charges. I also put in a call to Detective Myers. He had told me long ago that he would check in on "Jordan," to make sure "he" was staying on the straight and narrow. Obviously, neither of those adjectives applied here. To Myers' credit, although he must have felt vindicated Miss SmartyPants Housewife had been wrong all along, he never rubbed my nose in it.

I knew "Jordan" was coming back up to Portland. "He" and Abbey still wanted to go to the ROTK premiere at their old haunting grounds, despite the Tentmoot disaster. Bob and Sue had no intention of returning to San Dimas, so they ordered Abbey and "Jordan" to bring up all of their personal items (particularly Sue's bedroll, which served as Jed's luxury accommodations). I explained all this to Myers. He told me to call him back if I ever pinpointed a specific location for "Jordan," as he would like to have a little talk with "him." I told Bob and Sue to get in touch with me if "Jordan" showed up on the doorstep with their stuff.

I was chatting online with MissTree when Bob called me at 10:00 Monday night. His voice was an excited whisper; it seems that Amy and Abbey were unloading his things from their van right there in his driveway—and Bob was standing in front of a uniformed policeman, Officer McCormick of the Portland Police Bureau.

"'Jordan' told this cop 'he' had to return my things, but 'he' was scared I might get violent," explained Bob. "'*Jordan*' asked the *cop* to come here. Do you believe this?!"

"Lemme talk to the cop," I said.

At first, the officer didn't want to take the phone, but Bob knew he had to persuade McCormick to talk to me, or face alone the irresistible force that was *me on a mission*.

I told the officer, "Listen, about those two in the van, one of them is named Amy Player. I talked to the sheriff here today. He said when she showed up, he wanted to know about it. Please, just check her out on your computer, there should be something in there about her."

While McCormick surfed the police web in his cruiser, Bob spoke of the cold December night. He was outside in his shirtsleeves, freezing, but didn't dare go in at this point, not even for a second. I IM'ed MissTree with updates as fast as I could type. Bob took a closer look at his cell phone, which had just been returned to him by Abbey; he realized Sean Astin's phone number, which Sean gave to Bob at Project Elanor, was deleted.

Finally, the officer returned to tell Bob all he could find was some old missing person report under the name Amy Player. Bob once again forced McCormick to take the phone, lest my fury cause his cell phone to combust.

"Officer, you need to speak directly to Detective Myers of the Marion County Sheriff. I don't know what he had planned, but it must not be in the computer yet."

I gave McCormick the pager number from Myers' business card, the same card I'd pulled from my screen door a lifetime ago. McCormick reluctantly agreed to page him. Over the sounds of Bob's chattering teeth, I could hear the officer's phone ring, and I crossed my fingers and listened to the play-by-play from Bob.

"Okay, he's moved over by his car. I can't hear him anymore. Damn, I'm freezing. I wish I had my coat. Now he's heading over to the van. He's talking to 'Jordan.' Asking 'him' to step out of the car. Jordan's getting out. They're talking. Abbey's still in the car. *He's arresting 'Jordan!'* He's got out the handcuffs. YES! He's walking 'Jordan' over to his car. In you go, bitch. Don't bonk your head! Now he's going back to the van. He's talking to Abbey. Ooh, look at 'Jordan.' The handcuffs are hurting. That's right, bitch. Squirm around a little. It won't help."

I couldn't type the IMs fast enough. MissTree was on AutoSquee and so was I.

Bob had his and Sue's possessions from LA. Amy was in handcuffs. The next day was the big Line Party for ROTK. It looked like "Jordan" would spend the grand opening of the movie, the one we all waited years to see, in jail.

CRUCIO! Best served cold, indeed.

THE AFTERMATH

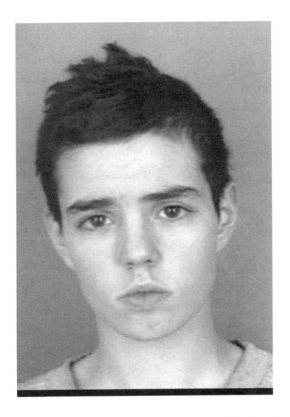

Booking photo for Amy Player, courtesy of Marion County, Oregon, Sheriff's Office.

Alas, the overcrowded Women's Division of the Marion County Correctional Facility just couldn't keep Ms. Amy Player, aka Jordan Wood, aka Victoria Bitter, for more than nine hours. Myers interrogated her, let her sweat a bit, but he eventually had to cut her loose. She got sprung from the slammer in time to make it to the Line Party.

Amy and Abbey arrived just in time for John and Talisha's wedding, which was held in the parking lot of the cinema. Rob Bob, the theater manager, put up a lighted tent just for the ceremony. Sue and I scrambled that afternoon to deck it out with colored lights and candles; it was hardly the beautiful Convention Center, but we all made the best out of what we had. The cold and damp couldn't quench the radiant bride or the lovestruck groom, and though the setting lacked fancy frills, it had plenty of genuine warmth.

We even acted with cold civility towards Abbey and Amy, for the sake of the bride and groom; after having their wedding pulled right out from under them, they certainly didn't need a brawl during the ceremony. Abbey and Amy mugged for the news cameras that showed up to film this übergeek celebration, but the camera guys were more interested in those of us in costume—not just disguised as male.

Tentmoot had come to an end, but the exposé was only beginning. Over the next two months, the Prancing Pony became a hotbed of information, as people learned of the scandals and came forward with their own stories, dating all the way back to Project Elanor. Some, like MissTree, tried to post their grievances earlier, but these always disappeared immediately. But this time around, "Ninja," the tech guru and SQL database manager of the Prancing Pony message board, eliminated Abbey and Amy's deleting privileges, so everyone at last had a chance to tell their stories.

Three weeks later, when Bob booted up his computer (which was returned to him that cold December night), he found "MrFrodo" had left open her connections to the Tentmoot email box and BoE's private message system. Suddenly we all had access to the original documents Amy sent to all the celebrities, businesses, and volunteers involved in Tentmoot. We'd caught the express train right into the Grand Central Station of lies.

With the firsthand correspondence, reports from dozens of outraged people, and contact information for all the parties involved, I was able to slowly piece together just how Abbey and "Jordan" fooled everyone. Along the way, I learned new terms like "headdesk," "wank," and "pastede on." I met trolls who were smugly delighted to tell me what an idiot I was for falling for such an "obvious scam." I met sardonic strangers that made me laugh so hard it gave me the strength to ignore the trolls. Friends became enemies, acquaintances became friends, and help turned up in unexpected places and forms. The Pony and my new LiveJournal became a microcosm of all that is finest in humanity, even as they detailed the banality of the common sociopath.

Wanna take a look?

AIR NEW ZEALAND

After assuring everyone for months that the Tentmoot travel arrangements were taken care of, Amy finally set to work on Air NZ.

Date: Fri, 28 Nov 2003 19:51:14
From: "Tentmoot 2003"
Subject: Rings fans need a miracle

To whom it may concern-

WHO WE ARE
BitofEarth.net has grown from a 17-member online mailing list to the world's fastest growing Tolkien fan group in less than two years, and successfully completed a wide variety of projects in cooperation with the creative forces behind the Lord of the Rings trilogy. You can see more about our organization and what we do officially at our website: *http://www.bitofearth.net*

Unofficially, our core staff are a group of six individuals who have had our lives profoundly changed by the Lord of the Rings trilogy and are trying to give back (see attached article from the Oregon Herald to get a better idea of WHO we are).

WHY WE'RE NOT JUST ANOTHER FAN CLUB
We feel that love has come to be far too defined as money - the best fan is just the one with the biggest collection of merchandise and fanciest costume. We believe that this needs to change...that fans need to contribute to their culture, not just consume it.

Peter Jackson and the cast and crew of the Rings trilogy epitomized this spirit in the amazing dedication they showed to bringing Peter's fannishness to beautifully realized life. Using that inspiration, we are harnessing the energy and resources of fandom to community service and charity fundraising projects.

By far our most audactious so far is TentMoot 2003 (tentmoot.bitofearth.net) taking place from December 11-15 at the Oregon Convention Center in Portland. We have managed to get over 50 vendors, the largest venue in the Northwest, and almost 20 celebrities to work with us to raise money for Reading is Fundamental and Future Forests in a completely grass-roots fan effort...but we now find this in jeopardy.

Over half of our celebrities are flying in from New Zealand...and we have just lost our airfare.

WHAT WE NEED
A donation of airfare: round trip from Aukland to Portland, OR for the following individuals, departing December 10 and with return dates listed in dividually:
Lawrence Makoare-Dec 18
Sala Baker- Dec 15
Brian Sergant-Dec 15
Bret McKenzie-Dec 19
Matt McLeod-Dec 19
Rich Christie-Dec 19
Shannon Williams-Dec 19
Daniel Weetman -Dec 19
Barnaby Wier-Dec 19
MichaelAugust-Dec 19
Lee Prebble- Dec19
Alexis French - Dec 20

Also, two craftsmen, one each from Weta Workshop and Weta Digital. Weta does not know who they will be sending until at most the day before they fly, due to the insanity of the schedule over there at the moment. Is there any way to get corporate tickets that they could pick up with their Weta ID and a letter from BitofEarth saying that yes, they're the appropriate technicians?

WHY SUCH SHORT NOTICE?
We had secured a donation of airfare from a local businesswoman who is the mother of one of our staff members and owner of Wenatchee Nail, one of the largest hardware wholesalers in the state of Washington. Unfortunately, her husband just filed for divorce this week, and the business and all her personal assets are now frozen pending the lawyers assessment.

This puts us in a very difficult position, as it is far too late to throw any extra fundraisers, so quite honestly, we are now crossing our fingers and praying for a miracle. Of course, the production itself is infamous for it's own generous share of miracles, and BitofEarth has seemed to inherit that luck, perhaps through our own pure stubborn ness,so we have hope...

WHAT CAN WE DO FOR YOU?
You will be displayed on all of our advertisements and promotional materials, and we will place a link to Air New Zealand on the website permanently. In addition, we would like to offer you a display table free of charge *http://tentmoot.bitofearth.net/moot/merchants.html* where you may promote your beautiful country and exceptional service to over 1,000 convention attendees per day. Rings fans are currently the

#1 tourist draw to New Zealand, and this would give you a great opportunity to connect with many of them in a very hands-on fashion. You would also be displayed prominently on the event t-shirt and thanked explicitly and profusely at the beginning and end of each celebrity appearance. Please help us make a miracle happen.

With Hope
Jordan Wood
Celebrity and Media Relations Director

This letter has been reproduced in its entirety, right down to the grammatical errors and typos. Surprisingly, this particular letter does not state BoE is a non-profit entity, but it does manage to align BoE with RIF and Future Forests. These names were used without the agencies' permission.

Diane is the owner of the hardware chain Amy cited. Her husband Jeff (they were not in mid-divorce as claimed) confirmed Amy had indeed asked them for a half-million dollars. Jeff explained he just laughed in her face. Abbey even slipped and admitted to me that the core staff had discussed that option, but it never got off the drawing board.

Air NZ responded politely and clearly with this letter:

1 December 2003

Dear Jordan

REQUEST FOR FLIGHT ASSISTANCE

Thank you for your letter requesting help from Air New Zealand for flights from Portland to Auckland return. I'm sorry to hear about the loss of your previous sponsor and her position.

We unfortunately must advise you we are unable to assist on this occasion.

While we are involved in a number of sponsorships of national non-profit bodies and organisations, we are unable to consider, at this stage, those requests outside our annual sponsorship commitments. Our website, *www.airnz.co.nz* has further information on sponsorship and the process for applications.

Again, I apologise that we cannot be of more assistance and wish you all the very best with fundraising to attend the events in New Zealand.

Yours sincerely
Sue Hart
Communications Co-Ordinator
Public Affairs

According to an email from Jenny Simpson, Amy called Ms Hart on December 1, 2003, after receiving the rejection letter. Amy "asked if there was anyone else in the airline she could talk to. Sue responded that it would fall into her department and we didn't have the budget to cover this." Amy must have spent the rest of the night inventing the tale of the organ donor tickets, which she dished out to me the next day.

Looking back, I knew better than to believe that story. No one knows when organs will become available for donation. That depends on all kinds of random factors like need, histocompatibility, and a helmetless motorcycle rider in the wrong place at the wrong time[4]. There was no way Air NZ could predict there would be exactly six organ donations in the month of December. At the time, though, I was caught up in outrage that Air NZ appeared to be screwing us so callously, and dismay that this festival I'd been waiting for was threatened. It didn't really register that Amy was saying something that didn't add up. It was just a detail that flew by in an overwhelming rush of other information.

The fact that Amy's story contained details such as the organ donor business was what made it all sound plausible. Real stories are always rich with odd or irrelevant information, like, "My husband went to lunch at the cafeteria just like every other day and ran smack into Maureen, whom we hadn't seen in seven years. She was supposed to be my maid of honor but she got cancer two weeks before the wedding, and we didn't even know she moved here from California."

If Amy said only, "Uh, gee, they promised us free tickets and then, uh, they changed their minds," even *I* would know that was a crock. So she embellished it, charged it with emotion, put a little sugar on it so I'd take the bait.

On December 16, 2003, someone from Air NZ Legal declared they had no responsibility to inform me about the check-in status of the travelers or to inform the travelers there was a problem with their tickets. I told him that was not an acceptable answer, but he refused to discuss it further. He insisted Air NZ would charge me the full amount for their tickets: $9,830.70.

My attorney, Mike, wholeheartedly disagreed with Air NZ's conclusion. Air NZ had two hours to

---

[4] This, by the way, is why emergency room physicians refer to these as "donorcycles."

inform the travelers there was a fraud associated with their tickets. Mike felt Air NZ had a legal and ethical obligation to do what they could to mitigate the damages to all concerned: to me, the actors, and themselves! On my attorney's advice, I disputed the charges with my credit cards. If Air NZ thought they deserved payment, they were going to have to convince a jury exactly why *I* owed them money when *they* let three travelers fly on cancelled tickets.

It took some time and a number of formal letters from my attorney, but eventually both of my credit cards sided in my favor and removed all of the charges for the airfares. I braced myself for the inevitable trip to court, in the case of *Oregon Housewife v. Multimillion Dollar International Corporation*. But then the unexpected happened:

I got an irate letter from Donna the Travel Agent, because Air NZ turned around and charged *her* for Jed, Paul and Brian's tickets!

AIR NEW ZEALAND	Debit Memo	Memo Number 8960 180782		
Collections Department		Memo Date 4Feb04		
helena.aaker@airnz.com		Agency Number 2452301		CK 5
1960 East Grand Av Suite 900, El Segundo CA 90245		Ticket Number 0868573295130		
Fax: 310 648 7117		Date of Ticket Validation 9Dec03		
Phone: 310 648 7166		Your Report Period Ending 14Dec03		
If you have information which amends or cancels this debit, FAX details along with a copy of the ADM to 0600 737 077. NO phone calls will be accepted by the Fare Audit Team. All items NOT formally disputed within 21 days of the date of the Memo will be included on your next available bi-monthly Billing Analysis.				
Raised by: Air NZ Fare Audit		Passenger RANDALL/PAUL		
Reason for Memo:	Replacement Fare	Print Number 1 Original Issuing Unit aakerh LAX		
Frbk 00		Correct Computation		
We have been debited by mastercard for $6222.90. Transaction was processed without obtaining authorization. Please settle this adm with your agency check.		From/To	Via	Fare
	C2R	AKL/LAX	NZ	6099.00
		Total		6099.00

Donna spent eight hours putting together the airline tickets for BoE, with all of those date and guest list changes. She contacted Air NZ directly to apprise them of the emergency cancellation (even though they knew very well what was going on, since Rebecca and Jenny and other executives were actively involved all day). After all her work, she made no commission on the sale because it was cancelled. To top it all off, Air NZ sent her the bill for the travel, saying it was her responsibility because she didn't get my signature. Not theirs, for allowing three out of four people to fly on cancelled tickets, but Donna's, for not getting my signature on the credit card authorization.

Sue and I discussed this with Ted Stewart, Air NZ's "repo man" at the Baker, Govern & Baker Collections agency. He explained that by accepting this sort of transaction over the telephone without a signature, Donna had violated some rule of trade and was therefore liable for the charges. Air NZ was making a legal complaint that Donna did not obtain the necessary credit authorization.

Furthermore, as a travel agent, Donna had signed a standard industry contract in which she agreed to ensure payment for all fares she booked with Air NZ. In the world of legalese and business contracts, they were within their rights to hold her liable for the cost of the airfares.

That was all fine and good, but when it came down to *Right v. Wrong*, it seemed to me the folks who didn't stop three out of four travelers from using a cancelled ticket were a *tad* more at fault than the lady who didn't get the bill signed. Although Ted talked Air NZ into discounting the bill to $7,800, this was still a hefty chunk of change.

Air NZ gave Donna the choice of paying off the bill or losing all future business with them. This would not only take away a significant portion of her tourist travel business, but would also leave an ugly mark on her otherwise immaculate 30-year business record. They had her on the signature issue and Donna could not afford to lose her right to book travel on Air NZ. Her only choice was to pay up.

Allow me to summarize the salient points:

1. Air New Zealand refused to accept any responsibility for flying three LOTR celebrities across the ocean on cancelled tickets.

2. By disputing the airfares on my credit card, I invited them to sue me in court, to let a jury determine who was at fault here. Was it me, for purchasing the tickets and canceling them two hours before the flight, or was it Air NZ for permitting the cancellation, confirming they received the cancellation, stopping one of the travelers, but letting the other three fly anyway?

3. Rather than take me to court and lay all this out before a judge, Air NZ used a legal loop hole to dump the bill on the travel agent, who performed exemplary and thoughtful service to everyone involved.

More concisely: **Air New Zealand screwed the travel agent who sold me the tickets and threatened her business if she didn't pay up and shut up.**

Ultimately the fault for all of this belongs to the people who created this nightmare in the first place: Abigail Stone and Amy Player, aka Jordan Wood, aka Victoria Bitter. They were the ones who claimed

BoE was a non-profit entity; who used the name of legitimate charities like RIF without permission in order to gain support for phony fundraising events, for the purpose of attracting movie stars, so the two of them could indulge in some idiotic fantasy. However, suing the two of them would be what is known as "throwing good money after bad." They have no assets to seize, no wages to garnish, no money in the bank (at least that anyone knows of) to pay a judgement. They might be dead in the water in a courtroom, but what good would that do if there was no way to wring the money out of them? The airfare money would still be gone and the legal fees would just go tumbling after. Thus, the financial consequences of the air travel debacle came down to Air NZ, Donna, and me—and look who got the shaft.

But that wasn't all of Air NZ's noteworthy contributions. From talking to the travelers, I found out much later they tried desperately to get home after they found themselves sleeping on the floor of Abbey and Amy's filthy apartment. They understood me on the speakerphone that fateful morning and realized I would be charged for both halves of their airfares if they used their paper tickets for a return flight. But when they asked Air NZ to get them home, the best Air NZ would offer them were regular price one-way tickets, at $2000 each.

Again, let me summarize: Jed Brophy, Paul Randall and Brian Sergent had just lived through a nightmare, which could have *easily* been prevented by Air NZ. These three gentlemen waited in the Auckland airport terminal for two hours after I cancelled their tickets, prior to boarding their flight. At any time during those two hours, Air NZ could have paged them to the ubiquitous white courtesy phone and informed them there was a problem. The gate agents could have given the actors that message when they tried to board the aircraft. The people in General Reservations could have made sure this happened. The executives in LA could have made sure this happened. The executives in Auckland could have made sure this happened. But it didn't happen. "Tall Paul," "Snaga the Orc," and "Ted Sandyman" twiddled their thumbs in the airport for two hours with cancelled tickets rustling in their pockets and no one attempted to notify them. Then Air NZ declined to offer them a lift home.

When I talked to Ted the Repo Man, I pointed out these gentlemen all had speaking roles in the LOTR films, the same films that made New Zealand a worldwide tourism destination. In my mind, these gentlemen were, in a small but significant way, directly responsible for bringing in millions—if not billions—of dollars to Air NZ. I asked Ted if he really thought, under the circumstances, it would be in the best interests of his client to hound me, Donna, or the travelers themselves, for $10,000 in airfares. Ted said he would discuss that consideration with his client. The next thing I heard was that Air NZ reduced their total bill to Donna.

But the ticket agent at Air NZ apparently didn't see it that way when Paul, Jed, and Brian came straggling into LAX, exhausted from their ordeal without a penny left in their pockets. These gentlemen had no option but to use their paper tickets, sealing the deal for the total cost of the airfare.

One final point worth noting: These poor blokes spent roughly five hours drifting through LAX after their flight arrived on December 10, 2003. They tried to make their connection to Portland on several airlines, as they had no idea why the flight numbers listed on their itinerary were invalid. They tried to reach Abbey, but had trouble with the pay phone. After flying halfway around the world, they were reduced to wandering through the airport like lost waifs.

Fortunately, a compassionate lady at the airline desk said she could offer them some help through their "Stranded Travelers" program. They each were given a room at the nearby Sheraton hotel at a substantial discount, something around $50 a night for a room that normally goes for $200. The three stars from LOTR each got the priceless gift of a bed, a shower, and a phone to reach Abbey and finally get to the bottom of things, courtesy of . . .

. . . brace for impact . . .

United Airlines.

The airline originally booked for the stars' connection to Portland. The airline that never got a penny of their business, because the tickets on United were cancelled far enough in advance there wasn't even a service fee. The "Friendly Skies" apparently include friendly airports as well, because United had no particular reason to help these fellows out, other than the fact they were stranded and miserable and it was a really nice thing to do. A nice thing that apparently never occurred to Air NZ.

Makes you want to fly Qantas, doesn't it?

THE SUICIDE ATTEMPT

Clarification: Amy has faked many suicides, but this chapter refers only to the alleged attempt on December 9, 2003, after the cancellation of the airfares.

The threatened loss of $10,000 has a profoundly nerve-wracking effect on someone who is a tad high-strung under the best of circumstances. I therefore kept detailed notes every day after the Crash and wrote down as much as I could remember about the events leading up to it. I then organized my lists by cross-checking the events against time stamps on emails and the long-distance charges on my phone bill. In short, I compiled a record of Tentmoot Crash of suitable precision to gain a spot in the Anal Retentive Hall of Fame.

I called "Jordan" to demand an accounting of "his" story at 3:49 PM on December 9, 2003. "He" was supposed to call back in 30 minutes with the name of the person who would prove "he" had not lied about the free tickets. At 4:26 PM, I called again and reached the teenager, who indicated "Jordan" was locked in the bathroom. By 4:52 PM, I had been transferred to every empty office at Air NZ headquarters and tried "Jordan" again. No answer. I called their cell phone (which has caller ID), and got no answer. I made a final attempt at 5:15 PM: no answer. When Abbey checked in with news of the suicide attempt, I guessed it must have happened at 4:45 PM or thereabouts, when they stopped answering the phone.

Unbeknownst to me, Bob was also checking in with BoE headquarters that evening. I knew Sue flew to Portland in November, 2003, to take care of local details, and I had been told Bob was in Portland, too. I had no reason to believe otherwise; nothing indicated that Bob was in the apartment when I talked to Abbey or "Jordan" on the phone.

In fact, Bob was in San Dimas the whole time and flew up to Portland on December 9, 2003. Of course, Bob had observed "Jordan" discussing the travel arrangements, but was never told there were problems with the funding. No wonder Amy always picked up the phone on the first ring.

On December 9, Bob arrived at LAX around 3:00 PM. He bummed around, had a snack, then decided to call home just before boarding his 3:50 flight. When Bob explained this, I suddenly recalled the other phone ringing in the background while I was ripping "Jordan" a new orifice.

Abbey told Bob all hell was breaking loose, because I had suddenly cancelled the celebrity travel. She told Bob to check back in, as they were still in the recovery phase. There was nothing for Bob to do but hang up and numbly board his flight.

Bob's jet landed in San Francisco at 4:50 PM, and he plowed down the jetway to hit a payphone before boarding his connecting flight. He reached BoE at 5:00 PM, and was told yes, the travel was screwed up, but Abbey and Amy were taking care of things. Thus, at the same time they were ignoring my phone calls, they picked up for Bob and indicated things were under control.

By 7:00 PM, Bob arrived in Portland, checked in, and heard "Jordan" was in the hospital. Sue confirmed with neighbors that an ambulance arrived and carted "Jordan" away at some time that evening.

I garnered the impression, based on their failure to answer the phone, that "Jordan" attempted suicide at 4:45 PM on December 9. At 5:00 PM, however, Abbey reassured Bob that things were under control. It is pretty unlikely anything was under control, since, at that point, Amy had less than two hours to come up with $18,000 in airfares.

Amy was found by the paramedics in a pool of vomit containing some partially dissolved pills. She appeared to be unconscious, but apparently the paramedics were not impressed by the depth of her "coma." There were no sedatives in the house at the time of the attempt, a fact confirmed that night by Abbey and later by Bob. There was nothing, therefore, that would have led to loss of consciousness. In fact, there were only aspirin, Advil, vitamins, and Tylenol. While it is possible to kill oneself with those drugs, it takes more than a few pills that are vomited up before being digested.

How interesting. No body, no lethal weapon, inconsistent symptoms, and an inconsistent timeline of events. Something tells me this "tragedy" was no more than a drama.

THE CREDIT CARD CON

A number of people had comments to make about the events of December 9, 2003.

- **Zinnia**: When I became aware that Turimel charged her credit cards for the airline tickets for tentmoot, I got a call from Abbey asking me to do the same (actually, she mentioned "holding" the tickets on my credit card until the Tentmoot funds were released after their nonprofit number came through). She also asked me give her contact information for other ponypals, which I refused to do.
- **Primrose**: I did get a credit-card requesting call from them about then. She told me it was only to "hold" though in my case it was supposedly a requirement for band instrument rentals the first call and for airfare the second call.
- **Della**: On the Monday before Tentmoot started, Orangeblossom called and said that New Zealand Air had canceled the tickets they promised for the celebrities. She said that the tickets were canceled because BofE would not be officially non-profit until the 15th of Jan. Orangeblossom said that if they had a credit card to hold that they would fly everyone over. I refused to give her my credit card number. It just didn't feel right and even though she said my credit card wouldn't have been charged, "just held" I was uncomfortable with the plan.
- **Voontah**: Somebody from BOE also called me early in December for my credit card number for the flights. Luckily I'm naturally suspicious and didn't give it.
- **Tini**: OB also called me with the same story about the non-profit status and that my credit card would be "held". I took that to mean that it was a

back-up plan rather like co-signing a loan for someone... it didn't really matter to me what she called it, I was not going to do it. I said "I'm afraid my credit card would not do you much good... it doesn't do *me* much good!". She did not press the matter after that. She definitely stated that my card would not be charged, just "held"...

I was crystal clear with Amy that I needed credit card numbers to *pay for* the remaining domestic airline tickets. Amy told me they would call BoE members and get credit card numbers for that purpose. Abbey contacted these five people (plus who knows how many more), intending to charge their cards to the limit with airfares and told them they *would not be billed.*

Do you suppose when these folks got their bills and saw all those airline charges, they would call Abbey in a fury, only to be told poor Abbey didn't have anything to do with it, that nasty Turimel (me) must have billed the cards?

FLIGHT OF THE KIWIS

So just how *did* Abbey and Amy manage to drag three movie stars halfway around the world to their door? Why, the typical smoke and mirrors, of course! They got their foot in the door via Lawrence Makoare. Their initial contacts are not in the Tentmoot mailbox, so it's hard to say how they talked him into it. Amy is very good at begging without looking like she's begging. Lawrence could not be reached for comment prior to this printing.

By November 19, 2003 they were using Lawrence's private email address and were on first-name basis with him. Once Amy developed a somewhat casual, friendly relationship with Lawrence, she used him to put the moves on Paul Randall and Sala Baker. On December 5, 2003, she told Lawrence, "We have been trying to follow up on Sala and Paul, but have been unable to get through to their representation. Would you mind re-sending their email addresses?"

Lawrence had already mentioned Tentmoot to his friends. He knew they were interested in more information, so he gave Amy their personal email addresses to circumvent those oh-so-unhelpful representatives. Within minutes, Amy dashed off letters to each of them.

To Sala Baker: I spoke to your manager, Mr. Joiner, about this approximately 5-6 weeks ago. He said that you would be happy to come. I have tried several times to contact him since then and clarify the details, but he has not returned my messages, and has never answered the phone at his office. The day before yesterday, Lawrence, whom we have been working with directly, delivered quite the bombshell. He said he had talked to you at the premiere and that you knew nothing about this[5].

To Paul Randall: I was unable to find any representation for you, and finally spoke to Three Foot Six who said they had contacted you and that you were not interested. The day before yesterday, Lawrence, whom we have been working with directly, delivered quite the bombshell. He said he had talked to you at the premiere and that you knew nothing about this. And that you *were* interested.

The Jason Joiner story is probably hogwash, but Amy really had emailed 3 Foot 6. They didn't give her any information, but she enhanced that fact a little in her letter to Paul. As she undoubtedly intended, Paul was a bit indignant that "someone at 3 foot 6" turned down the initial offer without even consulting him. He had never been to a fan convention, and despite the late date, he thought it might be a fun "opportunity into that whole world." He also liked the concept that his appearance would raise money for charity. His friend Lawrence was going, and he was able to get time off work, so he decided to go for the gusto.

Although Sala Baker could not be reached for comment, Bob confirmed Sala also liked the idea of hanging out with his friends at Tentmoot and the

---

[5] Amy had put this post script on an unrelated email dated 11/19/03: "We have also confirmed with Sala Baker, if you would like to coordinate your appearance for the same day." How interesting that Sala was contacted in October, confirmed in November, and heard about Tentmoot for the first time in December.

ROTK premiere. Sala called BoE on December 8, 2003, leaving a message that he was willing to come. Amy told me Sala was *so* excited about Tentmoot, he bought his own international ticket to LA, so all he needed was a flight to Portland.

As for the other Kiwis, Brian Sergent and his agent expressed interest in Tentmoot on November 26, 2003, presumably after receiving one of Amy's standard invitations. Jed Brophy heard about Tentmoot from his friend, Bruce Hopkins (Bruce's BoE mishap is recounted in a later chapter).

Like Lawrence, Bruce was going to Tentmoot and thought it would be fun to bring some friends. Jed agreed, and contacted BoE to see if he'd be welcome to join the party. Amy was so busy trying to ensnare the "big name" stars that she didn't even recognize Jed as an actor/stuntman and never posted his name on the guest list. She assumed he was from WETA Workshop and simply bragged that WETA was begging to send someone to Tentmoot.

Once Amy had these fellows on board, it was just a matter of getting their airline tickets. Lawrence and Paul were both leaning heavily on Amy for flight information and she strung them along as best she could.

•[The "donor"] has had a lot of confusion about the date line...what is OUR 10th vs. YOUR 10th, but since she is donating over $70,000 worth of airline vouchers...again, we haven't had a lot of choice.

• If it is not in my inbox when I finish sending this email, I am going to call Air NZ myself and not get off the phone until I have it, if I wind up needing to put it on my OWN credit card.

Per the last sentence: Yeah, Right! The ruse must have worked: all four of them showed up to fly to the States. Only three of them flew, though, and Lawrence was not a happy camper when he wrote to Abbey:

There better be a damn good reason WHY!!!! my ticket was cancelled when I got to the airport! I gave up a good paying job to do this for charity and now look what happened! Not only has my time been wasted going to and from the airport, but my family as well, who took me there only to turn around and come back and pick me up as soon as they got home. I live an hour away from the airport, and was so embarrassed when they came back that it just pisses me off!

I just hope my bro, Paul is alright. He was on the same plane and hoping to travel with me. I've emailed him and told him to get on the next plane back home. Same with Sala!

I really don't need to hear any crap about a last minute sponsor that failed to come through with the goods. Cause I feel that it's bullshit! It just boils down to Really, really BAD Management and organisational skills! You may think this is harsh, but believe me, if I was there in person, it would be a hell of a lot worse. This just takes the cake.

Despite the spike in his blood pressure, Lawrence was ultimately the lucky one. After Paul, Jed, and Brian landed in LA they were stuck at the airport for five hours, roaming from airline to airline and trying to find out what was going on. United Airlines finally put them up in the hotel, and after a rest, they took a walk through Hollywood with Abbey and Di. Abbey had boasted that she "took the boys sightseeing," but according to Jed, the boys gave her "no choice but to take us where we wanted to go as we were fairly pissed off by then."

When Abbey offered them the free condo, Jed & Paul were relieved by the prospect of a cheap place to stay. Brian's relative had a small apartment without enough room for all of them. They were completely unaware Sala Baker was frantically emailing and calling BoE to offer them a place to stay ever since Lawrence had told Sala they had gone without him.

Jed and Paul checked out of their hotel and waited hours for Abbey to pick them up in the van that Paul accurately described as "a rusty old piece of shit." She drove them back to San Dimas, then discovered the condo was not available after all[6]. Abbey was polite and friendly, so they decided to ride things out for the time being. They ended up buying dinner that night, since their "hostess" was utterly broke. Finally they decided to cut their losses and turn in for the night, only to discover their "bed" was the floor.

Believe it or not, it got worse! Amy was released from the hospital the next morning and attempted to cook breakfast. Jed and Paul were forced to buy everyone *yet another* meal after "Jordan"burned the bacon to charcoal. At that point, they'd had enough,

---

[6] Sue is certain there never was a condo. They had lived in San Dimas for all of two months and didn't know anyone in the area, much less someone with a spare condo to lend them.

and when I told them via Speakerphone they could get home with their paper tickets, they promptly made Abbey drive them back to LAX.

Jed and Paul confirmed Air NZ made no attempt to contact them as they waited in the Auckland airport before their trip. Paul was eventually reimbursed by BoE for his expenses in Los Angeles, but Jed only received about half of what he spent. Jed also told me,"We were led to believe you were responsible for the whole event falling over"

I had expected as much. In January, 2004, when I found Paul's email address in Tentmoot mailbox, I sent him a long explanation of what really happened. He replied:

> Thanks for the update - what a story!! Sorry I had to take the initiative and get us away from those mad people, thereby costing you the return flights. As for Jordan, we were confused about her/him the whole time. You certainly cleared that up.

Bless your sweet, tall heart, Paul. You're welcome.

SOAKING THE BLACK SEEDS

Photo used with permission from www.theblackseeds.com
(more photos—and music—available on the website).

Matt McLeod is the manager of a large reggae/ funk band called The Black Seeds. They are a red-hot, high-energy live act in New Zealand, but that wasn't what caught Amy's eye when she was lining up talent for Tentmoot. She was honed in on one of the musicians, Bret McKenzie, who became a fandom icon after his three-second portrayal of the delectable elf, "Figwit," at the Council of Elrond scene in FOTR. Bret's good looks were noticed by some very funny fangirls, who set up a snarky website in homage to the elf who made them sigh, in the middle of Frodo's grim acceptance of the burden of the One Ring, "Frodo is great...WHO IS THAT?" Bret became an unwitting LOTR celebrity, eventually earning a speaking part in ROTK.

Matt explained that in November, 2003, he received "the dream call from the states saying that

The Black Seeds and Figwit were to perform at Tentmoot." The prospect of opening up a whole new market for their music was naturally exciting, but Matt had some doubts.

> We realized that the costs of bringing a band over for just one show were extremely high and therefore never got our hopes too high. I always said 'we'll believe it when we get on the plane.'

> About 8 days before we left, I called Jordan (having still not received itineraries for our flights) to again %100 confirm that it was all still going ahead.

Of course, "Jordan" had a snappy reply.

> Back in early November, we got all the tickets for Kiwis donated from Air NZ. Five days ago, Air NZ called and said that they were very sorry, but with the huge rush of tourism for Return of the King, they were cutting back on the number of tickets they could give away. So we mustered the troops, scrambled like crazy, and managed to get a SECOND donation from a private travel agency, who ALSO agreed to fly everyone free of charge. They also weren't too keenly aware of the concept of an international date line.

> At 2:30 this afternoon our time, we got a call from the travel agent, asking for our tax number so they could write it off. We told them that our tax number was being processed by government, and would be re-issued on January 15. They then suddenly told us that we would have to secure it all on credit cards. IMMEDIATELY. Which meant coming up with $70,000 American in less than 12 hours.

We have called around like crazy, up to and including maxing out personal cards and calling in
well-off relatives, and have come up with about
$13,000 of it so far. This would be enough to fly
everyone, including Bret, EXCEPT for the Black
Seeds. We have a lot of screaming crazy Figwit
fans...

It's up to you where you want to go from here. If
you have any ideas, PLEASE, PLEASE share
them. ANY ideas, no matter how crazy, would be
welcome here.

Whew! That email was stuffed so full of lies, you
couldn't pack another lie in there with a crowbar.
Matt was pretty upset that Air NZ would treat them
all so callously (a familiar tune, *n'est ce pas?*).

We have 9 people who have re-organized the next
2 weeks of their lives for this trip. One thing I can
do is go to the papers tomorrow in N.Z. and try
and get huge media about the Air N.Z. situation
and get them an enormous amount of bad press.
This would possibly force them to reconsider but
would most likely be too late.

Amy backpedaled pretty fast when she heard
that!

It would be too late, and it's something we've been
considering from this end too. I would ask you
not to, for the same reason we've decided not to.
As it stands, they are very very sweet and sorry
and know they owe us a big one, and the next
time we need airfare, they're ready to bend over
way backwards and kiss anything that needs kissing. If we make them angry, I'm afraid that they'll

get obstinate, dig into "it was a corporate decision and they were lucky to even have it offered in the first place" and we'd never get anything from them ever again. It's very dicey trying to intimidate big people, and we're worried about getting burned. If you feel confident about it, though, let's talk.

That last lie was really a top-of-the-line model. *We don't want to screw up our relationship with Air NZ, but if YOU would care to screw up YOUR relationship with them, let's talk.* By inviting Matt to call her bluff, Amy took the opportunity to sound perfectly sincere, without any risk that Matt would actually follow through and catch the lie.

Matt grumpily accepted that the debut in The States was off, but that wasn't the end of the screwing. Stan Alley, a friend of Bret's, was making a documentary about "Figwit," and he personally booked a flight to Portland to film Bret at his first fan convention. Another band member booked a side trip to Canada after Tentmoot. Matt noted, "fortunately, they were both able to get full refunds so financially, we haven't lost anything, apart from some disappointed Black Seeds."

In the meantime, Amy was spreading the word about the sudden removal of Tentmoot's headliner band. She gave me this explanation.

Bret McKenzie and the Black Seeds are out. This is actually not a whole lot to do with the money issue, that was just a bit of a final straw. They gave us this massive list of band equipment needed, we jumped through the hoop, and now, about every other day, we've been getting more emails saying "oh yeah, and we need this expensive deedlyhopper too." Bob is out for blood, and

148

when we said they should have put it all out there
for us in the first place...

This letter looked remarkably similar to another
one "Jordan" sent out at the same time.

Bret McKenzie [and the Black Seeds] are not coming. About which Bob made great rejoicing. As
people, they're great. As a band, they had a personality clash with Bob.

In other words, the Black Seeds lost their opportunity to play their *first gig* in the States because they
couldn't get along with the stage manager. Sure
makes them look like nitwits, doesn't it? Like a
bunch of unprofessional divas that couldn't set aside
personal differences in order to take advantage of a
fantastic opportunity. Not a very nice thing to say
about the Black Seeds at all . . . especially considering this was the explanation Amy sent out to the
other Kiwi celebrities about why their friends from
the Seeds would no longer be joining them at
Tentmoot.

This is another interesting example of how Amy
couched her lies in a way that minimized the chances
she'd be caught. If the Kiwi actors believed her lie,
they would probably not discuss it with anyone in
the band—who would want to bring up an embar-
rassing topic like that? Only a *very* close friend would
say, "Geez, how could you Seeds blow off your first
gig in the States because of a personality conflict?"
She was banking on the fact that the victims of her
lies were too polite to check out her story—at least
long enough for her to get what she wanted out of
them.

149

After the Crash, Abbey must have realized she'd better snow Matt a little more, in case BoE had an opportunity to ensnare the Seeds again.

There was some miscommunication between our organization and Air New Zealand. We had arranged for a donor to sponsor what tickets we could manage... The donor called us and told us that she had spoken to Air New Zealand, and they were giving her different information than we were and that she was canceling the tickets.

Jordan Wood was the primary contact, both with the celebrities and with the travel. I can say that everything I heard from this side was consistent with what he has told everyone else. I don't know what happened, and it is difficult to clarify everything at this time, because shortly after receiving the news, Jordan attempted suicide.

I am very sorry that this event has ended so badly; it was coming together so beautifully, and could have been a wonderful thing for the fans, and done some good for charity as well.

Matt is such a genuinely nice person he offered Abbey his condolences.

Myself and the band want you to know that we have a lot of sympathy for what's happened!! We have had a few problems of our own due to the cancellations but they are nothing too serious and we have absolutely no anger towards you, Jordan or the festival. Please keep me up to date with Jordan's health!! Despite all of this, we would definitely consider working with you again in the future and I really hope everything works out O.K.

After seeing Matt's letter in the Tentmoot Inbox, I knew I had done the right thing by making sure nothing worked out O.K. for Those Two. I was filled with a warm sense of accomplishment when Matt later said, in a reply to me, "I've already wasted enough time dealing with those ****** idiots!!!"

Original cost quoted to fly 14 people from NZ to Portland: $70,000
Bye bye, Black Seeds.
Amount Charged to My Personal Credit Card for International Travel: $15,581
Amount Refunded when I cancelled all the international tickets: $5,676
Seeing Abbey and Amy lose their website, credibility. and connections: priceless

It's true, the best things in life are free.

MORE BULLSHIT FOR FIGWIT

The Pony discussion about the Black Seeds eventually caught the eye of a friend of the band, "Prokyon." Prokyon also had a friend named "inDUHvidual," who was one of the comediennes responsible for the hype that is Figwit. Prokyon emailed me and mentioned inDUH had a story of her own I might find interesting.

And what a story! It seems that "Jordan" invited inDUH to chip in for Bret's appearance at Tentmoot.

> We have the hotel, rental cars, and food covered from our end, but we were wondering if Figwit Lives would be willing to help us sponsor the airfare. We would be able to get a few of your people a private dinner with Brett and the band. Interested?

InDUH wasn't so much interested as amused. For one thing, Amy spelled Bret's name wrong. It seemed fishy to inDUH they would be seeking sponsors with only one month to go. InDUH was a student, therefore poor, and could barely afford to keep FigwitLives.net on line. Prokyon recalled they "had a tremendous laugh that [inDUH] was approached to pay for something even a site like TORn might be hard-pressed to pay for. If Mr. F/Amy had done any research, he/she would have realized inDUH had already met and spent quite a bit of time with Bret on two different occasions and that such an offer was really quite pointless."

InDUHvidual politely declined and even thoughtfully suggested "Jordan" might invite Bret's two-man comedy music team, Flight of the

Conchords (FotC), instead of all nine members of The Black Seeds. In addition to being a smaller act, inDUH also thought the Conchords would really appeal to the LOTR crowd. "They're intelligent, subtle and funny. The essence of geekdom, really."

As usual Amy wouldn't take "no" for an answer.

We actually were hoping that the Figwit Lives fan community could help-not the webpage staff specifically. There have been other fan communities that have helped with things like this before...they usually either put up a Paypal "donate here" for the members, or hold a few fundraisers.

Unfortunately, Brett is no longer with Flight of the Conchords. They have added several members and become the Black Seeds, whom we have invited, and who will be playing every night.

InDUH went straight from amused to appalled. "I couldn't believe Mr.Frodo actually wanted me to ask people for money. They obviously screwed up by not taking care of this earlier and I was not about to ask my mostly young and penniless visitors to pay for it."

Your cause is worthy but I feel a little insincere about asking the Figwit fan community to sponsor something they will not have the opportunity to be actively involved with.

Flight of the Conchords is a comedy act duo- Bret McKenzie and Jemaine Clement. The Black Seeds are a reggae-funk band that Bret is a part of.

Amy just had to get in the last word. "We spoke to Bret's manager, and it seems that he is no longer a member of FotC." This was totally false, but inDUH simply had to be put in her place for being so impertinent as to correct the almighty "Jordan."

Prokyon also had a personal brush with Abbey and Amy a few weeks prior to Tentmoot. She heard of Tentmoot and was thinking about going, even though she lived in Los Angeles. But then she attended a fête at a Neiman-Marcus department store to unveil their LOTR window display. Several LOTR celebrities attended the event, so of course many fans showed up. Prokyon was standing in the crowd when she overheard the people next to her chattering away and realized they were calling themselves Orangeblossom and Mr. Frodo.

Mr. F/Amy was under a very wrong impression Bret's other musical endeavor, Flight of the Conchords, had broken up, added a few members, and turned into the Black Seeds. I tried to set him/her straight but he/she wouldn't listen at all. I didn't reveal that I know Bret.

Apparently inDUH's affront got under Amy's skin, such that she felt compelled to reinforce her lie to others. Too bad it's such a small world she only succeeded at making a jackass of herself and scared away a potential attendee from Tentmoot.

HIJACKING BRUCE HOPKINS

Photo by Megan Worthy.
Bruce and his producing partner, Rebecca Kirkland, smiling in the face of adversity.

Bruce Hopkins played a supporting role in the LOTR films, the character of Gamling, guardian of The Golden Hall of Meduseld. His reputation in fantasy preceded LOTR for his roles in TV shows like Xena and Hercules. On top of that, he is popular at conventions because he's a pleasant, fun person. Excitement was evident on the Tentmoot mailing list on November 6, 2003 when "Jordan" stated Bruce was confirmed to appear on December 11 and 12, 2003.

Some people noticed, however, that Bruce was on the schedule for another event at that time, The Gathering in Toronto, Canada. One fellow was concerned enough to point it out to TORn.

11/21/03 Hopkins NOT Attending Portland Con.
Xoanon@3:35 PM

Corsair writes: You may be interested in knowing that the TentMoot people are incorrectly listing Bruce Hopkins as a confirmed celebrity at their event, when he in fact will be attending elsewhere. Another group has a written contract with him at an event on another coast entirely... and the actor has since informed organizers that he is definitely NOT attending TentMoot, and has told the TentMoot people so some time ago.

You may want to check this out... or get someone else to do so. It would be a shame if Ringers were misled by incorrect information.

When I saw that on TORn, I called "Jordan" and asked what the *HELL* was going on. BoE reacted immediately, sending this email to Xoanon.

No one contacted us before making the post, and the information was not only incorrect, but slan derous. It was implied that we are somehow running a scam against Ringers, which is patently absurd. There is no possible way that we could gain by misleading people with our events, as we do not even make any money from them...EVERY penny over and above our overhead costs goes directly to charity.

As for what happened with Mr. Hopkins, he WAS confirmed with us AND the Gathering. He was planning to fly from New Zealand to Portland, appear at TentMoot for one day, and then fly on to Toronto. BitofEarth and the Gathering were going to split the airfare, but the Gathering did not provide us with the necessary confirmation numbers to do so with Air Canada, and did not return our phone calls. Because our calls were not returned, the window of time to set Bruce's flight to Portland passed, and Bruce had to cancel with us. We IMMEDIATELY removed his name from the site.

All of the people we have currently listed as confirmed attendees or video appearances are just that: confirmed attendees or video appearances as of the time they are posted. We update the list DAILY to keep it accurate.

We are asking that a retraction and apology be posted by 3:30pm PST. Otherwise, we would have to call New Line and the representation of the pending artists today and inform them that we are being slandered on TORn with inaccurate information.

Abigail L. Stone

Another high density lie letter. This one came so close to a Critical Lie Mass that it nearly set off an uncontrollable ThermonucLiar Chain Reaction. TORn didn't buy it, but they diplomatically gave BoE the benefit of the doubt.

Update: BoE states that Bruce's name was in fact taken off their list of confirmed celebrities for the event some time ago, but the Sponsor a Celebrity page had not been updated for some time. Bruce's event schedule can be found on his personal site - Bruce-Hopkins.com.

TORn was far too generous. Amy had four days to update both pages of the website since receiving this from Bruce's PR representative:

Mon, 17 Nov 2003 18:41
Hi Mr. Frodo:

I don't want people to still think he is attending this event and book their tickets - can you please make sure that his name is taken off your confirmed list asap?

Thank you,
Rebecca

Ed R, president of The Gathering of the Fellowship, was kind enough to explain what really happened.

Bruce Hopkins signed on with us in mid-2003. We paid for his flight from New Zealand. After some discussion within our staff, we agreed that if Bit of Earth were able to arrange a change of flights directly with Air Canada, then we would allow it, as long as they covered all the extra costs involved. We asked Mr. Hopkins and his agent to have Bit of Earth contact us directly for the necessary details.

After a while, Bruce contacted us and said "never mind - I will not be diverting my flight". A few days later, I was left a telephone message from a female person, saying that she was from Bit of Earth, and that their computer had been down, and that as a result they received our communication late. She left me a telephone number to return her call. Since at that point we had already been contacted by Mr. Hopkins, telling us that he would not be changing his itinerary, I ignored her message and did not return her call.

I don't know what constitutes Abigail Stone's definition of "confirmed", but ours is the possession of a SIGNED agreement by all parties involved. There was NO agreement made between Bit of Earth and the Gathering, since there was no direct communication between us. The attempt to take advantage of Mr. Hopkins while he was already in North America (courtesy of us) was ill-advised and insulting, from our perspective.

Ed's letter was confirmed by Ginger W, VP of Programming for GOTF.

I concur with all that Mr. Rodrigues relayed to you.

And by Trish T, Treasurer for GOTF.

I was aware of the situation with Mr. Hopkins as described most aptly by Ed. I just wanted to confirm his details are correct, to the best of my knowledge.

AND by Robert P, Programmer for GOTF.

When this was first brought up in mid Oct, I sent an email to MR Frodo, in which I gave the phone# for the Air Canada help desk, Confirmation#'s for Bruce Hopkin's flights, and suggestions on change of flights with cost breakdowns.

Bruce's agent emailed me at the end of Oct, asking how arrangements were going and were the new tickets purchased? I informed her that I had not heard from Mr Frodo. I checked with Air Canada and TentMoot never called them to check on any changes.

2nd week of Nov, Bruce emailed that he would not be attending TentMoot as they had not made travel arrangements in a timely manner. 2 days [later], I heard from MR Frodo informing me that his computer had been down and he never got my 3 emails. [He asked] how could we work this out, and could we pay for the flights and then he would cut us a check after his event? I gave him [Ed's] email address as I was not going to do this.

Amy was up to her usual routine: wait till the last minute, beg for a freebie, promise to pay it back knowing full well there were no funds, and hope people feel sorry enough to give it to you.

She appears to have been preparing something new, however, when she sent this message to Matt McLeod just after canceling the appearance of The Black Seeds:

You might also want to talk to the Gathering of the Fellowship, because I know that they were working with Air Canada, and if one of your boys has a date and a ticket, they might be interested in swinging something last-second with Bret or with all of you to give their event a little extra oomph and to help you out with the "we were pre-pared to be gone all this time" angle.

What a kind gesture. At first glance, one might think she was trying to mend fences with the Seeds by helping them get another gig. But with the reference to the ticket on Air Canada, I have to wonder if she was setting up to re-snare Bruce. I can imagine a letter to TGOF, along the lines of, "Look here, we bought this ticket for Figwit, we'll share him with you if you'll share Bruce."

After all of Amy's secrecy, it was incredibly refreshing to receive such a professional, open response to my query to The Gathering. Each of those emails had been copied to other people on TGOF's board—they were clearly unafraid to have their words reviewed by others. Thus the difference between keeping things confidential versus outright concealment.

Of *course* it was appropriate for Amy not to hand out sensitive material willy-nilly; things like Sean Astin's phone number or Lawrence Makoare's personal email *should be* kept private. But *everything* was clandestine with "Jordan," every detail kept tight under wraps. This was because Amy had so many lies spinning at once, she had to ration out what she could tell any given person, lest the whole web fall to pieces. The letters from The Gathering demonstrate How It Oughta Be Done—with open communication and full disclosure.

Bruce's tale also exemplifies the way so many people went out of their way to help Abbey and Amy. It was incredibly generous for The Gathering to agree to pay the lion's share of Bruce's travel, yet give up some of their time with him to BoE. Not only were they willing to do this, Robert even made it easier on BoE by offering suggestions for rearranging Bruce's flights. Any competent, reasonable person, given that much assistance, could have produced a wonderful event out of it all. BoE received gift after gift of this nature, the good will and labor of hundreds of rock solid nice people. Abbey and Amy just squandered it as though they had an unlimited supply.

161

KIRAN SHAH'S BRUSH WITH EVIL

Kiran & Kit Shah, who are too sweet to snarl at a camera.

Chaitan 'Kit' Shah received a fax on November 25, 2003, forwarded from his uncle Kiran's agent. It was an invitation for Kiran to appear at TentMoot. "Bit of Earth is gladly offering to facilitate all transportation, accomodation (sic), meals, and other travel needs. We are anticipating attendance ranging between 4,000-7000 people over the course of the week." It included a description of BoE and Project Elanor, and of course mentioned Sean Astin's appearances. Kit invited "Jordan" to give him a call and tell him more about Tentmoot.

"I thought 'Jordan' was a bloke," Kit said, in his jovial British accent. "They had good attendance projections. The website was very well organized and professional, and the venue looked beautiful." He noted "Jordan" seemed disorganized and wasn't always clear on details (such as when Kit asked specifically about insurance), but this didn't bother him too much. "I blamed it on the size of the event," he said, and who wouldn't? "Jordan" couldn't possibly be on top of every detail for a festival that large. Even when the airline tickets didn't arrive, Kit wasn't alarmed. "Kiran hadn't done many conventions, and none for LOTR, but we'd been through big events before." It was unusual, but not unheard of, to have air travel pending until the last minute. Amy even reassured him the delay was expected:

> The package the airline is giving us, as it is a donation, is a bit odd. They can guarantee the days of the flights, but they say they can't guarantee the times until the day before, because which specific flight is dependent on the one with the most open seats.

Kiran offered to forego his usual autograph fee and allow BoE to donate it all to Great Ormand Street Hospital Children's Charity. Amy invited Kiran to officiate at John and Talisha's wedding—the two of them arranged all the paperwork needed for a layman to perform the ceremony. Kiran couldn't possibly pass up such a quirky offer, which was certain to result in some positive PR! He did pass up other invitations for paid appearances on those dates because, ultimately, Tentmoot sounded like a lot of fun.

Kiran and Kit received notice Tentmoot was cancelled on December 10, 2003, via this email from Abbey.

> We had arranged a private donation of the tickets, and everything seemed to be progressing wonderfully. Then at approximately 4PM US time, our private donor informed us that she had spoken to Air New Zealand, and their information differed from ours, and thus she was pulling her

donation and canceling the tickets. This was a devastating blow, and quite simply the death knell for TentMoot 2003

Of course, there was a slightly more comprehensive explanation as to why Kiran couldn't attend Tentmoot:

Dear Jordan,

Owing to our present economic climate, I regret that British Airways is unable to offer you complimentary flights for Mr Shah. The airline is facing turbulent times and it has become necessary to introduce a number of cost cutting measures to match the business climate.

Best wishes,
Jackie.
Community Relations Co-Ordinator.

HOW THEY SCREWED JOHN HOWE

© 2004, www.john-howe.com

"Me by Me," by John Howe. Used with permission of artist.

John Howe's name appeared on the Tentmoot guest list on October 27, 2003. "Jordan" announced John would be coming to Tentmoot, barring any unexpected interference or emergencies. Many people were excited by the prospect of meeting the artist who beautifully illustrated many of Tolkien's tales. John was touted as a live appearance (as opposed to the less exciting "exclusive video").

John said he could scarcely remember the Portland incident, but he recalled he was first contacted by Amy "during the summer or early fall [of 2003]. It was possible I would be in Vancouver [at the time of Tentmoot]...finally said I couldn't make it, but accepted at that point to do a video appearance if it could work for everyone."

Some of John's correspondence remains in the Tentmoot mailbox. On November 11, 2003, John notified "Jordan" his appearance in Vancouver was cancelled. Although John did not explicitly state he would therefore not be attending Tentmoot, that point certainly seemed obvious to me. One would think the directors of Tentmoot would want to clarify this point right away, but Amy did not reply to John until November 25, 2003. "Does this mean you would be unable to attend TentMoot?" asked Amy. "BitofEarth would be more than happy to provide all travel expenses, or to facilitate the filming of a video appearance if at all possible. It would be a true shame to lose you."

John immediately replied that he would be in Berlin and Paris during Tentmoot week, but if "Jordan" could get a video crew to his home in Switzerland, he was game to give a video interview. Amy saw fit to wait until December 6, 2003, to arrange the video crew.

> We're looking for a European ringer who is willing to meet John Howe in Germany or Switzerland within the next three days to tape a private interview for TentMoot 2003. Interested? Know someone who is? Know someone who knows someone who might be?

John couldn't recall exactly how he got a copy of this message, which was clearly not meant for him to see. " I discovered the professional video team was actually going to be a random crowd of fans off the street armed with a video camera. That's the point where I stopped thinking it was a good idea."

John confronted "Jordan" about the message; this was her reply:

It was actually just to the TORn staff, whom we work with professionally and switch out camera crews with, to see if they had anyone who would be in closer proximity to Switzerland for the filming...

We didn't want to say too much about what it was for, however, as TORn has a sometimes trouble-some habit of posting anything that comes into their inbox without looking at it. We were burned on a previous event by someone knowing that we were going to tape an appearance with a ce-lebrity and then going to their people without our knowledge and saying "I'm the BoE camera per-son, I need to know where to meet Mr. X." They wound up not only getting a private meeting with that person completely falsely, but making us look quite bad in the process and losing US the ap-pearance. We didn't want that to happen again.

We knew we'd be filtering through the TORn staff who are just plain fans, but we'd rather do that and either get a TORn-cooperative professional cameraman (or know to call in our German crew) or someone else trustworthy from TORn than risk having a repeat of the previous fiasco.

Fascinating. I wonder if the TORnies were aware they made BoE look bad by helping some "just plain fan" glom onto a celebrity.

Despite having been caught in mid-lie, Amy con-tinued to push John for a video session in Berlin. He replied, "I already have 3 film crews hovering around me for the whole time, I don't think I could get New Line to authorize a 4th." This, I believe, is Swiss for "I'm far too polite to just say *leave me alone, you fucking lunatic.*" However, Amy finally got the message, and with less than a week to go before Tentmoot, she finally downgraded John's guest list status from "live appearance" to "video."

It turned out John was in no danger of being pestered in Berlin. "Jordan's" German contact already responded to the call to arms.

> Mr. Frodo wrote to me (and others) on Dec. 6. (un)Fortunately I was busy otherwise – I went that weekend to a premiere in Hamburg and met Christopher Lee and Cate Blanchett. I came back on Dec 7 and that was too late anyway. I wrote an email to Mr. Frodo that he/she asks a little late to do such a thing, because it needs some good preparation. He/she never answered this eMail. Now I know why.

And now we all know why.

THE SHORE/SHAH WANK REDEMPTION

Date: Tue, 25 Nov. 2003

Jordan

I know for a fact that Howard Shore, Miranda Otto and Ngila Dickson are not attending Tent Moot- yet they are on the confirmed celebrity page.

============

Wendy Rutherford
New Line Cinema
Director, Interactive Publicity and Promotions

Even *I* find that email somewhat intimidating. It may be only three lines long, but there is a volume stuffed between those lines—a tale of high-priced attorneys, Hollywood black lists, and scathing condemnation of BoE that would be both widespread and credible. However, Amy felt up to the challenge of snowing New Line itself.

Tue, 25 Nov 2003 15:05

Ngila was going to be coming in person up until this past weekend, and we are working with her people regarding whether she will be appearing with a live satellite feed or on video.

As of Thursday, when last we spoke to Miranda's people, she was also confirmed to participate. It was suggested to us that although unlikely, if she concluded the filming of her current project in time,

169

a personal appearance might still be possible. We felt it would be better to wait and fill that in than to waffle back and forth.

As for Howard Shore, I will personally call immediately to find out if there has been a miscommunication, and if that is the case, his name will be removed immediately and I give my sincere apologies.

Ngila Dickson got dragged into this in the following fashion:

• **November 6, 2003**: Amy sent the usual email to Ellen Nicholson, inviting Ngila to appear at Tentmoot.

• **Nov 20:** Ellen briefly replied that Ngila would be in New Zealand at that time.

• **Nov 21:** Amy asked if a video appearance could be arranged.

• **Nov 25:** Ellen told "Jordan" to take this question up with Ngila's assistant, Sophia. Amy informed New Line that Ngila was being switched from "confirmed live" to "confirmed video" status.

• **Nov 26:** Amy asked Sophia if a video could be arranged.

• **Dec 5:** Amy reminded Sophia she would like to arrange a video.

• **Dec 7:** Sophia replied, "If it is possible for you to organise a video feed, then perhaps we could do it, pre-recorded by your camera crew."

Ellen spoke to my publicist about the matter on July 20, 2004 and couldn't even remember sending these letters. They were completely insignificant at the time. Ngila never even heard of Tentmoot; Sophia obviously didn't waste Ngila's time even mentioning it, since she never heard back from "Jordan" with the "plans" for "his" "video crew."

"Ngila was going to be coming in person up until this past weekend . . . " Amy never had a penis, but she sure had some big brass balls. One wonders how she sat down without clanking.

There was no correspondence about Miranda Otto left in the Tentmoot mailbox, so the truth of that tale will probably never be known. But Amy apparently realized it would look more professional if she followed up with Wendy regarding her scam of Howard Shore.

Date: Wed, 26 Nov 2003
Wendy-

I have spoken to my assistant, Samantha, and to Mr. Shore's representation at Gorfaine-Schwartz, and we have successfully figured out what happened!

We are handling multiple celebrities at this time, including Kiran Shah. We keep track of where things stand with whom by having a large list on the wall with four columns, "Ready to Fly," "Confirmed: Book Flight", "Pending", and "No," with the names being shuffled from one column to the next as things develop.

Samantha had received the email declining Mr. Shore's appearance, but not yet had a chance to speak to me that day, as we were both on the phone. Before she had a chance to do so, she heard me yell "YES! We got Shah!" Meaning Kiran. She thought I said "We got *Shore*," meaning Howard, and, assuming that I had talked the agency over since the email she'd received, moved the name on the board accordingly. Because we don't move the names without confirmation, seeing his name in that column lead me to believe that Samantha had, indeed, received confirmation, and I authorized the page update.

Sue confirmed this was a gigantic crock of crap—there was no such message board. Abbey and Amy simply weren't that organized! Furthermore, although the initial contact from Kit Shah did arrive on Nov. 25, 2003, his initial spark of interest hardly amounted to "getting Shah."

Lying through her teeth right to New Line Cinema . . . Daddy must be so proud.

WHAT'S QUENYA FOR "BITCH?"

David Salo was the linguistic consultant for the LOTR films. His correspondence abounds with exquisite Old World elegance that harks back to the letters of JRR Tolkien. Furthermore, he and his wife Dorothea out-snide me so fiercely that I genuflect before their side-splitting emails, crying, "I'm not worthy!"

David received his first invitation to Tentmoot on October 25, 2003. "Jordan's" letter stated, "Although we cannot provide an honorarium, BitofEarth.net is willing to provide all airfare, accommodations, and other expenses." David must be regarded highly by Amy; the first part of that sentence was actually the truth.

David was too busy to reply to this inquiry. But Amy wouldn't take silence for an answer, and in a demonstration of resourcefulness *sans* tact, called Dorothea at her place of employment. Dorothea commented, "This person must have gone through considerable gyrations to find—not my correct work number, but the department's main number." Amy at least had the courtesy to invite them both to Tentmoot through this contact.

Dorothea remarked in her LJ:

> I might actually be able to swing that. I just have to get my project and my intro take-home exam in. My husband, however, has to take two finals and give (and grade!) one. I wouldn't give great odds of him being willing to do this con, even if this con hadn't managed to tick off his wife by calling her office. And of course they don't want me without him.

Apparently not; Amy's next solecism asked whether David could recommend his own replacement.

Novenber 18, 2003 4:03 PM
Mrs. Salo

We completely understand scholastic obligations, though we will regret your absence, but we were hoping that David might be able to recommend someone whom he considers of exceptional fluency in Tolkien's tongues who might be available.

David did not offer any suggestions, so Amy turfed the task of filling the Middle Earth Languages Panel to Cherie, aka Diamond. Her efforts are described by "NotAmused."

I am a moderator at a wonderful Elvish language website. DiamondTook frequented this site, and I occasionally visited BOE.

Diamond approached me, asking if would lead a panel on Elvish at TentMoot. I was terribly flattered (dumb, dumb, dumb) and said yes. Just as I was about to book plane tickets and a hotel room and the whole 9 yards, my husband ended up losing his job, and I had to cancel due to serious lack of funds.

Diamond was *very* upset with me, stating that I'd "agreed to appear" (even though I hadn't signed anything...). Not knowing what else was going on, I pled my case and she eventually "forgave" me for canceling.

How generous of Di. I chastised NotAmused for calling herself "dumb, dumb, dumb." What kind of Quenya aficionado could pass up a request to teach the language to other fans at a charity event? For the price of a plane ticket and a hotel room, she could spend a week doing something she liked to do—and for the benefit of charity! *Of course* she was tempted to join the fun. That's how Abbey and Amy operated, by exploiting people's eagerness to support RIF by doing something they enjoyed.

URBAN SNIPER

Amy approached Karl Urban's representative with a slight twist.

Wed, 19 Nov 2003
Troy - We have been working with Jenny Rawlings for the past three weeks regarding a potential appearance by Karl Urban, in person or by video at his discretion, at TentMoot 2003 this December. Unfortunately for us, Mr. Urban has recently transferred to your agency, and we have to start from scratch with fairly short notice.

This missive was sent to a woman named Jennifer Hahn. There's no telling why "Jordan" addressed Ms. Hahn as "Troy." Ms. Hahn replied immediately, "Unfortunately, Karl will not be available to participate...he is going to be in Europe working."

This simple answer was not enough to stop Amy. She sent Ms. Hahn her usual request for a video appearance (which of course included "the option of sending an autographed picture with the video appearance to be auctioned at the convention, with all proceeds going exclusively to his specified charity"). Amy followed up again on December 1, 2003, with her standard last minute video request.

Congratulations on the success of the Wellington premiere! I know that things must be fairly insane for you right now, and I hate to remind you of yet another thing on your plate, but I know how easily smaller things can get lost in the melee.

This isn't a "we need it yesterday" email, but I wanted to check in regarding the filming of Karl's video appearance for TentMoot 2003. As previously stated, we have crews available on short notice in LA, New York, the UK, and NZ. If it would be more convenient, Karl may also tape his own appearance, as his co-star Sean Astin is doing.

Amy even submitted six questions from the Prancing Pony for Karl to answer on his video. Ms Hahn's replies to these video inquiries are nowhere to be found in the Tentmoot mailbox and she did not respond to my request for comment. But for some reason, Amy took this rejection seriously. Four hours after mailing her last letter to Ms. Hahn, Amy sent this post to four "privileged volunteers," so we could explain to the rest of the food chain why Karl's name was suddenly off the guest list.

I HOPE KARL URBAN GETS FUCKED BY EVERY MOTHERFUCKING HORSE IN FUCKING ROHAN! INCLUDING THE ONE HE RODE IN ON! TWICE!

We've lost his video appearance now, at the last minute. Why?

Because he CHANGED MOTHERFUCKING GODDAMNED TALENT CUNT AGENCIES!! ONE BLOODY WEEK BEFORE THE FUCKING PREMIERE!

But he didn't just change agencies. No, precious! He left BWR. The one we've been dealing with for four months. So they aren't authorized to handle his schedule, book any appearances, or arrange any interviews. He joined Troy. So we talked to Troy. And Troy would love to help. But Karl has signed with them, so he can't handle his own schedule any more. EXCEPT he ALSO hasn't completed all his paperwork with Troy, so THEY can't handle it either.

Meaning that no one, INCLUDING KARL DUCK-FUCKING URBAN, can book him for anything. Peter Jackson had to personally fucking vouch for him to get into the premiere of his OWN CUNT-TURKEY MOVIE!

The strange part is, Ms Hahn did in fact work for BWR, so this lie doesn't even begin to hold water. Something must have really frosted Amy's flakes, for her to make up such a careless and unprofessional lie. Wherever you are, Ms. Hahn, I salute you.

To be fair, Amy stated on the top of that letter, "This message is not to be posted anywhere." Those of us who received it were apparently supposed to spread the news about Karl's ineptitude without referring to her original document.

Oops.

~Profile of Supported Charities~

Reading is Fundamental - The oldest and largest children's and family nonprofit literacy organization in the United States, RIF operates through a network of 435,000 volunteers and gives away 16 million books a year at schools, libraries, community centers, child-care centers, hospitals, migrant worker camps, Head Start and Even Start programs, homeless shelters, and detention centers.

The Riggs Institute - The Riggs Institute is a phonics-based multi-sensory reading and education program based locally in Beaverton and offering dedicated and custom-tailored instruction in the language arts. The methods used by the Riggs Institute have been hailed as nothing short of miraculous in turning students otherwise considered 'hopelessly' learning disabled into fluent, joyful readers, and we are proud to work with them in the true spirit of leaving no child behind.

Carbon Neutrality- Carbon Dioxide emissions produced by daily activities, ranging from home electricity consumption to driving and flying, are one of the primary causes of global warming, and the major production factors, such as fossil-fuel-burning cars are often environmentally detrimental in many other ways as well. BitofEarth is proud to announce that TentMoot2003 will be an entirely Carbon Neutral event.

Quoted from BoE.net website

THE CHARITY DISPARITY

December, 2002: BoE sponsors a party called Tentmoot 2002 in the parking lot of the Lloyd Center 10 Cinema, for people standing in line to attend the premier of *LOTR: The Two Towers*. BoE holds a raffle at this party, and "Jordan" states on the BoE message board that the raffle money is earmarked for Reading is Fundamental.

April, 2003: BoE sponsors a Special Screening of TTT at Lloyd Center 10, which is hosted by Sean Astin. Sean answers questions for 90 minutes from an audience of 600 people. Abbey proclaims (both on stage that night and on the BoE website) that $3,000 was raised for RIF.

Fall, 2003: BoE spams the celebrities of LOTR with invitations to Tentmoot. These invitations state explicitly that Tentmoot is affiliated with not one but *three* charities, and furthermore, BoE is a registered non-profit corporation (although they are still awaiting their "Tax ID number").

On December 22, 2003, I called the Donor Relations number for RIF in Washington, DC. I spoke to a very friendly fellow named Mike Nattel. It took him a while to recognize the name "Bit of Earth," but then the little light went on. "Oh, yeah! The garden! I remember them now. Say, did that ever get built?"

Ahem. "Um, yeah, last April. Didn't they tell you?"

"No, I wondered about that. It sounded like a great idea but they never really got back to me about it."

That pretty much annihilated BoE's prior claim, "a special action committee has been formed in the Portland area to facilitate the partnership with BitofEarth for Project Elanor." In fact, that action committee had been nixed in February, 2003, when someone from RIF took a close look at BoE.net and discovered Victoria Bitter's X-rated homoerotic fan fiction.

Mike Natell was pretty surprised to hear $3,000 was raised for RIF at Project Elanor. He checked their database and had no record of *any* donation, under BoE, BoE.net, Abigail Stone, or Jordan Wood. "RIF is a national agency, we don't really have local chapters," he explained. "In general, all donations come through this office. However, it's possible there was some local group affiliated with RIF. We do a lot of outreach in schools and libraries, for example, which might have received the donation. I'll do some checking."

I followed up with Mike in January, 2004, and he was glad to hear BoE.net had not paid their Internet hosting fees and would be falling off the Web soon. "Good! That means we don't have to bother with a 'cease and desist' order to BoE for using our name falsely on the website." How comforting to know BoE didn't ending up *costing* RIF money for a court order.

Mike never turned up any evidence of a donation. I checked in with Rob Bob, the manager at Lloyd Center 10, to make sure he hadn't sent the TTT proceeds straight to RIF. Rob distinctly recalled cutting the checks to BoE.

Mike conceded it was still possible BoE made a donation to an affiliate group. He had not been able to check out every agency in Oregon licensed to use

181

RIF's name and logo. About this time I mentioned the donation issue to Sue. "Oh, I know RIF never got a dime," she said. "I pinned Abbey down about that just before Thanksgiving. It took a while but she finally admitted it. She said there was nothing left after all the expenses of Project Elanor. I told her to prove it with the receipts, but then Tentmoot happened, and that was that."

This sparked some very interesting discussion on the Prancing Pony message boards, as BoE members realized the money they donated for RIF was not used for that purpose.[7] People started reporting their donations to Project Elanor, of both money and goods. Sue and I contacted businesses and followed up on long-lost donors. We had so many cans of worms open at once, it was a veritable nightcrawler convention. In the end, this is what we could reconstruct about the finances of Project Elanor:

Income And Donations
- $3,000 at the TTT screening
- $500 lunch money raised by members of the Prancing Pony
- $650 in sales of "personalized paving stones"
- $375 in sales of raffle tickets
- $100 from sale of Sean's ID badge at the end of Project Elanor
- $200 in T-Shirt sales
- Unknown amount of direct private donations
- Photography: all shooting, film, and developing costs

---

[7] The RIF money most likely went up in a puff of smoke from a clove cigarette.

- Video: all shooting, tape, and production costs
- Airfare: all but $444 of $1,093 donated by members of Prancing Pony
- Ornate Benches: Primrose purchased and donated these at no cost to BoE
- Materials: All plants, flagstones, and hauling of debris had known donors.

Expenses
- $510 for lunch from Gaffer's and No Fish, Go Fish
- $1,890 to Parr Lumber for the deck materials
- $444 for the Astins' air travel
- $72 to Lowes Hardware
- $385 to AT&T Wireless
- $263 to FlexibiliTs for T-Shirts

So let's see how that adds up.

(a) At least $4,825 in cash received by BoE.

(b) $3,564 in proven expenses for the garden.

(c) Amount left over for donation to RIF = (a) − (b) = $1,261

(f) Amount actually donated to RIF: $0.

Apparently Abbey went to the Enron College of Creative Accounting.

PROJECT HELLANOR

After Tentmoot crashed, I felt guilty about bailing Amy out of her incompetent handling of the lumber donation for the Elanor deck. If I had just let the lumber mishap proceed to its natural conclusion, maybe BoE would have been exposed for the fraud that it was, and would have never escalated into the fraud it became. But eight months after Project Elanor, when the Thought Police were barred from the Pony board, it became apparent that if I hadn't helped Amy, some other kindhearted person would.

My husband and I were the big suckers who went down for Project Elanor.

We were part of the 2002 Tentmoot, nine of us who came out of the *Two Towers* line party with one heck of a bond. All nine agreed to join Bit of Earth as official event staff. We spent many a happy weekend up in Portland helping to plan Project Elanor. About three or four weeks before the event, I volunteered to get the plants donated. My husband "Gandalf" volunteered to rent a minivan and be the official driver for Sean Astin.

I was given a list of different plants to acquire, a copy of the plans for the garden, and a promise from Mr.F. that I would have the numbers (how many of these and how many of those) in a few days. I then sat back and waited. And I sent emails. And I waited. And I made phone calls. And waited.

I did not receive a complete list until March 28, 2003. I took one look and almost fell out of my chair. I immediately let Mr. F. know there was no way I could get all those plants in a week. He gave me lots of email addresses and phone numbers for other Project Elanor volunteers, and many of them responded with an amazing fervor and zeal.

After lots and lots of pounding the pavement, we managed to acquire a majority of what was needed. Thursday evening, April 3rd, Gandalf and I trekked up to Portland and camped out at Mr. F's for the duration. Gandalf secured the minivan and we even got the rental company printed on the T-shirts and made sure they got a personal stepping stone in the garden. Many of the people who were promised a stone as part of their donation did not get one, and we felt really bad about that.

When we arrived, Mr. F. immediately asked me how the plants were coming. He then told us some of the plant counts might be different. Not only had almost all of the plant numbers changed, half of the plants themselves had been changed!

We had been in constant contact with Mr. F. the entire time through email and phone calls. Not a word had been said. The entire design was changed. It wasn't even similar to the plans I had been showing to the head honchos at the nurseries.

There was actually a logical explanation for this last-minute switcharoo. The Elanor Garden was built at the Riggs Institute, but that had not been BoE's first choice. Abbey and Amy had researched the Portland public library system and originally selected a small branch for the project site. They posted their find on BoE.net and obtained the services of a "prestigious Portland landscaper" to design the garden. The only problem was that they neglected to mention their ideas to the folks at the library.

The PR director of the library, "Bibi," (who requested I leave their name out of this book) couldn't recall exactly how she learned about the project, only that she was stunned to see her place of employment described on BoE.net as the future home of this garden project. She immediately called Abbey for an explanation. Abbey and "Jordan" came in for an appointment,[8] showed her the plans, and described the partnership with RIF and Sean Astin. Despite the brazen attempt to *literally* take over her turf, Bibi gave the matter a serious consideration and brought it up with the library directors. They decided although the garden concept was lovely, they could not take on the additional maintenance and liability that came with it.

Bibi explained this politely to Abbey and "Jordan." They countered with promises of perpetual maintenance from BoE and asked how they could get around the other issues. Bibi finally had to express herself more aggressively and tell them the answer was no. The next thing she knew, Abbey and "Jordan" were pounding the pavement outside the library doors with a petition, asking for signatures from people who agreed the library should have a garden.

---

[8] Regarding "Jordan," Bibi said," that was the only time in my entire life that I *could not tell* if that was a boy or girl."

Although most people would simply unleash the hounds at that point, Bibi escorted Those Two inside and gently pointed out that this methodology was not a very realistic or persuasive tactic. She gave them advice on where to look for alternate sites and how to approach them with their proposal. Her coaching must have worked, because they got out of her hair and latched onto the Riggs Institute.

There really was a "prestigious landscape designer," who drew up a beautiful plan for the original site at the library. Apparently when he learned he had wasted his time designing a garden for a library that didn't want it, he backed out of the venture. Abbey and Amy removed his name from the plans, then cut and pasted them to fit the Riggs property. They spent Elanor Day explaining to everyone that the garden was designed by a famous Hungarian, but he was so embarrassed by his poor English he chose not to attend. And of course, he was so humble he wanted his contribution kept anonymous.

Thus the sudden change in the garden plans that were thrust into Vanadriel's hands three days before Project Elanor. Her story continued from there.

> At this point, I panicked. I sent out frantic emails to all the wonderful volunteers who had been working their butts off to get these plants donated. I gave everyone the new plant list and numbers and apologized until I was blue in the face. I was angry and crushed—all I could think was "Great, these people are going to think *I* am sloppy and disorganized, *I* can't be counted on to hold up my end of a bargain."

187

But the volunteers shone through like nothing I'd ever seen before. They all stopped in their tracks, changed directions and kept right on going.

It was great. Back at base camp, Gandalf had a list of tasks to accomplish on Friday that looked pretty simple and straightforward. WRONG. We had no addresses, poor directions, bad instructions, and everything that could have gone wrong, went wrong.

We were supposed to pick up paving stones. We had awful directions to find the decorative stone place: "go to Canyon street and then ask someone else." It took us three hours to find the stone place, and then they had no idea what we wanted. Turns out we were supposed to pick OUT some paving stones. We didn't know how many, what kind, or what they were for. We finally gave up and told Mr. F. HE needed do that since we didn't know what we were doing.

That evening, I mentioned to OB I didn't know how much we were going to be able to get done on Saturday and we *might* have to make do with what we had. I never, EVER said "that's it, I'm done. Fend for yourselves."

Which is exactly what Mr. F. told the volunteers the next morning: "the woman who was getting the plants announced that she isn't going to work anymore." Lies! If I had heard about it at the time...well, I won't speculate on what I might have done. But they might have been short a minivan and a driver for Sean Astin.

On Saturday, we picked up Sean and his family at the airport. They were incredibly nice, down-to-earth, intelligent people. We got them settled at their hotel, then we went back to base camp—where I was told what Mr.F. said that morning. OB assured me it MUST have been a matter of miscommunication and they would NEVER say anything like that about me. Much later, I saw the email where Mr.F. said exactly that.

Next it was time for the TTT screening. Gandalf signed on explicitly to see the movie and the short feature by Sean Astin. Our sole job was to make sure the Astins got where they needed to be, when they needed to be there. We got Sean to the theater, dropped him off covertly at a side door, parked the car, and sat down in a staff-reserved seat. But then our security guy came rushing up and said the plans had changed: Sean was going to introduce the movie, say a few words, and then go back to the hotel.

Gandalf RAN across the parking lot to bring the van around, and I was hustled to the side entrance so we could move out as soon as Sean was done. Sean introduced himself and the short film, said he'd be doing a Q&A afterwards and sat down to watch. We all looked at each other and said "What?" We asked OB what the heck was going on. She broke down and cried, rambled on about how it wasn't her fault, all this work and now she wasn't even going to sit by Sean.

We waited through the short film, through the Q&A period, over two hours all together, outside the theater with the van. It was raining and cold. Finally we took the Astins back to the hotel and were dismissed for the night.

We didn't get to see either movie, we didn't get to hear Sean speak, nothing! We were furious and

189

heartbroken at the same time. OB and Mr.F. treated us like galley slaves for the rest of the event. After we got Sean and his family to the airport on Sunday, we got into our truck and fled as fast as we could.

Abbey posted her memoir of the TTT screening on the Pony. Her version was slightly different from Vanadriel's.

Sean finally notices me—introduced myself and shook hands. He gets interviewed by a really crappy reporter, then we talk for .04 seconds before we go into the theater. Sean goes first and the whole place goes nuts, people screaming and cheering and waving. I walk in behind him (talk about being in someone's shadow!) and get to the stage—we just stand there together while everyone stands and screams.

The crowd dies down enough that I welcome everyone and introduce myself—and everyone cheered! I thanked everyone and announced that we'd made $3,000 that night. Sean talked briefly about making *The Long and Short of It* and then we watched the movie. He took a seat on the aisle, first row.

Now, Orange had been promised a seat next to The Man, and she is not one to just not get it. So I plopped myself down on the floor next to him— and he said "I'll sit next to you!" and dropped on the floor next to me. We had a great conversation during the Long and Short of It about directing and filmmaking. Definitely my highlight so far.

After that, Sean got up and answered questions for 1 hour and 15 minutes. I was curled at the edge of the "stage" with my eyes glued on my hero, absorbing every word.

That was rotten enough to gag a maggot. Without those volunteers, Abbey would *never* have pulled off Project Elanor. They were helping make her dream come true and she rewarded them by making sure *she* got a seat next to the Movie Star while they sat outside in the rain. One would *think* that the Event Director would make a priority of keeping people informed of their duties, so everything would flow smoothly and according to plan. Abbey was too busy gazing at the movie star to *have* a plan in the first place.

Cameras were strictly forbidden at Project Elanor, so people would work, not snap photos of Sean. The volunteers were promised they would receive photographs and a video of the event, courtesy of professional crews who were donating those services. Although Abbey and Amy posted some cropped pictures to BoE.net, there was no opportunity to order prints or view the entire set of photos. There was no further mention of a video.

The photographer, Kate, had indeed offered to capture the event on film that day, but had not planned to donate the expensive supplies (i.e. film and developing). Abbey and Amy played the pity card until Kate agreed to finance those things herself. Yet Kate recalled neither Abbey nor Amy were particularly effusive with appreciation.

My cost was already well into the 200 dollar mark and I refused to spend any more. I was not much thanked by the 'evil twain' who only managed to complain that I had showed up way too early when I delivered the disks to their door. And I should try

191

to show up at a later time when delivering the next batch of film/disks. That show of gratitude was quite enough for me...

The video business was buzzard bait as well. There were no advance arrangements for video coverage of Project Elanor for the sake of the volunteers. Lucky for the liars, though, a few small local press crews heard of the event and showed up to film it. Folks generally assumed the crews were pros hired by the cons. One such crew, 3Dorks Productions, was actually invited to make an official video (after the fact).

> We learned about Project Elanor through TORn. At the time, we had thought we would just broadcast it as a segment on cable access networks. We were not making anything "official" until we spoke with Those Two later, just after PE.

> Post production was going slowly, but I was really pleased with it. Then they told us about their big plans for the rest of the year, HoF and Tentmoot, and there would be celebrity guests at each one. We were told we could film interviews with the stars. Even if we weren't fans, that kind of thing looks really great on your resume, so we agreed to do it for free.

> It was decided the Elanor video would be put on hold, to revamp the whole thing and make it into a longer documentary. At HoF, however, Abbey told us she was making her own documentary about BoE, that Sean Astin had promised to produce. She wanted to include our documentary as an "extra" on the DVD. I remember thinking at the time, "Where are YOUR cameras?" But also, "omg DVD produced by Sean Astin!!!"

After HoF, we could not get in touch with them. The time of Tentmoot rolled around, and we still hadn't heard a peep. We learned all the celebrities seemed to have dried up and Tentmoot had been scaled back to just one day, at the ROTK premier. None of us wanted to work at the premier, so we gave up. I rather wish we hadn't, as I think now the footage could be worth something for a different sort of documentary.

At the moment I am sitting on a nearly completed version of the Elanor Project video. If there are still people out there who'd be honestly interested in a short but glowing look at Project Elanor, I'd be willing to patch it up, polish it off and distribute it, if at all possible. I think those volunteers deserve SOMETHING!

Finally, MissTree was assigned to provide child care for the Astins during their stay.

I called BoE every HALF HOUR on Saturday, April 5, asking when I was supposed meet Christine. I got many different answers from increasingly rude voices. I was told Christine absolutely did not want to see anyone because she was tired and sleeping. 10 minutes later I was called by a different BoE staff member saying the Astins were out "seeing the town" and not even in the hotel.

When I finally met Christine later that night, one of the first things she asked was "Where were you all day?" Turns out she had been sitting in her hotel room with the children, waiting for me and asking people when I was going to show up.

MissTree was exasperated when I met her Sunday morning. I had my little son with me at Project

193

Elanor, since I was still nursing him. MissTree came over to cuddle him, saying she felt guilty because she was the child care volunteer but had no children to look after. She told me about her frustrating attempts to reach the Astins the day before.

I was surprised to learn there was a child care volunteer! OB never told me, and I specifically asked her about that. There were only 60 volunteers, so every hand was needed on the garden—and either MissTree or I could have chipped in if OB had simply coordinated the child care issue. OB knew darn well I was bringing my baby. If I had known about MissTree, I could have left the baby with her; I could also have looked after Sean's kids myself and freed MissTree up for work.

In addition, my five-year-old would have made a nice companion for Sean's six-year-old. He and Hubby spent Elanor Sunday at the Oregon Museum of Science and Industry. They would have gladly taken Sean's daughter along. Instead she was cooped up in the Riggs Institute building most of the day; there were too many power tools and heavy implements in the garden zone for her to help or play. She and her daddy planted a few sets of flowers together, but that was it. If she and MissTree hadn't clicked so well, that would have been one bored little girl.

At the time I chalked up the waste of resources to OB having too many obligations to plan it out better. But it seems more likely OB only cared about hanging with Sean Astin, screwing his family and everyone else in the process.

THE HALL OF FUBAR

After Ninja put an end to the Thought Police by removing the deleting privileges of Abbey and Amy, the bandwidth hummed from the release of pent-up rage. MissTree was at last able to defend herself from the accusations leveled after the Hall of Fire Music Festival.

When Hall of Fire came around, I BEGGED to be able to help. All Jordan ever said to me was "Go forth and get demo CDs from bands." I handed Jordan a huge stack of CDs with the contact info for each band written on the CD.

A week later Jordan claimed I'd never given him anything. However, about 12 hours later the roster for HoF was up and all but three or four of the bands listed were from my set of CDs.

So Hall of Fire actually comes around. None of the bands show up. I ask, "Why didn't you show? That's unlike you." A couple say, "We got an invite and emailed back saying we'd show and got no response." Other bands said they had NEVER been contacted to begin with.

About a day later I got calls and emails from several BoE members saying mysterious things like "I can't believe how you let BoE down" and "This is all your fault, I hope you're happy." Then some people slightly "higher up" in the echelons of BoE command called me very upset wanting to know why I hadn't gotten the permits for the event.

Hmmm...maybe because I was never asked to procure such permits?

I email Jordan, Abbey and the rest of the "senior staff." No response. I call them. I email again. The ONLY thing that happens at this point is that I am "accidentally" unsubbed from [the Prancing Pony] and all the BoE mailing lists I was on. After I re-subscribed, my posts had a strange penchant for disappearing.

MissTree lived in Seattle, four hours away from the Portland crowd; it wasn't likely she would directly confront Abbey or Amy. They could easily silence her on the message board. People generally knew MissTree really was involved with finding the bands, so it was not hard to believe she had other responsibilities as well. *Ergo*, she was the perfect scapegoat for HoF. Abbey and Amy laid the blame on her for such oversights as their failure to procure permits from the city, to invite and schedule musicians to perform, and to find out that groups cannot charge admission to events held in a public park.

Zinnia reported she was asked to arrange travel for Elijah Wood to appear at HoF. Zin handled the Astins' travel for Project Elanor in April, 2003. She had no reason to doubt "Jordan" when "he" asked her to book Elijah's flight. On July 9, 2003, she posted a request on the Pony for anyone with spare frequent flier miles to donate them for "a certain blue-eyed hobbit and his assistant." As they had with Sean, the Pony Pals came through and Zin was able to transfer enough miles into her account to get the tickets. It cost her $85 for the transfer, but the investment seemed worthwhile . . . until Diamond told her just a few days before HoF that Elijah would not be coming. Amy neglected to pass along this tidbit of information to Zin weeks earlier, when she learned Elijah was still filming in New Zealand.

Amy pretty much closed up shop on HoF once she learned Elijah couldn't make it. She didn't work on the venue or discover it required permits. She looked through MissTree's stack of demos[9] and sent out email invitations to the bands she liked, but never followed up with them. By all appearances, once she realized HoF wouldn't serve to ensnare Elijah Wood, she simply lost interest. The trouble was that Amy also planned to use this occasion to make Abbey's dreams come true, by having a *Movie Star Propose To Her On Stage*. Thus it was necessary to go through the motions of letting volunteers set up a stage, and pretending to be astounded when only a few bands showed up to perform.

The park ranger must have really thrown her, though, walking up in his short khaki pants and oversized walkie-talkie, demanding to see a permit. Amy was fortunate that she already had a lie prepared to explain the dismal turnout and lack of talent. When she learned she had also screwed up the permits, she already had a scapegoat handy. The trouble was, if she didn't go ahead and get these permits, there would be no stage for Sean to propose on, and that was not to Amy's liking!

Amy planned the movie star marriage proposal well in advance. She started networking online with BoE members a month before HoF. All four of the "hobbit actors" were rumored to be appearing at a fantasy convention, ComicCon, on July 19, 2003 in San Diego, CA. Amy had a slightly convoluted request for anyone who was going to ComicCon:

---

[9] Another Seattle volunteer was also asked to get demo CDs three weeks prior to HoF, so it is possible that Amy simply lost the CDs from MissTree.

> I need a Ringer to ask the guys if they'll do a favour
> when s/he's in the autograph line or at the Q&A. I
> want one of the hobbits to call during Hall of Fire
> so that we can hook the cell up to the mike...and
> I want them to help me propose.

HoF was scheduled for the July 26, 2003, so Amy basically wanted someone to discuss her request and pass on a written message to one of the actors. This message would provide the date, time, and wording of the marriage proposal. The actor would then call and make the proposal on the following weekend.

Amy wasn't able to find someone willing to waste their 45 seconds in the autograph line delivering her message, but a former Elanor volunteer, Tel, offered to bring it up directly with Sean Astin at a fan convention in Indiana called GenCon. This was even simpler, because GenCon took place on the same day as HoF, so Sean could just call Abbey right on the spot. Nonetheless, when Tel offered to approach Sean, Amy immediately IM'ed back, "Do you think he'd ask Elijah for us?" Alas, poor Amy had to settle for Sean Astin to deliver her dramatic proposal.

Obviously, it was absolutely necessary for the stage and the sound system to be ready for a call from Sean. Abbey just *couldn't* receive a proposal-by-proxy from a movie star in the obscurity of their living room! Who would know? Who would cheer, or applaud, or harbor a tinge of jealousy at Abbey's luck and "Jordan's" connections? Amy knew nothing had been done to ensure either performers or audience for HoF. Nonetheless, defying the protests of other volunteers, she dashed all over the city to obtain the necessary legalities at considerable expense. The permit from Portland Parks and Recreation was $1,835, Event Insurance was $665, and the remaining costs have been lost to obscurity.

But those weren't really Amy's expenses; she knew she could hit up the BoE community for donations to cover these checks. And she did just that, with great success. The Twins gave BoE $250, Sue cashed in $800—her savings for college—and the Pony Pals scraped together the rest to balance BoE's books. Amy and Abbey gushed with gratitude to their friends for rescuing BoE from bankruptcy and swore they had learned their lesson: "We will never again put out one more penny up-front than we can easily afford to lose without putting ourselves or the site in jeopardy."

That last sentence should actually read, "We now understand people will line our pockets with money if they believe they are supporting a good cause." Because that was the disposition of most of the money collected to "bail out" BoE from bankruptcy.

When Zinnia received a copy of the cancelled check from Portland Parks and Recreation, she accepted it as proof BoE spent (and lost) a lot of money on HoF. But after Tentmoot Crash, Sue decided to just check things out a bit at the Parks department.

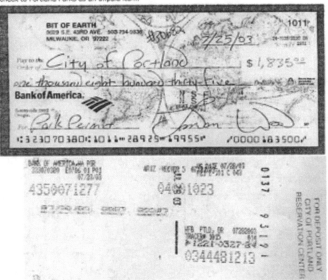

Reservation Center
Portland Parks & Recreation
1120 SW Fifth Ave., Suite 1302
Portland, Oregon 97204
Phone (503) 823-2525
fax (503) 823-2515

PORTLAND PARKS & RECREATION

Ensuring access to
leisure opportunities
and enhancing
Portland's natural beauty

8/6/03

Jordan Wood
9629 SE 43rd AVE
Milwaukee, OR 97222
RE: Unpaid check returned - Insufficient Funds

Dear Jordan Wood:

A payment for the below listed permit was processed at the Reservation Center on 7/25/03:

#30682 Hall of Fire Summer Music

A check was received in the amount of $1835.00 to pay for this rental. The bank has returned this check to Portland Parks as an unpaid item.

Letter and bounced check from HoF permits (on file at Portland Parks and Recreation).

Notice on the front of the copied check, the little letters "NSF." These stand for "Non Sufficient Funds." Notice also that the back of the check has two separate processing stamps from the bank. It is common practice for banks to process a check a second time if it bounces on the first try. I don't know why banks do this, other than to give themselves an excuse to charge more fees[10]. But in this case, the double run shows unequivocally that, despite raising funds to cover this expense, Amy never actually paid it.

But wait: Zinnia got a copy of the check—didn't she notice it had bounced? No, she hadn't, actually, because the check Zin received from "Jordan" looked like this:

Capture Date: 20030728 Sequence #: 4350071277   Mon Sep 08 16:26:11 CDT 2003

Same check number. Same handwriting and signature. But somehow the "NSF" stamp and the second processing stamp are missing. There are two possible conclusions one can draw from this evidence.

---

[10] Mojo Nixon says it best:"Finan-shoo-all Institutions/ Think they are so high-falutin'/Justa a bunch of coots inna three piece suits/try and steal all my loot.

1. Someone at Portland Parks doctored this check to make it look liked it bounced.

2. Amy and/or Abbey doctored this check to make it look like it cleared.

I know which one *I'm* inclined to believe.

One last observation: The lumber for the Elanor deck was actually paid for by two separate checks, both of which cleared to the satisfaction of Parr Lumber. The first, for $1,000, was sent to Parr in May, 2003. The second, for $890, was given to their friend Klyta for hand delivery to Parr on July 28, 2003. . . immediately after the "bailout" money came in. Klyta was unable to deliver the check that day—Amy sent her to the wrong address—but Parr eventually got it in the mail.

Thus it seems likely some of the money raised for the "bailout" paid off the Elanor deck. This is not terrible in itself, but it does mean $890 *more* dollars of the Project Elanor income went straight into Abbey and Amy's pockets. Regardless of the source, it was surely the same lovely green.

Amy probably felt exceptionally entitled to all that money and attention: the marriage proposal from Sean at the Hall of Fire Music Festival took place on her 20th birthday.

BILLYGATE

The Pony Pals had a funny feeling they had been misled about Billy Boyd's interest in attending the Lost Palantir Film Festival. It was no surprise that people had stories to tell about this issue as well.

Amy originally delegated the task of contacting Billy's representatives to "Eeyore," who lived in England and participated in BoE online. Billy's representative, Aude Powell, was based in London, so this seemed reasonable for phone bill and time zone purposes. Eeyore giggled over being dressed up with the lofty title, "International Celebrity Attaché."

Amy drafted an invitation to Billy Boyd and sent it to Eeyore, who in turn passed it on to Aude Powell. Eeyore left for a brief vacation and returned to find that Aude had replied right away. Aude had asked for an immediate call back with regard to Billy's participation, and this message sat unread in Eeyore's inbox for a week!

Eeyore forwarded Aude's message to "Jordan" sometime around August 22, 2003. At that point, Eeyore found her attaché status had been detached, as Amy immediately took control over contact with Aude.

On August 27, 2003, Amy decided she was ready for the next step. She called HeadDesk, who offered earlier to help by spreading the word about Billy on the BB.net Forum. Amy told HeadDesk, "We have Billy," and when HeadDesk asked precisely what that meant, "Jordan" responded Billy was confirmed to attend LP. Amy provided tantalizing details:

Billy was so interested in and excited about attending LP that he'd had his LA agent, Daphne, call him and wake him up (this was at about 3 a.m. Scotland time), and he had gotten on his own computer and reserved his own ticket for the event. All that needs to be done is raising the money for Billy's ticket.

Amy gave HeadDesk some information to post at the BillyBoyd.net Forum, inviting people who wanted to attend LP to donate toward Billy's $900 airfare. HeadDesk was concerned Stewart might not appreciate The Forum being used to announce Billy's agenda, but "Jordan" assured her Billy, Daphne, and Aude approved everything, even the fundraising. "Stewart won't be able to say anything about it," "Jordan" said. HeadDesk described her thoughts at that time:

> I knew Jordan and Abbey pulled off Project Elanor, with Sean's blessing and his presence. I had seen the pictures of everyone working hard and getting it done, and read reports from people who had been part of it and had a wonderful time. Because I trust and respect Sean, and I thought he trusted them, I thought it was safe to trust them.
>
> I wrote up an announcement and posted it on The Forum. Within hours, I had probably a dozen inquiries, and eventually four donations of $25 or less were made to my Paypal account.
>
> The next morning I found the thread was gone and I had a very strongly worded Personal Message from Stewart.

What happened next is still unclear. Several of Billy Boyd's representatives were invited to comment on the situation. Daphne has changed firms and could not be located. Stewart made some statements in August, 2003, but has since declined to comment further. Aude made comments that appear to conflict with Stewart's; it is impossible to determine which story is true. The concrete facts are as follows:

- Stewart privately told HeadDesk Billy wanted to attend LP, but he would not be "confirmed" until he had a paid ticket in his hand.

- Additional donors came forward, even after HeadDesk's post was removed, to help purchase Billy's ticket. A Pony Pal, "MST500," wired $500 directly to BoE via Western Union, based on her belief that Billy would be coming to Portland to host this charity event. Before the end of August, 2003, BoE had enough money to pay for Billy's airfare—especially considering that BoE probably had enough money the whole time, left over from the HoF bailout![11]

- BabyBlues serendipitously chatted with HeadDesk just prior to making a press release announcing that Billy was officially confirmed for LP. BabyBlues had no idea there were any problems with Billy—Amy hadn't mentioned this detail as they discussed the wording of the release.

I can wholeheartedly back up HeadDesk.
After that PM with HD, I called Jordan to

---

[11] It's quite possible that if Abbey and Amy had just used the HoF Bailout money to quietly buy Billy's ticket, Lost Palantir would have gone off without a hitch. I can only speculate that greed prompted them to take a second bite of the apple, which ultimately cost them Billy's appearance.

find out what was going on. Jordan's story was as HD said - "Stewart is an arrogant asshole and now we're having to straighten everything out." I got angry with that statement because I respected Stewart and knew him to do things in Billy's best interest. That's when I talked to my attorney friend. That's when I backed away from doing PR for LP. I PMd Stewart to let him know what I suspected and that I was no longer involved with Lost Palantir.

On the advice of her attorney, BabyBlues stopped communicating with BoE in early September. This was probably great advice for her sake, but the rest of us were left with one less apple of truth to bob for.

• HeadDesk didn't know what to make of things. She kept corresponding with Stewart, but he wasn't being particularly helpful. Nothing Stewart said contradicted "Jordan's" claim that Stewart was acting bullheaded. Then Stewart abruptly stopped communicating altogether. Another authoritative and honest voice jumped ship.

• I personally saw an email on "Jordan's" computer from Daphne. The gist of this email was that Billy would *no longer* be able to appear at LP. I have no idea now whether this document was authentic, but it appeared so at the time. I, too, felt this confirmed "Jordan's" story; Billy obviously had agreed to come but was *no longer* interested, presumably because of Stewart's meddling.

• Amy, as always, played the confusion to the hilt. She openly claimed to be working on this with Aude and Daphne, and made statements like, "Stewart is going down for this one," and this:

> "Appropriate Action" would be for him to lay off, and yes, I will call Daphne. This is not some random fan spouting off about an unsanctioned pipe-dream. We've got the confirmation, and Stewart needs to start double-checking before he layeth down the unjustified smack. He is NOT the first person to know when Billy does anything and everything, and just because he doesn't know yet - especially with breaking news - means he should CHECK, not just automatically get his knickers in a twist.

• Unbeknownst to all of us, other people saw Billy's name on the LP event page and called it to Stewart's attention as early as June, 2003. At least one person also sent an email detailing the unusual losses reported after Hall of Fire. None of these people received responses, but it is safe to say Stewart was supplied with information about BoE long before HeadDesk's post came up on The BB.net Forum. He had everything necessary at his disposal to conclude there was some very fishy fundraising going on at BoE.

• Amy told HeadDesk that Stewart was lying about BoE, calling BoE a sham organization and persuading Billy to stay away from LP. Amy apparently had no idea Stewart had been filled in about HoF and the "bailout." Thus Amy, thinking she was telling the truth, was actually telling a falsehood, namely that Stewart was lying, because she didn't know Stewart was aware of, and therefore telling, the truth.[12]

• HeadDesk believed Stewart to be a man of his word and smelled a rat at last. She sent one last message to Stewart to let him know "Jordan" was saying nasty things about him, and she, too, had doubts about LP. She refunded all donations that were sent to her PayPal account and warned MST500 to cancel her Western Union payment. Of course, this earned her a slot on the BoE Shit List.

• Amy initiated damage control by saying HeadDesk screwed up matters with Billy. She made up a story that HD altered the approved text of the donation request, making it "overzealous" and deceptive, which led Stewart to yank it from The Forum and condemn BoE. HeadDesk found herself receiving angry messages from "friends," lashing out at her for blowing their chance to meet Billy Boyd.

• HeadDesk recognized she now occupied the same scapegoat position MissTree was forced into after HoF. She already knew any attempts to explain the truth on the Pony would disappear like MissTree's. Stewart wouldn't chat with

---

[12] This reminds me of Heideggers's baffling credo that "hence also the will, as the will to will, is itself the will to power, in the sense of the empowering to power." It also reminds me of every William Faulkner book I have ever read. The budding author within me cries in anguish, "How did it come to this?!"

her any more either for reasons he wouldn't divulge. For HeadDesk, this began as a golden opportunity to participate in a wonderful BoE event similar to Project Elanor. It ended with the realization that "Jordan" was hanging her out to dry, alienating her friends on both BoE and BB.net, and she was powerless to stop it.

And in a selfish way, I was horrified whatever Stewart was being told about me, was getting passed on to Billy. I knew Stewart and Billy had been communicating about the situation, and the thought that Stewart and Billy might think I was somehow involved in a plan to extort money from fans, or promoting a fake film festival was simply awful.

• Back in Oregon, on September 4, 2003, Abbey and Amy claimed they called Sean Astin for "advice on how to handle this." They reported Sean wanted to attend LP, and tour the Elanor Garden with reporters from the E! Entertainment Network. Amy even claimed Sean volunteered to set things right with Billy.

Sean actually brought it up with us, as he'd heard about it from Billy at a photo shoot - nothing bad, just a lot of confusion on Billy's end. We told Sean about the miscommunication and Stewart's refusal to talk, and Sean immediately went into director mode. He talked about how "harnessing the power of the internet is important but mustn't get out of hand" and called Daphne. He confirmed our story with her, and instructed her to call Billy, as did he. She talked to Billy today, the

209

response, while we have no details, was positive, and she's working on schedule now.

- For the next two weeks, Amy led the BoE crowd on a bizarre roller-coaster ride. "Billy's still trying to make it." "Billy couldn't get out of his taping on Conan." "Dom, Viggo and Sean are interested." "None of them can make it, their schedules filled up with promos when the ROTK trailer was released." "They *will* be sending videos, we're sending Sue down there to tape them now."

- No one knew what was true then, and that hasn't changed, but Sean came through in spades with his warm and upbeat video in which he directly addressed "the audience of The Lost Palantir Film Festival" and referred to "Jordan" and Abbey by name.

- Billy Boyd did not appear on the Conan O'Brien show on or near September 20, 2003. He was photographed as a celebrity spectator at the Albert Hall in London on that date, during the Disney Channel Kids Awards.

It seems Amy really managed to sink her hooks into Billy at some point, just as she did with so many other celebrities (and even more chumps like me). Fortunately, Billy had the benefit of a watchdog like Stewart to keep him from falling into the cesspit with the rest of us.

It is encouraging that Billy Boyd was truly interested in supporting an amateur film festival to raise funds for charity. Perhaps when things started to look unsavory, he and his people deliberately used

Conan or the Disney event as an excuse to graciously back out of LP. It is also only natural for his publicists to shelter him from the fallout that BoE generated. But I found it very disconcerting when my own publicist received this missive:

> From: Brunskill Management Ltd.
> Sent: Monday August 09, 2004 8:22AM
>
> For your reference we at no time committed Billy to appear: only that we would pass on their request and if Billy was able to commit, we would be in touch. He was not able to, and therefore we did not commit him.
>
> However, our files indicated that a liaison was picked up with Daphne/David Lust at Patricola-Lust Public Relations. However they too were informed by us that he was unable to commit to this event.
>
> Ms Aude Powell

Did Aude just say Billy was never going to appear? The same Aude who requested an immediate phone call in mid-August, 2003, to discuss his appearance? Meaning Stewart was telling a bald-faced lie to HeadDesk two weeks later, which only added fuel to this bewildering fire? Or did she just pass the buck to Daphne, à la "if Daphne said Billy was committed, she did so without our authorization?" Or is this some Clintonesque usage of the words "we" and "commit," to downplay the fact that *Billy* agreed to an appearance that *Brunskill* later turned down?

After reading Aude's statement, I emailed Stewart to ask if he would comment. At first, Stewart said, "I would like to see your questions, see what is going on, get Billy's permission and take it from there." But after I sent my questions about the missing details from this chapter, his tone changed. "After consideration I feel that it is best that any information relating the the BoE incident is best served through Billy's representation."

Any self-respecting fangirl knows Billy and Stewart have been best friends for ages, and Stewart is infamous for his blunt-but-honest demeanor. I sent another message to Stewart, telling him I was very uncomfortable with the conflicting information I now had about Billy's intent. I begged him to clarify things, even if only "off the record." He replied, "I have stated, quite clearly, that I cannot talk about this unless instructed by my client. You have to go through [Billy's representative Aude Powell] to ask permission for me to talk on this." Stewart is unable, or unwilling, to approach Billy himself? Or is he suggesting that Aude ordered him to clam up, lest it leak out that Amy had, in fact, been able to wrap yet another celebrity around her finger?

Something seems rotten in Scotland, and although I hate to vindicate Amy Player in any way, she could teach these people a lot about "working the story." Although it's obvious we will never know the full extent of it, it sure appears that Amy Player successfully pulled *something* over on Billy and his PR people.

THE FALSE PALANTIR

Even without the celebrity scams, LP was stinkier than expensive cheese. One problem was that Amy never advertised this event. When it really looked like Billy Boyd would attend, it was reasonable to feel confident about tickets selling well. Portland definitely contained 700 people who would line up around the block for an event hosted by Billy Boyd, even if the news was spread strictly through the grapevine. But later, when Amy knew Billy's appearance was tenuous at best, she still found excuses not to advertise the film festival itself.

"Jordan" said Rob Bob forbade any advertising "until Mr. Boyd's appearance was confirmed." I told "him," "You should at least make some posters and put them up around town, or in the film departments at local colleges. Leave Billy off the poster entirely; just announce an amateur fantasy film night."

"Can't do it," said Amy. "Rob Bob said no advertising."[13] "Jordan" assured me "he" wasn't concerned in the slightest about attendance, because 400 tickets had already been purchased through Ticketweb.

Despite Amy's confidence, a grand total of 63 paid guests showed up and munched on popcorn at the Lost Palantir Film Festival. A number of BoE "staff" were less than thrilled by the turnout for this "fundraiser." "Jordan" explained Ticketweb screwed up the reported ticket sales, so BoE had no idea they needed to advertise more aggressively.

---

[13] Rob told me, months later, that this was a lie, Rob had been worried about the turnout and had *encouraged* Amy to advertise!

The lack of advertising was hardly "his" fault anyway: "BabyBlues," BoE's new PR person, was in charge of that. If anyone had a complaint, they should take it up with her, and—big surprise—she was somewhat scarce after the event. Unlike previous scapegoats HeadDesk and MissTree, BabyBlues was not being censored from the message boards by the Thought Police. BabyBlues was deliberately avoiding any association with BoE to protect her professional reputation.

BabyBlues tried to advertise LP, but was undermined in the usual fashion by Amy's laziness and incompetence. When the battle with Stewart took place, BabyBlues "couldn't risk being further involved with what seemed to be an increasingly corrupt organization."

She did come back and attempt to make professional press kits to distribute at LP. Amy didn't manage to bring the proper folders for the kits to the theater, so BabyBlues ended up frantically assembling the kits during the festival with inadequate supplies. She was willing to do this, however, for the sake of the E! reporters. As a PR professional, this was a great opportunity for shmoozing, and she was excited to showcase her excellent work to a potential Industry Contact. But after all her effort to assemble the press kits, she was furious to learn the E! crew didn't receive one.

It turned out Amy misrepresented the reporters anyway. The following message was sent to me on January 7, 2004, by one of the crew, "NotE!butNice."

I do not nor have I EVER written for E! or ET. I got introduced as being from E! by Jordan. I kept correcting him/her on this.

I attended LP because I was already scheduled to be in Portland for other reasons. We wanted to do a story on the film festival and the fan-fundraising concept. I never wrote my story because I didn't believe the charity line either.

I was not even approached about going to the garden until I was leaving. I turned Jordan down because I was so fed up with her. I am so mad to know he/she/it made promises on my behalf. I am so sorry Jordan used my presence at the festival to get more work out of you.

I walked away that night convinced BoE would all just implode on itself. I just thought it would happen in a few days, not on the grand scale it did.

I wondered briefly why NotE!butNice didn't voice those opinions at LP, but I quickly realized that was impossible. Amy manipulated the situation such that the only way NotE! could convey her observations and disgust was to make a scene. For example, I tried to approach the crew and show them the ceramic Palantir I made for the grand prize. "Jordan" swooped in like a ravenous vulture, intercepting NotE! and monopolizing the conversation. "He" made damn sure NotE! didn't have a chance to speak to me alone and blow "his" story.

If all that weren't enough, the film contest itself appears to have been rigged. There was a very low-quality film on the playbill that had obviously been shot as an afterthought on some sort of web-quality streaming video camera. Although it did have the requisite LOTR theme via the costumes, it had no real beginning, ending, or plot. It looked for all the world like someone turned on their camera at a fantasy convention, recorded the passersby, then slapped on beginning and ending credits.

A friend of one of the entrants, "Thorin," visited the LP web pages to see if her friend won anything. She had never seen BoE before, and was stunned to recognize the description of aforementioned poor quality "movie" as one that she had appeared in. This "movie" was simply a memento another friend recorded on his camera phone. He posted it on his website just to share it with his friends in the video.

Thorin discussed this with her "co-stars," who confirmed none of them had submitted it to LP. She put out a plea on her own LiveJournal, asking people who had gone to LP to get in touch with her. She quizzed the people who responded about what they saw at the theater, and confirmed that the film shown at LP was the same one from her buddy's website.

Thorin decided to find out just how this film got submitted to LP. She called Abbey and "Jordan" and got into what she described as "an extremely bizarre, hour-long phone call, which was the biggest display of an attempted fandom pissing contest."

> They were basically trying to impress me with what "Big Name Fans" they were. Even at the time, knowing nothing about them, there was lots of eye rolling on my end. [For example], they were making such a big deal that "they've seen the LOTR costumes," and I could ask them any questions about the costumes I wanted... Ummm... If I have questions, I'll just ask Richard Taylor.
>
> The gist of the conversation was that the movie was submitted over AIM, and they were unwilling

to look through their AIM logs to see who it was from. Which was kinda interesting, considering that if we had "won something," wouldn't they need our contact information? Our first thought was that someone submitted it just to get the "prize" themselves... but if they had, they would have been sure to leave contact info!

We garnered the impression Abbey or Jordan had taken it off our website (or knew who had) and then proceeded to lie to us about it.

That made sense, because most of the entries for LP came from the BoE household. Perhaps, in a rare lapse in their typical self-absorption, Abbey and Amy realized it might look a bit narcissistic if the Film Festival consisted mainly of their own entries. They probably culled this entry off the Web to fill out the schedule a tad—and conveniently stacked the deck in their favor for the contest, by selecting a film that was never intended to be of competitive quality. Thorin agreed.

I really don't think some random person would snag a film like that and submit it—I mean, if you're going to submit a phony entry, at least pick one that has a chance of winning, right? I just thought you might like to know Abbey and Amy were dishonest not just about big things, but even the small, day to day stuff that betrayed and took advantage of other fans.

217

DOMINIC: CON AGAIN

Siri Garber was Dominic Monaghan's PR representative at the time of the Lost Palantir Film Festival. On January 6, 2004, I called Siri at Platform PR and explained how Amy tried to send Sue over to Dom's house to get his video greetings for LP.

Siri didn't sputter, but I could tell she really wanted to. "There was never any agreement for anyone to meet with Dominic to make a video."

We discussed Amy's claim that Dom was sick and miserable that day because he had his wisdom teeth pulled. Siri remembered that day, because Dom really was sick and miserable because of his teeth. She was absolutely certain Dom never arranged to meet Sue at any time, for any purpose.

The same was true for Viggo Mortensen. I called his PR representative at BWR as soon as I hung up with Siri. I never caught the name of the person I spoke to, but she confirmed there was never any arrangement for Viggo to meet Sue on either day. She was vehement that Viggo would have nothing to do with BoE.

BoE paid for Sue's airplane ticket to LA, but Sue blew $120 of her own money on cabs and food. The tape from Sean could have been Fed-Ex'd by Sean or his representatives for about $17.

This scenario is primarily about the abuse of Sue rather than Dominic Monaghan, per se, but Abbey and Amy managed to stick a different stiletto into Dom. To wit: the Oregon Attorney General investigated BoE and their fundraising tactics. The investigation is discussed in Part III, but one small part is worthy of mention here, as Abbey and Amy attempt to defend their claim that BoE supported the charity "Future Forests."

> BitofEarth.net was seeking an environmentally-based charity or cause to be supported by future projects and events. Mr. Dominic Monaghan, who plays the character Meriadoc "Merry" Brandybuck, began campaigning in late fall 2002 for carbon neutrality in various print, internet, and television media. He was not presenting the organization as a for-profit business at all, but rather encouraging that fans make donations towards the purchase of sustainable forest in a manner consistent with the customary solicitation of charity funds. Upon hearing about Future Forests, we examined their website, which we found to be extremely confusing, but did hold up the appearance of a not-for-profit organization. By this time, several other fan groups were preparing donations to Future Forests [at] Mr. Monaghan's behest, and if we were in fact in error as to the precise nature of Future Forests, we wish to apologize, as well as suggest that any other prominent fan sites associated with Mr. Monaghan or the hobbits should likely be contacted, as this is a commonly held conception in fandom, to prevent them from making the same error.

Let's break that down sentence by sentence.

1. BoE wanted another charity to "support."[14]
2. Dominic encouraged people to support Future Forests (FF).
3. Dominic didn't explain FF was a for-profit corporation.

---

[14] Apparently they felt that RIF didn't deserve such largesse.

4. Abbey and Amy were too moronic to glean that fact from FF's website.
5. Everybody else was doing what Dom said and they all probably thought FF was a charity too.

So, BoE's false representation of itself as a charity fundraiser is . . . all Dominic Monaghan's fault? Welcome to the BoE Scapegoat Club, Dom.

IF YOU TELL THEM, THEY WILL COME.

Project Elanor was meant to be a small event. Only so many people can safely crowd into a construction zone like the garden plot, and the number of volunteers was deliberately limited to 60. The TTT screening Sean hosted on the previous night was an order of magnitude larger, although the theater was not filled to capacity.

The screening was not scheduled until the last minute, because it was uncertain whether Sean would be able to come up to Portland early enough to host it. It was therefore impossible to advertise the show through newspapers or radio. The turnout for the screening was obviously the result of word-of-mouth and news blurbs that were posted on TORn.

Right after such a successful venture, Abbey and Amy might have legitimately believed that traditional advertising was unnecessary. They drew plenty of warm bodies in the theater without any advertising, so why waste money or time on ads when the Web was good enough *and* free?

There was a problem with this rationalization. Project Elanor had been a feature on the Internet since September, 2002. It was mentioned on TORn multiple times in that six-month period and the TTT screening itself was mentioned daily on TORn from March 28, 2003 to April 4, 2003. There had been plenty of time for news of the event to spread—and the event *always* promised the possibility of Sean Astin. In the end, despite Sean's confirmed appearance, months of hints, and a week of daily reminders, word-of-Web wasn't enough to fill the 700-seat theater.

One could still give Abbey and Amy the benefit of the doubt after the flopped Hall of Fire festival. Amy maintained the park would surely have filled if Elijah Wood had been the emcee. Alas, if only Elijah wasn't forced to back out at the last minute (leaving poor Zinnia stuck with an unused airplane ticket). An appearance by Elijah would guarantee good PR on TORn. It was reasonable to expect a mass of squeeing fangirls storming the gates to ogle the young, single Elijah.

Amy reassured everyone BoE learned its lesson, made connections, and found a wonderful new PR representative in BabyBlues. Everyone anticipated that the Lost Palantir Film Festival would benefit from her expertise. It certainly could have, if Amy had chosen to take BabyBlues' advice.

I recommended an initial press release about a month prior to the event. That release went out to about 25 radio stations, the 4 major TV stations in Portland, and 8 Portland area newspapers. No guarantees, just statements that BoE was in contact with celebrities from the films and possible attendance. I heard nothing from Jordan. I DID hear back from a DJ who was a HUGE Rings fan and wanted to help promote it.

Shortly after that, the whole Billy fiasco blew up and I told Jordan there was no way I could put my professional reputation on the line for BoE.

About two days before LP, Jordan asked if I would please write and distribute press releases stating there was still a chance for Billy's appearance AND they would have videos from Dom and Viggo. I tried to explain the futility of such an effort at that late date, but I did end up writing a release.

I questioned Jordan about whether or not they had permission from the celebrities' press agents to publish a press release WITHOUT their reviewing it for accuracy. Jordan said Mr. Boyd's agent laughed and just said "so long as it's factual, we don't care what you write." Um...I've been in Marketing and PR for more than 12 years - I found that statement VERY hard to swallow. Obviously it was a ruse to prevent me from forwarding content to the agents for review. Jordan also wanted me to change the PR contact name and info to MY NAME. Not just no, HELL NO!

I spent the next day and a half distributing the releases, writing bios for Dom and Viggo, and cleaning up the Sean bio that Jordan sent me. I spent my own money to produce a quantity of releases and bios (in color) so that press kits could be put together "on the fly" at LP. I told Jordan EXACTLY what folders to bring, and when I arrived with the press materials, there were no folders. He sent someone over to the mall to buy some folders (which were the wrong thing) and I had to assemble the press kits on my hands and knees. For nothing. I don't believe the reporter even got one. My supposition is because Jordan couldn't back ANY of what was said in the press kit.

Whether the radio, TV, or newspapers did anything with the releases, I don't know. I was so disgusted I didn't follow up with any of the media to see if we got any coverage.

And of course, "Jordan" told NotE!, "BabyBlues was to blame for the lack of media attention."

223

Fortunately, NotE! was savvy enough not to believe a word "he" said.

Another volunteer, Della, tells a similar story about the advertising for Tentmoot.

I agreed to send faxes for Jordan about Tentmoot. On Oct. 28th I was sent the information and faxed the requests for the various stars to either attend Tentmoot or send a video tape. He even had me send one to Leonard Nimoy's agent requesting an appearance.

I have done some PR work, and I know a "pat" celebrity answer when I hear one. Where Jordan heard a "yes," I heard "please leave me alone."

Jordan once said to me these charity events were to be a springboard for his career. I thought, "not as selfless as it had seemed, but still it was worthwhile."

I didn't hear anything from him until the end of Nov. We made up the Tentmoot Press Release. I did a good job. It is 12 pages long! Then Thanksgiving week, I received fax numbers for newspapers, TV and radio stations for California and Oregon. I started faxing the pages on Thanksgiving day.

Thanksgiving fell on November 27, 2003. Tentmoot was scheduled to open two weeks later, on December 11. Amy did not begin advertising Tentmoot until two weeks prior to opening day, even though this method resulted in not one but two dismal failures earlier in the year. Amy also knew full well that six months of Internet teasers and a week of daily posts on TORn could not draw more than 600 people to see Sean Astin host the TTT screening.

Despite this knowledge, Amy projected attendance figures for Tentmoot at 4,000 to 10,000. She mentioned these figures on all her invitations to celebrities and to businesses like the Convention Center and the Doubletree Hotel. She claimed this figure was based on the 5,000 people who attended Tentmoot 2002.

However, she neglected to mention that Tentmoot 2002 was a free party, held in the Lloyd Center 10 parking lot on the night before the premiere of TTT. She somehow overlooked the fact that those people came to stand in line for the movie, and "attended" the party because it was already taking place around them.

To summarize: BoE did nothing to advertise (or even organize!) HoF, once they determined Elijah Wood could not attend. BoE did nothing to advertise LP, most likely because they were making false claims of celebrity appearances. But BoE did nothing to advertise Tentmoot, even though not all the celebrity appearances were phony. I believe I detect a pattern:

1. BoE invites a celebrity to a festival.
2. BoE secures a legitimate place to hold the festival and spends money on the appropriate permits (even if this is utterly futile). Every thing looks good on paper.
3. BoE does *not* advertise this festival to the general public.
4. BoE blames some hapless volunteer for "screwing up" the advertising.

If Billy, Elijah, or the Kiwis made it to Portland, what would they have encountered? An appropriate venue, all the necessary paperwork, a banner out front saying "Welcome, Fans!" but no actual fans in attendance. No one but Amy, Abbey and a handful of BoE volunteers. If they were put off by the pathetic turnout, "Jordan" would just shrug "his" shoulders and say, "We did our best, this kind of thing happens when you have to rely upon volunteers to handle the advertising."

It would seem there was one goal all along: to attract celebrities to Portland for Abbey and Amy to fawn over, while other people paid for it all. When I mentioned this to Sue, she cocked her head a moment and said, "'Jordan' did say once that Abbey had a fantasy of meeting the entire cast, and 'he' was going to make it come true for her."

THE CHOICES OF MISTRESS DIAMOND

Cherie Deuvall, aka Diamond, aka Emily Sharpe, aka Crystal.

Cherie "Diamond" Deuvall hauled, shoveled, weeded, planted, and otherwise flexed and bent heroically at the Elanor Garden. She and Bob were the only "hobbit kids" to maintain steady employment while they lived together in Portland. She kept the same work ethic in LA, immediately getting a job as a telephone canvasser, then switched to a barrista position at a java joint called Koffee Klatch. Even Tall Paul, during his misadventure in LA, felt Di "seemed to be the sane one and quite unaware of what was going on."

When Tentmoot crashed, Di seemed just as shocked as the rest of us. She stayed behind to work when Amy and Abbey came up to Portland for the Line Party. She was tearful whenever she checked in with her friends up north. Like all of us, she was uncertain of the truth, but unlike everyone else, she was completely emerged in Lie-Lie Land for all but those few days when Abbey and Amy were in Oregon. Those Two might not have been able to fool everyone else, but they still had a chance to work on Di.

Di was willing to give them that chance, too. She didn't want to hear my story of the Air New Zealand situation, but asked me to put it in writing. Abbey and "Jordan" gave her a different version of events and she wanted to give each side an opportunity to present their story.

> Abbey and Jordan have until January 1st to hand over their proof to me. While I doubt that they will be able to do so, even a court of law gives a suspect a chance to give proof. How can I do any less? I must treat this as a court case.

I forwarded the emails from Air NZ so Di could see the proof of "Jordan's" lies. She sent me contact information for Tall Paul and Jed Brophy, so I could speak to them myself. Di and I exchanged several calls and emails. I encouraged her to confront Those Two about the nonexistent donations to RIF. I said, "Tell them to SHOW YOU THE MONEY, Diamond! My guess is that they can't. And will have a billion bullshit stories about how the check was never returned, and the receipts were lost in the move, and their ledger caught on fire from a cigarette ash on that entry, etc etc etc."

January 1, 2004 came and went, and Di was still "undecided" about whom to believe. I reminded her

228

she had given Those Two a reasonable deadline to prove themselves legitimate, but she told me she wanted to give them more time.

The three of them drove to Oregon for Amy's arraignment for identity theft on January 13, 2004.[15] Sue told Abbey and Amy to bring up the rest of her things from the San Dimas apartment and return them to her at the courthouse. Unfortunately, Sue and I were directed to the wrong courthouse that morning. We quickly discovered our mistake and rushed across town to the correct place. We arrived 15 minutes late but Abbey, Amy, and Di had already left. Di posted news of that trip in her online journal.

> Jan 14, 1:41 **BWAH?**
> Arrived at the courthouse to find that those who said they would be there were not there. Where was all this proof that was supposed to send J to jail? Obviously the detective couldn't even find it. But thank God!!! J is a free man. We went and celebrated with breakfast. Go us!!!

> Jan 14, 1:55 **HAH!**
> Take THAT, you fuckers!!!

> Jan 14, 4:22 **YOU ARE THE ONES WHO ARE THE BALL LICKERS!**
> Just talked to Bobbie at Parr lumber. They said they were paid with the check [Abbey and Jordan] said they'd paid them with. Does safety dance of happiness. And I forgot, we were running to Mexico, huh? So why did we show up and they didn't?

---

[15] This matter is discussed in detail in part III.

Obviously, Diamond succumbed to the Dark Side.

It was nonetheless a huge surprise to receive a call from Wells Fargo Collections on January 28, 2004. Four months earlier, I drove Di to Wells Fargo and cosigned a loan for her—a loan that *all* the kids needed in order to afford their move to Los Angeles. I assumed she was handling her financial responsibilities to Wells Fargo. She had income and the monthly payment was very affordable. Wells Fargo hadn't mentioned anything to me before, and I never imagined Wells Fargo would hesitate to speak up if there was a problem.

There was a problem, however. Di's first payment was due October 1, 2003, and monthly thereafter. Wells Fargo tried to call her in January, 2004, but the number in their records was disconnected. The phone was in Bob's name and he refused to pay for Amy's $1,700 in calls to PR agencies in New Zealand. That put an end to Di's *old* phone number.

I tracked down Di's parents, only to learn she hadn't given them a new number—and she only called in when she needed money, using the old "Hi, Daddy!" routine. Fortunately, Wells Fargo had Di's work number and I finally reached her.

Di said "Jordan" was supposed to take care of the payments—she always turned her paycheck over to "him" as the household financial manager (something Sue and Bob were asked to do, but refused). She pleaded ignorance—she hadn't known payments were due because she hadn't received any statements.

I asked, "Did you ever send Wells Fargo your new address after you moved to LA?"

"Uh, umm…"

I interrupted her in mid-lie, having learned from this adventure how to spot one in the embryonic state.

"Cut the crap, Di. That was incredibly irresponsible of you, not to keep them current. I am so disappointed in you I can't even describe it." I asked her flat out, "Are you planning to stick me with the payments on this loan?"

"No," she said flatly.

I gave her the toll-free number for Wells Fargo. Collections and she promised to call them first thing in the morning. She didn't call. She put 116 minutes on the prepaid calling card Helen gave her for emergencies, but she didn't call Wells Fargo.

Once again, I had to track her down. I didn't know if she even *had* a phone at home, so I tried the manager of their apartment complex. This woman was so incompetent she gave me two separate wrong numbers for her tenant. Then she refused to walk over and knock on Di's door for me[16]. I gave up on

---

[16] I believe these shysters were able to get an apartment from this woman because she couldn't find her ass with both hands. I agreed to cosign their lease, but never actually did because they never sent me anything to sign. They talked the manager into letting them move in anyway, explaining that they were sure I'd send back the paperwork ASAP.

When Bob and Sue moved out, this same woman let Abbey, Amy and Cherie move into a smaller unit on the property, and gave them back *the entire deposit* on the original apartment! Even though five people had been on the lease, she gave all the deposit money to those three. THEN she did not make them put down a deposit on the new unit! Needless to say, they never paid another penny of rent and had to be evicted in June, 2004.

I own the fact that I decided to give these kids money without verifying the stories they were telling me, but this gal gave them a freebie apartment after the sheriff came pounding on

that route and called the San Dimas Sheriff. They grumbled a bit, but were willing to send someone over to knock on the door. Although no one answered, I knew the three of them were slithering around behind the curtains, trying not to breathe too loudly between "This is the Sheriff," and "Open up, please."

The visit from the sheriff proved effective, as Cherie called Wells Fargo an hour later and arranged to make some payments. The representative explained that Di agreed to pay off the past due amount over time, and noted that very few Wells Fargo customers ever sic the sheriff on deadbeats. I diligently sent Di gentle reminders before her payment due date over the next few months.

- I am going to hound you ALL I WANT until you PROVE to me that you are capable of paying the money you agreed to pay. And it's not harassment, it's BUSINESS. Get it? You welch on a loan, I have the right to make sure you're not ripping me off. Period.

- You go on back to your little world of denial—just pull your head out of it long enough to make that loan payment. Which, by the way, is DUE at the end of the month. That means it needs to AR-RIVE at Wells Fargo BY Feb. 29. That is a Sunday. Mail doesn't come on Sunday. And Wells Fargo is a bank, it won't be open to process your check on Saturday. So it really needs to be at Wells Fargo by Friday Feb 27. It takes a couple

---

the door. Remember the last time you went through a hassle of paying for a credit check and deposit on a new apartment? Amy could sell the Pope a double bed.

days to get through the mail. That means you need to mail this check by the 23rd AT THE LATEST, or you'll need to do another check-by-phone. Is there anything here you do not understand?

- I will call Wells Fargo before I leave for LA. If they have no record of receiving a payment from you by then, I <u>will</u> be coming to visit you, to extract cash from you to pay the debt you owe. And after that snippy letter, I may just come to Koffee Klatch as a customer, just to force you to wait on me. If you don't want me to do that, then PAY YOUR BILLS ON TIME. It's that simple. And don't get snotty with me any more, young lady. You're out of your league.

- Every time you watch the LOTR movies, you can bask in the delight of knowing everyone you see on the screen despises you. Boy, I hope the friendship with Miss Jordan and Abbey is worth all that. Pay your Wells Fargo bill.

- Do you understand that you are now officially white trash, Di? Are you prostituting yourself yet? Addicted to crack? Got AIDS? So much to look forward to...You will never be able to buy a new car or house or get a credit card—in short you're going to end up with nothing but filth, squalor, and second-hand garbage.

The pep talks worked for a little while. Di got the loan all caught up by March 2004. Then she stopped paying again. She quit her job, got evicted from the apartment, and apparently planned to disappear without a trace. Sue and I had to go all the way to Portland and check the public record at the Department of Justice to get her contact information and turn Wells Fargo loose on her again.

The sad part was that, out of all my communications with Di, even early on, there was never an iota of responsibility from her. Not a single "Gee, Jeanine, I screwed up. I'm sorry I got the loan into a mess. I should have let you know I was having trouble paying it off." Not even so much as an "oops." The acolyte was learning to snatch the pebble from Master Amy's hand.

SEAN ASTIN

"Jordan," Sean, and Abbey at Project Elanor.
Sean, Wash Yer Hands…

Sean was invited to comment in this book about the BoE situation. "My people" provided "his people" with a list of specific questions, to clarify how this philanthropic man unwittingly lent his name and reputation to a pair of grifters that misused, abused, and milked it for all it was worth. He has declined to comment, and who could blame him: he trusted Those Two and got burned to the core, why on Earth should he confide in yet another fangirl?

Sean's involvement is obviously the most extensive of all the celebrities and this narrative would not be complete without his story. Some of it can be pieced together from scraps I have gathered along the way.

Sean's father, John Astin, teaches in the theater department at Johns Hopkins University. One of his students shared some insights with me.

John's got a ridiculously high level of self-esteem and self-confidence. You could say he's got an ego. I think Sean might have "inherited" that from John. They're both remarkably self-assured.

However, John is also a remarkably caring and giving individual. He's constantly doing volunteer work, forever giving up personal time to help students, and is the first person to ask you what's wrong and offer to help if you look even the slightest bit down. John has worked himself into sickness and exhaustion for his work and his students. Considering that his name alone attached to the theater program has people throwing in their support left and right, he doesn't need to do that. He's just a passionate guy, throwing himself and his energies into something he feels strongly for.

He's said repeatedly in and out of class that if you're going to do something, you have to stand behind it 110%, that nothing is ever beneath you, particularly not hard work and discipline. He always says he was raised that way, he's raised his kids that way, they're raising THEIR kids that way, and he hopes his "other kids" (students) will take it to heart, too.

I've only met Sean once, and fairly briefly. He came to visit his dad and wanted a tour of campus. Sean was very relaxed, very casual, and he wasn't put out to be surrounded by gobsmacked students. Everyone was very impressed by how forthcoming and sociable he was. He didn't preach about his projects, or make pseudo-political statements. He just yakked with the students about lacrosse, the shows we were working on, the campus landscaping, silly topics. And he was actually interested, asking questions and listening. We were all quite impressed that someone who's achieved so much acclaim could seem so, well, normal.

On September 11, 2002, Sean Astin delivered a speech in Washington, D.C., about the value of community service. Amy Player, a beautiful young woman, approached him with admiration in her eyes and appealed to him to help her realize her dream: to build a garden where children could read. She was asking a man of generous nature, with a particular passion for literacy, to put his money where his mouth was.

You can bet this convergence of events was no coincidence. Amy could have approached Sean about Project Elanor in the autograph line at a convention, in a letter, or via formal contact with his representatives. But she knew Sean could hardly ignore her request under these circumstances! He would have to listen to her at the very *least*, or he would risk looking like a hypocrite. And amidst the rush of emotions from speaking to the public on the anniversary of the terrorist attacks on the United States, the circumstances were optimal for Sean to give her what she wanted.

Dustin Hoffman played an autistic savant in the movie *Rain Man*. His character could barely accomplish the mundane activities of daily life, but he could—without even trying—perform feats of mathematical genius. Amy's aptitude for telling lies and manipulating people is similar to the "genius" of a savant. Her lies flow easily and spontaneously, without a trace of guilt or mischief in her eyes. She intuitively recognizes situations that can be turned to her maximum advantage.

Amy surrounds herself only with people of a certain nature. Her victims have to work hard and independently so she can easily isolate them from one another, lest they compare notes and expose her lies. They have to be humble and polite, because she can't risk a public confrontation with an aggressive loudmouth when she makes a rare mistake and reveals a lie. They must have a strong sense of fair play and insist on reviewing all sides before passing judgement. That way, if a lie gets exposed, Amy can delay and obstruct communications, to get what she wants before her marks wise up to her schemes.

Sean fit perfectly into the mold of Amy's ideal victim. His work ethic and leadership are lauded to the point of good-natured teasing on the LOTR DVDs. There was no chance he would be comparing notes with any of her friends, either online or in real life. He is also known for his level head and kindness toward fans. And on top of it all, despite Amy's imaginary penis and lesbian orientation, she frequently stated she was "hot for" Sean Astin.

Gibson Patterson was Sean's representative at Patricola-Lust Public Relations. I called her on January 6, 2004, to make sure she and her client were aware of the problems within BoE. Gibson had just returned to the office after nearly two months of worldwide ROTK promotions with Sean. I told her RIF never got a penny of the money raised at Sean's TTT screening. She gasped and blurted, "I was against this from the very beginning!"

I told Gibson I had a summary I'd made for the police, which explained some of BoE's scams (and included proof), and she asked me to send it to her. She wanted to forward the information to Sean, his wife Christine, his attorney, and other appropriate parties. I sent her two files, which she received and passed along that night. The next day, she left PLPR and took a job at a new firm.

Aghast, I had to ask Gibson if she left (or lost!) her job on account of BoE. She replied:

> Monday, January 12, 2004
> NO WORRIES! I have been planning on leaving for a few months. I did take some clients but not Sean. Continue to contact David Lust at PLPR about this matter. I think the more correspondence with David about this the better. I spoke with Sean before I left and he was definitely appreciative of the information that you and others have forwarded.

It was comforting to know Abbey and Amy didn't get this woman fired from her job. However, it seemed oddly coincidental that Gibson left after realizing she was right on target in her assessment of BoE and her client had turned down her advice.

On October 15, 2003, Sean Astin's assistant, Michael, called Detective Myers. Michael noticed an Oregon news release about "missing person Amy Player/Jordan Wood." He discussed it with Sean and offered to assist the detective, although at the time, neither of them knew how to get in touch with "Jordan."

Later that same day, Detective Myers discovered both Sean and Christine Astin left him voice mail messages about this missing person case. Myers described their subsequent conversations in Amy's missing person case file.

> Mr. Astin stated when he was first contacted by "Bit of Earth," they were soliciting his assistance

in making an appearance at what he described as a park renovation function in the Portland area. Mr. Astin stated they were what he described as a disorganized group that needed direction to succeed, and described himself as providing this to them. Mr. Astin stated he thought the group had potential and agreed to make the appearance. Mr. Astin stated that [Project Elanor] was when he first met Jordan Wood. Mr. Astin commented, "When I first met him, I thought he was a she."

In my conversations with Sean Astin, he was asked if he knew how to get in touch with the person he knew as Jordan Wood, and he referred me to his publicist, Gibson Patterson. I called Gibson Patterson. She indicated she was instructed by Sean Astin to provide any information that would aid in locating the person known to him as Jordan Wood. (Amy Player) and provided an address and two phone numbers.

Sean indicated to Myers he felt that he could lead BoE into achieving its potential.

Zinnia heard Sean mention at Generations United that his colleagues wondered if he was indulging in some sort of ego trip, hanging out with adoring fangirls.

On April 23, 2004, Sean referred to Project Elanor in a chat session sponsored by www.whitehouse.gov.

It is great to find time to volunteer because it feels so good. One project I was involved in was transforming a parking lot into a garden. I flew my family out and we all worked on it together. There are some pictures of this on seanastin.com. My family was there with me and we had a great time. It is sacred family time as far as I'm concerned when you volunteer together.

Whatever the reason Sean took interest in BoE, he found the egg he cradled and warmed contained a cobra that delivered a venomous strike. Everyone touched by BoE felt that same sting when they realized they had been lied to and manipulated. They had all thrown away their time and money to a couple of swindlers with silky tongues and a selfish agenda.

Any one of us could have—and *should* have—called RIF to determine whether the garden was being built with their blessing. Any one of us could have—and *should* have—followed up with RIF regarding how much money they actually received. Anyone could have called "Jordan" on "his" bizarre identity story, rather than politely overlooking the fact that "he" was a she. The "if only" list goes on and on. Many of us are painfully aware we had the tools to expose their lies at our disposal the whole time, but we didn't think to use them. Zinnia spoke for many when she commented:

> It is amazing how even when I was becoming increasingly concerned about Abby and Jordan, I still jumped at any chance to do anything involving Sean - which [is] why most of us continued to remain involved. I so highly respect Sean, and I trust him and his judgment. I felt I was doing something positive, and Sean spoke so positively about [Project Elanor] at nearly every fan event he attended.

Many good people helped BoE out of one incompetent failure after another, enabling Abbey and Amy to save face and move on to con another day. My hope for all the victims—including Sean—of Abbey and Amy is that they are able to ignore the arrogant jeers of smug spectators and move beyond the "how could I be so stupid" self-deprecation. We trusted, we helped, we overlooked, we rationalized, but none of us acted out of maliciousness or intent to impose our will upon others. Only the deceivers have reason to be ashamed.

PART III:

BACK AGAIN

THE AFTERBURN

According to the Prancing Pony guru, Ninja, "OB and the crew did a rush job just after the TentMoot cancellation, changing the passwords of every server account to something only they know." Bob and Sue no longer had access to the staff email box, so we could only guess what Abbey might have told the celebrities.

As soon as Amy was released from the hospital, she and Abbey drove up to Portland for the ROTK Line Party, bringing Bob's computer with them. Abbey's machine had been rendered inoperable by a virus months earlier. When they returned home, they no longer had a computer in their apartment. They had no way to get to the Pony to delete incriminating emails or posts. Then Ninja nixed their privileges just in case. Finally, after Bob settled in and booted up his computer, he discovered that although Those two locked the doors to the Tentmoot mailbox, they left the keys in his machine.

One dayt the Prancing Pony was rerouted to an unrelated site, and we all thought that was the end of it. However, the hacker had not exceeded Ninja's expertise and he restored the Pony for more fact-finding.

BoE.net was chronically in debt to their web host, and the site was kept afloat solely by contributions from Pony Pals. Ninja attempted to bill the credit card Abbey left on the account, but the charges were denied. BitofEarth.net and the Prancing Pony died of natural causes in mid-February, 2004, when the host finally suspended it for non-payment. Neither Orangeblossom nor Mr Frodo ever posted to their website again.

They must have read the Pony though, because on February 23, 2004, I received a Federal Express envelope containing three things:

1. A check for $50 toward the rent money they owed me.
2. A notice that "Jordan Wood" was now a legal name by common law (it did not specify to whom this common law name belonged).
3. A Cease and Desist order from Abbey, Amy, and Cherie.

At twelve pages, this last document was far too long to reproduce in its entirety, but noteworthy excerpts appear below.

CIVIL INJUNCTION TO CEASE AND DESIST

SECTION I: DEFINITION OF TERMS

Issued by Abigail Stone, Jordan Wood and Cherie Deuvall on behalf of themselves and the organization "BitofEarth" hereafter known collectively as "The Issuants." Issued against Dr. Jeanine Renne, Hereinafter known as "The Recipient."

SECTION II: STATEMENT OF CAUSE

Be it stated that the Recipient has been committing acts of libel, slander, unauthorized computer access, harassment, conspiracy to commit malicious prosecution, and business defamation. These acts have caused harm to the Issuants, both material and intangible, in the form of defamation of character, malicious destruction of business and professional contacts, malicious destruction of personal associations, financial damages of no less than $2,843.15, and emotional pain and suffering.

SECTION III: CEASE AND DESIST

The Recipient is hereby ordered to cease and desist relating to all individuals and organizations, public and private, the following libelous statements verbally, in writing, on the internet, and by all other methods.

1) That the Issuants removed from or caused to be removed from the Recipient a large sum of funds, including but not limited to the sum of $10,000, regarding the purchase of airfare for TentMoot 2003 celebrities in December of 2003.[1]
3) That the Issuants have publicly claimed that "Baby Blues" was responsible for advertising difficulties with the Lost Palantir Fan Film Festival.
9) That the balance of the money due to Parr Lumber ($890.79) was paid with funds gathered at the Hall of Fire Summer Music Festival.
12) That Cherie Deuvall, acting alone or in collusion with the Issuants, has caused severe damage to the Recipient's consumer credit rating.
17) That the Issuants requested 25 tickets be donated from Air New Zealand for TentMoot.
18) That the Issuants appropriated funds intended for charity and/or event expenses for their own personal use.
24) That it was impossible for the Issuants to successfully meet the costs for TentMoot 2003 prior to its cancellation.

---

[1] Not all 78 demands have been listed in this excerpt, just the interesting ones.

44) That the Issuants have forged or have intent to forge documents to support the existence and validity of BitofEarth.net events.

53) That Mr. John Howe had at no point expressed interest in and/or agreed to appear and/or provide a video appearance to TentMoot 2003.

58) That fraudulent actions have been definitively committed against and with intent to cause or disregard of harm towards Mr. Sean Astin.

61) That "MissTree" was blamed by the Issuants for the lack of attendance at the Hall of Fire Summer Music Festival.

66) That the Issuants directly and knowingly instructed a volunteer to violate the terms of posting on the message boards at http://www.billyboyd.net

67) That neither Mr. Dominic Monaghan nor his representation at any time expressed interest in or intention to attempt to assist, have association with, and/or participate in the Lost Palantir Fan Film Festival.

71) That Jordan Wood spent the night of December 15-16, 2003, in a female penitentiary.

78) The Issuants have, are, or have intention to stalk and/or harass Mr. Sean Astin and/or Mr. Elijah Wood.

SECTION IV: REPARATION OF HARM

The Recipient is hereby further ordered to take the following remedial actions:

1) Remove all libelous and damaging statements from all public and electronic forums, including but not limited to LiveJournal (http://www.livejournal.com), Greatest Journal (http://www.greatestjournal.com),and SANET (http://www.sean-astin.net).

2) Contact all personal and professional associates of the Issuants previously libeled to and re-

248

tract and renounce all libelous statements. These contacts must include but are not limited to the following:
Reading is Fundamental
New Line Cinemas
Air New Zealand
Mr. Robert Bob
Mr. Kiran Shah and all relevant representation
Mr. Paul Randall and all relevant representation
Mr. Jed Brophy and all relevant representation
Mr. Brian Sergent and all relevant representation
Mr. Bret McKenzie and all relevant representation
Mr. Matt McLeod
Mr. Lawrence Makoare and all relevant representation
Mr. Karl Urban and all relevant representation
Mr. Bruce Hopkins and all relevant representation
Mr. Elijah Wood and all relevant representation
Mr. Billy Boyd and all relevant representation
Mr. Sean Astin and all relevant representation
Mr. Dominic Monaghan and all relevant representation
[Total of 54 names on this list, including all major cast members of LOTR]

Copies of this document will be sent to all specified relevant parties.

There was much more, but it hardly deserves more space. It included a demand for repayment of losses of $2,843.15 to BoE within 90 days, and a "restraining order" forbidding me to contact the three of them in any way, shape, or form—and not only that, I may not contact anyone they know or *will meet*! Finally, they gave me all of three days to contact everyone who ever read my LiveJournal, as well as the 54 celebrities and businesses they listed, to retract my statements.

I immediately posted this ludicrous document to my LJ. This missive was not signed by a judge and my attorney confirmed such "stream-of-consciousness pseudolegal gibberish" was not worth the paper it was printed on. However, as an example of unmitigated gall, it is priceless.

Online observers found it hilarious that I was asked to censor all of their personal and community journals by none other than the "dead parrot" herself, Victoria Bitter. They squealed with delight that maybe they, too, would receive a Genuine Fake Legal Document from BoE. Perhaps it would be printed on fake paper, made from the same stuff as "Jordan Wood's" fake penis: Veebonium!

The general consensus was that reading this letter left people's jaws resting on the floor of the flat *below* their own. One person suggested I taunt Abbey and Amy into having a real judge sign it, so they could perjure themselves on what was essentially their confession. NotE!butNice wrote, "You have my express permission to contact me! Jordan and Abbey have no right to dictate who I can or cannot be contacted by."

Some comments were just too damn funny to paraphrase.

- **Anonymous**: Is it telling that in the 95 Theses here, they never say the statements were false, only libelous?
- **Cleolinda Jones**: This is the loveliest thing I've ever seen. It's like the *2001: A Space Odyssey* of wank. "It's...full of stars!"
- **Ixcer6**: This proves that stupidity and deter-

250

mination are NOT a good mix.

- **Essielte**: I especially love the phrase 'libeled to.' Hey, we've been libeled to!
- **Sagralisse**: Does "malicious dissemination of personal and private information" cover talking about Mr. Frodo's miraculous penis?
- **Anonymous**: Yes, I think "dis-semination" is the appropriate legal term to use when discussing an imaginary penis.

The REAL shock came when we discovered BoE had, as promised, mailed copies of this letter to each and every member of the cast and crew of LOTR. Once again, the online readers kept me in stitches with their biting commentary.

- **Kym_chanur**: Actually, there isn't much they can do to top this, is there? Unless Ms. Stone and Ms. Player file a lawsuit against Turimel for not complying with the C&D.
- **Elfy**: I think an equally fake lawsuit would really rock my socks with this wank.
- **Cleolinda Jones**: Oo! Oo! I know a really good fake defense lawyer!

This jocularity was a restorative elixir at times when I was ready to give up. I realized Abbey and Amy were spotlight addicts, seeking attention both from movie stars and chumps like me—and every time they succeeded in enraging me was just a victory for them. But laughter, mockery, and exposing the truth would rankle them to the core, even though spending a night in jail, losing their home(s), and being estranged from all of their loved ones didn't bother them in the slightest.

251

Several LJ readers wondered if Those Two suffered from mental illness, and therefore may not deserve condemnation for their actions.

- I've known Abbey for 18 years, and am more concerned about her mental well-being than your court case. Anyone who interacted with them for more than five minutes should have been able to tell the depth of the delusions they were dealing with.

- I never got to know [Abbey] on any significant level but she seemed like a nice person. A little melodramatic, a little self-important, but a genuinely nice person.

- I never really said anything after leaving BoE about Amy's increasingly strange behavior. But the few people I'd tried to talk to about it on the BoE Yahoo group were very dismissive (of course, Abbey was one of them. Duh.)

- As far as I can tell from the Padawan Sidious mess, VB somehow managed to convince Orangeblossom that she (VB) is Elijah Wood. Isn't playacting him, isn't a whole lot like him, but that she is *actually Elijah Wood.*

- Abbey told me, "Amy gave over her body to Elijah. She is tired of channeling all the different people, and the Amy personality is tired. Elijah said he'd take over, and Amy agreed to let him."

- [I] was concerned about Abbey three years ago when I first heard her tell me that hobbits spoke to her through her head . . . Don't think I can't see a disassociative schizophrenic break when I see it manifesting in aural and oral hallucinations.

I cannot even begin to guess whether Amy or Abbey have a legitimate psychiatric diagnosis. They obviously never expressed themselves honestly with me. Furthermore, I was interacting with them as a friend, not a doctor. But I am comfortable making some comments about my observations of their behavior in general.

I never saw either of them display any evidence of "impaired reality testing," such as claiming to hear voices or responding to internal stimuli. In other words, no one channeled any hobbits in my vicinity. Psychotic symptoms can wax and wane, but from a medical standpoint, it seems very unlikely that the two of them both recovered their "sanity" at the same time, without any medications.

By early 2003, Abbey discarded all of her friends from the "hobbit channeling" days, including her husband. Online and "real life" friends alike were antagonized with unfair and vicious accusations, until there was no one left that knew about the channeling. One possible interpretation is that Abbey and Amy realized this channeling nonsense could cost them their budding relationship with Sean Astin, so they deliberately alienated everyone who could embarrass them by bringing it up.

In February, 2003, when the Prancing Pony was redirected to the exposé of "Jordan's" true identity, Abbey and "Jordan" vehemently denied "he" was Amy. On the one hand, it is possible the two of them were so deeply enmeshed in their mutual delusion they really believed Amy was a man. However, they were manifesting no other delusional behaviors at that time. One could expect two people who were psychotic enough to genuinely believe that a woman was a man would show other signs of failed reality. Indeed, I would expect them not to perform basic hygiene or carry on a coherent conversation if they were truly that ill. Yet this was the time they were successfully manipulating others into supporting Project Elanor and interviewing Sean Astin over the phone. These efforts may not have been honest and forthright, but they required a great deal of organization, much more than would be expected of someone suffering from serious mental illness. It is hard to believe they could accomplish all that while under a delusional belief that Amy was really a male.

Did Amy really believe she was a man? It seems unlikely. When she was hospitalized for the alleged suicide attempt, the "Jordan Wood" tale never even came up. If it had, the staff psychiatrist would have kept her locked in and pumped her full of Thorazine. There would have been a harsh and immediate consequence of her story about being a man—and *just* at that point, she stopped telling the story.

The same holds true for her arrest in Portland. A delusional woman would demand to be housed in the men's division of the jail, for example, and would insist her name was Jordan Wood, even if it meant additional charges of obstructing justice. Amy simply sat down and calmly gave Myers a full confession. She recognized she would get in real trouble if she kept up the phony stuff, so she immediately told the truth. Truly psychotic people cannot just turn it off like that. Sociopaths, however . . .

Was Amy delusional at all? Her lies were so detailed, and she clung to them so tenaciously, one might suppose everything did was fueled by delusions of grandeur. In my experience, however, while psychotic people do come up with bizarre and

254

detailed stories, these aren't usually very "organized." Their thoughts wander, they often fixate on some irrelevant detail, and perhaps most tellingly, they *don't* always have a logical answer for everything. When faced with a cold hard fact that contradicts the delusion, a psychotic will typically deny the fact (against all reason), ignore it, or become puzzled and upset. Amy consistently made up new lies to fit in with the facts. The Shore/Shah tale is a prime example. Amy recognized when her story did not match reality and she changed her story immediately. A delusional person would demand that reality change to make sense in their story.

The only diagnosis I would consider for Amy at this point is a personality disorder, perhaps one or more of the "Cluster B" types described in *DSM-IV*, a manual commonly used to diagnose psychiatric illness. Cluster B personality disorders are characterized by grandiosity, deceit, and utter lack of empathy.

A personality disorder does not involve delusions or impairment of reason. People with these disorders know full well what is going on and understand the difference between right and wrong. They simply do not *care*. They take no pride in doing good, honest work and they feel no remorse if they hurt others. It is of no concern to them when their actions are harmful, irresponsible, or illegal. If they lived on a deserted island, they would be just fine—they would have no one to hurt and they can take care of their needs. They get into trouble when they interact with society, which frowns upon the chaos they create with their deceits. There are currently no effective medical or psychoanalytic therapies for personality disorder. [2]

With Abigail, it is more difficult to pinpoint how much was deliberate, and how much may have really been mental illness. Looking strictly at her behavior, some of it could be described as reckless or destructive. She lost a good job, divorced her husband, gave the boot to all her friends, all for the sake of her "hobbit hobby" and Amy. Such ineffective coping and unsound prioritizing is certainly seen in cases of real mental illness. It is also seen in "normal" people when influenced by charismatic or menacing "leaders."

The hobbit channeling appears at first glance to be psychotic: "hearing voices" is a textbook sign of schizophrenia. Looking closely, however, there are suggestions that this was not truly hallucinatory in nature. For example, Abbey described her "difficulty" channeling in the beginning. She frequently complained about not being able to hear the hobbits as easily as Amy. She asked for guidance as to how she should meditate properly and so forth, to clear her mind for the hobbits. Most schizophrenics are somewhat taken by surprise to find they can hear voices no one else can hear, and while their feelings range from upset to completely blasé about the voices, I have never known one to actively try to amplify them.

Abbey also shared Amy's ability to turn off the voices when it was expedient to do so. She described

---

[2] In some ways, these people are analogous to rabid dogs. They wander through polite society spreading chaos and pestilence, unchecked until Atticus Finch comes along...

an incident at work, where she hid in the office supply room during lunch. She sat there in the silence and meditated, willing Pippin to manifest in her mind. Eventually he did and the two of them shared a banana while he snooped through her memories. In Abbey's words, "Then someone came in to shred something and startled me back to 'reality' for the remainder of lunch."

Hallucinations have no respect for interruptions by co-workers. This strongly suggests Abbey was primarily indulging in flights of fantasy and imagination and not succumbing to a psychotic disorder.

Ultimately, there is absolutely no doubt Amy and Abbey were both aware they were doing wrong with regard to the BoE scams. They covered their tracks in complex ways. For example, they deliberately altered the check to Portland Parks and Recreation to hide the truth about BoE's finances. If they were not fully cognizant of their actions, they would have defended themselves with nothing more sophisticated than a basic fight-or-flight reaction. Instead, there was no deception too complex for them to employ during their attempts to acquire the shiny baubles they wanted.

A summary by Lauren covers it all:

[Amy] has used and manipulated and then hurt and tossed aside people from all over the globe. I don't really care if she's fully aware of how much damage she's done. I don't care if she needs a swift kick in the ass or lots of hugs and lithium every day. She needs to be stopped, because she is, basically, a charismatic sociopath.

THE CRIMINAL CHARGES

When Detective Myers interviewed me in my living room on October 10, 2003, he alluded to crimes Amy confessed in her "suicide letter." She claimed she stole $11,000 from Abbey and her husband back in January, 2003, and then managed to pin the blame on him. She also wrote that she had trafficked in drugs.

Myers did not tell me any details, since evidence must be kept private until the trial. I inferred from his hints, however, that Amy had swindled her way across the country, leaving a swath of emptied apartments behind her. He wanted to impress upon me that he was looking for a Bad Bad Person. It unfortunately convinced me that Myers had the wrong guy.

However, when it became painfully clear that Amy had conned me, I called Myers and helped him locate and arrest her. Based on my earlier impressions, I thought he had an iron-clad case against her for multiple thefts and narcotics trafficking. Unfortunately, he only had her confessions to such crimes in a phony suicide letter, with no proof as to whether she really committed them or made them all up to convince her parents that she was better off dead than on the run from the Law.

The probable cause for Amy's detainment on December 15, 2003, was identity theft. Amy created yet another tale of her origins: she was Jordan Gabriel Wood, a male, born and raised in a "fundamentalist Pagan" commune in Estacada, Oregon, called "Circle of Light." According to "Jordan," this commune did not utilize such things as official certificates of birth or public schools, but "he" did have some documentation to back up "his" claims.

258

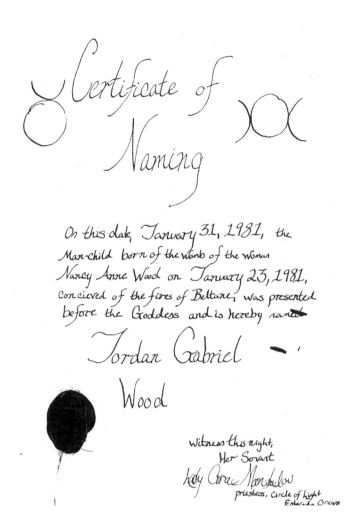

Certificate of
Naming

On this date, January 31, 1981, the Man-child born of the womb of the woman Nancy Anne Wood on January 23, 1981, conceived of the fires of Beltane, was presented before the Goddess and is hereby named

Jordan Gabriel
Wood

Witness this night,
Her Servant
Lady Circe Moonshadow
priestess, Circle of Light
Esperada, Oregon

"Jordan's" Pagan birth certificate, from "his" Social Security application. The black smudge is a wax seal.

Amy applied for a Social Security card as Jordan Gabriel Wood. Social Services were suspicious of the commune story, despite the extensive documentation from "Circe Moonshadow," high priestess, a partially-burnt immunization record (with the word "tetanus" misspelled), and a check-out form from Emanuel Hospital in Portland, indicating "Jordan" and Mom departed safely after "his" birth.

Amy went next to the Department of Transportation, where she was issued an ID card. She wasn't able to pull off her full story: the ID was under the name Amy Jordan Gabriel Player Wood, and still noted she was female.[3] You can see that Amy approached these chores in a deliberate and organized fashion.

To Do

Kinkos {
- Naming Certificate
- Hospital Refusal
- Immunizations
- Homeschooling Letter

- Go home & get work ID
- Go to SS office with all plus
   - Death Certificate
   - Work ID
   - Mail
- Go to DMV

STE 530
530 Center St. NE

---

[3] Her next step would presumably be to use that ID to apply for a new one, with the story that she'd divorced and shortened her name back to Wood. Then that ID could be returned to a different DMV with her complaint that some idiot had checked "F" instead of "M" under the "sex" column...

Thus Amy was detained for questioning on the night of December 15, 2003. Unfortunately, petty crimes of property were not sufficient to justify holding her until the arraignment. Myers couldn't even find an excuse to keep her in jail long enough to miss the ROTK premiere the next day. Rather than let someone with blood on their hands go loose to make room for Amy, they released her and even permitted her to go home to California. She was to return for her arraignment on January 13, 2004.

Armed with my story about Air NZ, I set out to register some additional complaints. The sheriff's office informed me that, because I live within city limits, this was the purview of the Salem Police Department. I gave a statement to Sergeant Keith Blair of the property crimes division and waited for the charges to add up.

I'm glad I didn't hold my breath. Sgt. Blair wrote up my complaint and reviewed it with Don Abar from the Marion County District Attorney. Don decided that although Amy misrepresented Air NZ and lied to me about having sufficient funds for reimbursement, it didn't sound to him like "theft by deception." Don Abar told Sgt. Blair that fraud has a strict legal definition, which requires the crook receive a direct financial gain from the crime. If Abbey and Amy had taken my $10,000 and stuffed it into a Swiss bank account, that would be fraud. But Amy and Abbey didn't run off with my money, they merely enjoyed $10,000 worth of celebrity entertainment at my expense; ergo, this wasn't a theft.

My attorney was dubious about that decision, but what could I do? The DA (District Attorney) is responsible for prosecuting criminal charges. DA (Don Abar) declared these were not criminal activities, so he would not permit the police to level charges against Amy. I raised a loud protest, but it soon became obvious that a certain DA (Damned Asshole) wasn't about to let some *housewife* tell him what was fraud and what wasn't.

Grrrr. Well, at least the identity theft charge was still on the books, thanks to Detective Myers. Sue, Vanadriel, and other Elanor / BoE friends planned an ArraignMoot in the parking lot at the courthouse on January 13, 2004. We could at least have the satisfaction of seeing her charged with identity theft, and if she pled guilty, we could share a round of high-fives.

Don Abar pooped on that party as well. Despite the fact that Myers hand-delivered a 200-page report to Don's desk, detailing the activities of Amy Player and submitting them for prosecution, Don decided to ignore the charges. Not drop them—*ignore* them, formally. Amy moved to Los Angeles; she was no longer Salem's problem. If the district attorney charged her, Marion County would have to take her to trial and punish her as well, which would mean spending its own time and money on her. Now who would want to do a thing like that? Show of hands? I wanted my taxes back.

And besides, according to Don Abar, Amy was a "first-time offender."

Don Abar placed the charges in a "no action" category. This means that if Amy returns to Marion County, and becomes *our problem* once again, the charges can be reactivated and levied against her. But as long as she stays far, far away, her record will stay shiny and pristine. Sgt. Blair put it succinctly: "Welcome to the Criminal Justice system."

Don at least had the courtesy to tweak Amy a little, by making this decision at such a late date there simply was no time to send a letter announcing the arraignment was cancelled. Amy, Abbey, and Di drove up from LA in their rickety van to appear at a nonexistent arraignment, on a fool's errand of their own for a change. Although paying for the gas and having to get out of bed early was probably more painful than jail would have been for Amy, that was her only punishment. The whole episode must have validated her belief that she was above the law, and if her lies fail her, all she needs to do is make a fresh start in a new town.

I told Sgt. Blair I had evidence of false advertising and using celebrities' names to promote Tentmoot and LP without permission. He wearily said, "That's not my jurisdiction." This was not an attempt to pass the buck. Blair simply understood perfectly the limits of his reach. The false advertising was for events in Portland, so that had to be taken up with the Portland police. The celebrities needed to file their own complaints that their names were used without permission. And with the relatively small amount of money involved, and no large-scale TV or print ads, it was very, very unlikely anyone would bother taking the time to complain.

I called Sgt. Blair again when I received the Cease and Desist order, hoping he could find evidence of extortion, threats, or practicing law without a license. He commented that it was obviously written by "someone with no job and *way* too much time on the Internet." He described it as cagey, but not criminal. For example, extortion charges require a direct threat to person or property, but the C & D only vaguely threatens to "take legal action." Abbey and Amy were pushing the limits, but they stopped *just* at the edge of a criminal act and thumbed their noses in disdain. Sgt. Blair confided that this sort of thing is the reason the frustration level is very high among policemen.

Why should people like Those Two have any respect or fear of the law, when they know damn well it is rarely enforced? They got away with everything they did—and not because they were terribly clever and covered their tracks perfectly like the sneaky villains on TV. No, they mailed out a confession (in the form of a fake C & D) to all the people they hoodwinked and still walked away as free as farts in a windstorm.

THE CIVIL CHARGES

As I was calling various businesses in Portland to let them know they were conned by a phony nonprofit organization, someone at the Doubletree Hotel suggested I bring this up with the attorney general. That sounded like an interesting idea. I wondered what that was, exactly, and how it differed from the district attorney. More gold stars on the lapel? Being an ordinary law-abiding citizen, it had never even occurred to me the DA and the AG were not the same thing.

Sure enough, they had different phone numbers. Fancy that! On December 22, 2003, I called the AG's office and spoke to Steven Christensen. He listened to the nutshell version of the saga of BoE, reattached his jaw to his face, and told me he wasn't sure this would fall within his purview—it sounded criminal in nature. Having heard from the Criminal Justice people that this was strictly a civil matter, it was a challenge to coherently explain that contradiction without going supernova.

Steven agreed to look into it further and have someone get back to me. The Christmas holidays were imminent, and were followed by a major ice storm, during which every public office in the state went into low gear for two weeks. *Joyeux noel.*

On January 12, 2004, Sue and I walked into the attorney general's office[4] and discussed Bit of Earth with Jan Margosian, the head of public relations for the Oregon Department of Justice. Jan, whose heart

---

[4] Such is one of the benefits of living in the state capitol. We also get really good fireworks at 4th of July.

is as kind as her will is strong, brought us up to speed on the ins-and-outs of making trouble for trouble-makers.

The DOJ, she explained, could not represent either of us as individuals; it was concerned with the welfare of the State of Oregon. She thought it sounded like the state had an argument against BoE, since hundreds of citizens donated money to Project Elanor and other events under the assumption they were contributing to charity. She couldn't tell us any details about the DOJ's intentions, because so many laws are in place to protect the privacy of "alleged" wrongdoers. She did say she would look into our case herself. We left her office that gray, cold afternoon feeling as though we'd been given a late Christmas present—a guardian angel in the DOJ.

Although we didn't find out until seven months later, we were correct beyond our wildest dreams. Jan had the phone off the hook before the door whapped our behinds on our way out. She called RIF and confirmed BoE sent them no money, and further learned BoE had no authorization to collect funds in RIF's name. She typed up a summary for the Charitable Activities department, noting that perhaps it had not fully appreciated these women were acting as unregistered professional fundraisers. She sent it on to Harvey Kirk, the chief investigator for Charitable Activities, with an added note.

I'm kinda worried about this case. Amy Player, who is not 21 but has a dozen akas, fake IDs, birth certificates, etc., has been doing this sort of thing for several years and no one seems to be able to stop her. Lots of odd things about this case but it appears the Sheriff, Police or DA might not take any action and then we are the only game in town.

Go, Jan, go! After reading that in the case summary, I feel better about my taxes.

As it turns out, Bit of Earth was already safely on the radar of Fiona Harpster, an investigator for the Office of the Attorney General, Oregon State Department of Justice, Charitable Activities Section. While I hope I never see a title of that magnitude on a letter addressed to *me*, when addressed to BoE, it read, "Valiant Knight in Shining Armor" from my point of view.

Fiona contacted the Convention Center, Ticketweb, RIF, the Riggs Institute, Lloyd Center Cinema, and all of the other major players from Elanor and Tentmoot. Sue and I spammed her with links, phone numbers, copies, and summaries of material culled from the Prancing Pony. She patiently put up with our ranting, and with the quiet subtlety of a bow hunter closing in on a 12-point buck, she unraveled the tangled deceptions of BoE.

Fiona sent Abbey and Amy a letter on February 9, 2004, describing the evidence she had gathered, and invited them to voluntarily submit evidence and explanations to the DOJ. She added a caveat: "If you choose not to comply on a voluntary basis, the Department may seek formal legal action to compel your compliance." Those last three words still send a shiver down my spine.

Although Fiona's letter specifically requested a response by February 27, 2004, Abbey and Amy did not reply until March 5, 2004. Excerpts of their defense appear below.

- We are very concerned to hear about the formalization of these accusations which had been previously maintained – where we feel they belong – only in the world of internet rumor and gossip. We have nothing to hide.

• Our business computer, upon which all records, notations, copies of letters and documents sent, and many other items have been kept, has been rendered utterly inoperable as of 12/5/03 by one of our departing staff members, and the data has been irretrievably lost.[5]

• We have been blocked from access to our business email account by Dr. Jeanine Renne, who gained unauthorized access as of 1/7/04 and changed the password to keep us out.[6]

• Most importantly, BitofEarth.net was not originally intended to be a charity organization.[7] We did not see the need at that time to keep particularly careful records.

• Our event structure was very much of the spirit where if we needed something, we would hand a volunteer a $20 bill and send him/her for it without a second thought.[8]

Abbey and Amy went on to provide incorrect amounts for both the net income and net expenses of Project Elanor. They claimed RIF essentially authorized BoE to use their name for

---

[5] The only staff members that departed from San Dimas were Sue, who left in November, and Bob who left on december 9.

[6] This is an example of libel. Bob was an authorized user of Tentmoot e-mail account, and he voluntarily shared access with me. I have never changed the incredibly long and obscure password that Bob supplied for the account.

[7] This is the most unimpeachably true statement ever written by Amy Player.

[8] "Moerwen," a volunteer from Hall of Fire,confirmed that Abbey and Amy often handed her a twenty and said, "Go get me a pack of cigarettes," or " I need a latte."

fundraising purposes over the phone (when in reality they require written contracts). Finally, they attempted to implicate Dominic Monaghan in some sort of vast conspiracy to defraud fans via Future Forests.

Fiona didn't buy a word of it. On April 16, 2004, the Department of Justice sent BoE an Assurance of Voluntary Compliance. This document explained that the state believed Abigail Stone and Amy Player violated specific laws under the name Bit of Earth. The State of Oregon intended to protect its citizens from phony charity solicitations, so the DOJ forbade either Abbey or Amy from fundraising in Oregon again—even for a legitimate non-profit agency. If Abigail or Amy wished to contest the state's observations, the matter would be settled in court. Otherwise, if they accepted the state's mandate (without necessarily admitting guilt), they could pay a fine and return the signed, notarized AVC.

The AVC outlined in exquisite detail exactly which laws had been broken, and the penalty amounted to a fine of $9,000. However, if Abbey and Amy returned the AVC and a $500 fine, the remaining $8,500 would be suspended. If they were to violate the terms of the AVC, the suspended amount plus up to $25,000 per violation would be levied against them.

For the price of a $500 fine, they were able to keep all the monies from Project Elanor (at least $1,261), Hall of Fire ($2,500 by their own admission), and Lost Palantir ($630 in ticket sales). Abbey claimed many times on the Pony that various people made donations directly to them; those amounts will never be accounted for. Not a bad profit at first glance.

On the other hand, it also cost them every friend they had, any possibility of a Hollywood career, their website, their home, and the esteem of their idol, Sean Astin. I'd say crime didn't pay.

SO WHERE ARE THEY NOW?

Sue, Helen, Klyta, and I went to Los Angeles for the Academy Awards in February, 2004. Sue hadn't been lucky enough to get a ticket to TORn's "Return of the One Party" before they sold out, so she went to an alternate gala, "Into the West." The Twins and I attended the TORn bash and had a fantastic time, watching ROTK win eleven Oscars and celebrating with the cast and crew after the ceremony.

Sue's evening started off wonderfully as well, but her overall enjoyment was dampened when she looked up and realized she was ten feet from Abbey, Cherie, and Amy (in full "Jordan" costume). She recalls, "At that moment, I understood (for the first time in my life) how one human being can kill another." Paralyzed with shock and rage, she stood back a moment and listened to them explain to some unimpressed guests that they were *such* close friends with *so many* of the cast, especially Sean Astin, who helped them build a garden. Abbey and Diamond wandered off to annoy someone else, so Sue replaced her jaw, walked up to Amy, and said hello. Slick Amy could do no more than gape and run from the room without a word.

Sue had no desire to let them ruin her evening, after all the misery they had already caused. She quietly let the security staff know that if any celebrities showed up, there were three people who needed to be removed immediately from the party. It turned out that Primrose, one of the gardeners at Project Elanor, was one of the party's hostesses, and she had already given Security the same orders. No stars showed up; they all spent the evening at TORn's party.

We later found out that Those Three expected as much, and tried to gatecrash TORn's party. Fortunately, TORn's security recognized them and flatly denied them admittance. I can only imagine their frustration, *knowing* all their objects of desire were contained within those walls but they couldn't talk their way in.

TORn expressed interest in writing an article about BoE's mischief within LOTR fandom, as a cautionary tale for fans worldwide. Two TORnies, "Demosthenes" and "Maegwen," put forth an incredible effort to investigate the scandal, interviewing many of the involved parties (including Abbey and Amy, who maintained they were completely legitimate and the Tentmoot failure was all my fault). But there was so much information, so many points to cover, and the two of them have real jobs beyond their volunteer work for TORn. The article proved too unwieldy to complete before this book went to print.

BitofEarth.net and the Pony are gone, but I preserved the story on a LiveJournal, *www.livejournal.com/users/turimel*. The former Pony Pals who originally took interest in the story spread the word to friends, and new readers have joined in like compound interest. They often share their own reports, such as Thorin's discovery of the improperly "submitted" Lost Palantir entry, or Prokyon's encounter at Neiman-Marcus.

In May, 2004, I got an unexpected email from "SecretSpy," a casual follower of the story. SecretSpy works in a shop on Hollywood Blvd in Los Angeles.

There are professional celebrity impersonators, hired by Universal / Hollywood Wax / Commerce that pose with tourists, give out info, whatever. Because they get tipped it's attracted a certain amount of street people. I saw a new girl working. She was a bit rotund, wrapped in a white sheet with a kinda kooky headdress on. It looked like a bad Halloween costume. I approached her to get her story. Right away she started talking about her 'boyfriend' who does Harry Potter, and how he did a great Frodo. Then she pulled out a card and handed it to me.

Harry Potter? Or Tom Riddle? You decide.

"Jordan" claimed to have a master's degree in English literature when "he" applied for this job at Starfire. They were impressed by "his" talent and signed "him" up for party appearances right away. "Jordan" proved very popular and the manager slated "him" on the fast track to stardom, saying, "We knew we could take 'him' all the way to the top."

Soon after, though, BoE's exploits were reported in a Portland newsmagazine, *Willamette Week*, and

Starfire was not thrilled to learn they hired a girl with a civil suit on her record.

Abbey, Amy, and Cherie were evicted from their San Dimas apartment on June 1, 2004, for failure to pay the rent. Amy was obligated to keep the Marion County Sheriff apprised of her whereabouts, so she sent in a false address, apparently to give the appearance of compliance. SecretSpy heard the three of them moved in for a time with a Shrek impersonator.

Cherie's father reported in August, 2004, that Di had a falling out with Abbey and Amy and moved in with some new friends. One can only wonder whether she finally realized they were creeps and left, or whether they decided they'd wrung all they could from her and gave her the heave-ho.

The Elanor Garden remains on the Riggs Institute property and has become a beloved local hangout. Many people enjoy their lunches in the serenity of the deck and children play among the flowers. One can only hope that RIF, as well as local schools, churches, kid's clubs, and the like, will come forward to both enjoy and maintain this beautiful community resource.

A group of original Elanor volunteers formed a new organization to continue the upkeep on the garden. "One Small Garden" (OSG) has already held several weeding, replanting, and tidying events. No movie stars, press, or video crews were invited to these—just people who love to garden and are happy to simply chip in.

On April 3, 2004, OSG held an Anniversary Work Party in the garden.

Hard at work at the one year anniversary

Many of the gardeners had served at Project Elanor and new people joined in too. It was a gorgeous spring day, mid-70's and sunny, and the garden was in dire need of a good pruning and an even better weeding. We planted new flowers in bare spots, spread organic fertilizers and weed controls, cut back overgrown plants, and prepped the deck for sealing (a task Abbey and Amy never bothered to complete).

We also pulled out Abbey's stepping-stone from the pathway and replaced it with one from Northwesternesse, a Tolkien fan club in Seattle. Sue lit some ceremonial bundled sage[9] and carried it through the garden to excise any spiritual remnants of Those Two from the local space-time continuum.

OSG hopes to focus the energy of Tolkien fans onto projects that embody his ideals. We plan to build more gardens, restoring underused urban

---

[9] This strongly resembled a Cheech and Chong movie prop, much to my amusement.

spaces to lively, organic, and sustainable retreats for the enjoyment of all. And unlike BoE, there will be no cancer wreaking havoc under the surface.

APPENDICES

APPENDIX A

Channeling Hobbits

The following online chat transcript took place between Amy Player (as Victoria Bitter, V) and Abigail Stone (as Orangeblossom, O) sometime in mid-2002. Abbey gave this document to some of her friends to explain her attraction to Victoria Bitter. One of them passed it on to me. At times they refer to Abbey's husband as "Strider." Note that Abbey complains of her difficulty "channeling"the hobbit voices, and that Amy encourages her to keep trying. Amy also takes advantage of Abbey's disappointment over being infertile, by promising contact with "The Great Mother."

V: Do you ever try to stand back and tell yourself it's just a movie, just some books, just an actor?
O: Daily. Don't work for shit. Its *not.* If it was .
V: *sigh* So good to hear I'm not alone there.
O: No. You are not alone in this.
O: I am not joking on LJ and in posts when I say I'm genuinely questioning my sanity.
V: *hugs* Me too, sometimes.
V: I look at my priorities sometimes and just cry, because I realize that I have a packet of ramen and a can of tuna in the cupboard, I'm sleeping on the floor of an empty apartment I've been evicted from as of two days after I get back, I have no transportation other than my own two feet, and am overdue on half my academics .but I just spent twelve hours on a piece of hobbit smut and am dropping 300 bucks on this convention.
O: But that is what makes you happy .isn't it .
V: It is, and that's what I tell myself, but when my shrink

looks at me and says "does it really make sense as an adult to let your hobby take over basic living needs and academics?"

V: Well, it's hard to answer.

O: Yes. I know, I understand. Whn I try to explain myself .to others .I can't.

V: And you wonder if you're maybe not a little bit nutters.

V: Because quite honestly, if you were someone else, you'd tell them they were.

O: Or a LOT bit nutters .

V: Well, the LOT bit nutters comes when fic flows into your fingertips like the pulse of blood through an open wound.

O: Yes.

V: When you hear them whisper behind your thoughts and open your eyes on their memories.

O: When you're awake at two in the morning and you're seeing through their eyes and hearing their thoughts and saying their words for them .

V: When you strike his hand and wince in pain, and when his tears flow with your sorrow mingled in false pain and real saltwater.

O: When for a while you're not sure where you leave off and he begins .

V: When you speak with his voice and he beats with your heart and you vomit his pain upon the page so hard that nothing of your own life can curl within the space you've created, and it can fill only with more of itself until you wonder if really you're left at all as you, or if you have become a shell of flesh, a vessel possessed by a being that neveralwaysnow existed.

O: I cannot even put into words what its like to read that, and know *someone else has a fucking clue what I mean*

V: Been there, done that, Orange sweet. *hugs*

O: *hugs back*

O: ITs still frightening at times.

V: If you're mad, then it is a madness in which we walk together.

V: And what is reality but a delusion shared by the majority?

O: with friends .there are many of us on this road, it seems .

O: Indeed

V: My Master says that some of the creatures of Middle Earth - Elves, Dragons, Dwarves - existed much as described, as beings Other than Man - long ago, because there are artifacts found beyond the capability of the cultures they are found in, and there are just TOO DAMN MANY myths from tribes that never knew each other, countries that never collided that are *all the same.*

V: There must be some basis in reality, even twisted as it is by thousands of centuries of myth.

O: I agree, I really do.

V: I know a lad who was a dragon in a past life.

V: It's no different than my Master's brother having been a horse.

O: I need to find a Master .

V: I talked to her about this, actually, if you don't mind.

O: *interested*

V: She says that the surge of interest in Tolkien's Middle Earth has created a huge explosion of creational energy, which is a powerful force, not only through the fans, but through the thousands of deeply devoted people in the production itself. That energy has been directed so strongly towards the ideas of Elves and Ents and such that the *real* star-spirits and tree-spirits are reacting to it, reaching out in return.

O: Ohhh!!

V: But no spiritual energy or spirit can manifest purely in the mind of any but the most deeply trained and gifted, so like any spirit or God or divine, they come through a form we can comprehend. This is why the Gods of any culture resemble the bodies and customs of that culture. In our case, they reach to us through the most closely identified aspects .hobbits.

O: *nodding .*

281

V: She says I'm being contacted by the warrior-spirit - he's been called everything from Thor to Ares to Seti over the ages - trying to use Soldier!Merry as an avenue to tap my creational energies.

V: She says that just reaching lightly towards your signature through me, she's willing to be you're being touched by Athena/Eaestar/Isis - the Goddess of children, protection, fertility, wisdom, and youth - manifesting as Pippin (though she thought from 3000 miles and having-never-read-LOTR away that his name was Pelican)

O: *wide eyes*

O: As Pippin?

V: She said that she was touching you "oddly, possibly a bird in the form of a little man?" I asked why a bird, she said "I'm getting "Pelican." I asked if it could be "Peregrin." and she gasped. "Very young."

O: Wow .

V: She thought he was a child.

O: "they would look, to you, as one of your children ."

O: I have The Great Mother reaching out to me .?

V: She also nailed that you've been in pain lately, both physically and spiritually, about the subject of your own fertility.

O: I just .this is so amazing .I wish .I envy you having a Master, one who *gets* this .I wish I had access to that .

V: You do. My Master says that She feels your pain over your empty womb and seeks to comfort you, but you are very spiritually closed, either through upbringing or ignorance, and She is left trying to touch you through the strongest symbol of youth and innocence that is tied to your creational process.

O: I want so much to open to it .

V: Which winds up being Pippin, and She's not so thrilled with that - would rather do it directly - but this is better than nothing.

V: Once I knew it was the Warrior, I *know* that energy, so I was able to basically meditate early this morning and say *really, Mars, if you'd wanted my attention, there are* *easier ways than siccing a hobbit muse on me.*

O: *nodding* its just .its something I've sought so .I've tried .

V: Turns out He's pissed off at me for letting myself become so weak over the Eye of Sauron and accompanying emotional mess, and become too creationally-centric. But then, He's always thinking He has to overcompensate for my womb to keep me on track as a Warrior-spirit myself. He's suspicious of women, always has been.

V: I know, but you can't do it alone.

V: Mars is so moody. That's the name I use for Him when he's like this. *rolls eyes*

O: fascinating .Its just .its like bitter comfort.

O: To have been reaching for The Mother, seeking her, praying to her, lighting candles .and to find out *she's trying to reach me and I can't hear her!*

V: That's the first thing you'll learn once you start touching the Energies. They're not some plastic Jesuses. They're like the Gods and Goddesses of pagan legends .moody, fallible, fickle.

V: *hugs* She found a way.

O: But those are the kinds of deities I've believed in

O: but her as Pip is odd .but then again, maybe its not the who but the fact that it knocked open a door .

V: And you *did* hear her, you just heard her speaking with the voice as a little hobbit.

O: But the Pippin thing .it .I can't see the tie to The Mother in what I went through with Van .

V: She was just touching your creational energies. It wasn't as direct a communication as what I had with Mars - where you can see the concerns about weakness and purpose manifesting bloody direct in Last Standing and Displaced - but more like .let me remember my Master's metaphor .

O: *very attentive*

V: Like electricity. You were dealing with a bulb of creative energy working at 100 candlepower running off your own batteries. The Mother is trying to reach you, and she sees that the type of power you're using to make that bulb light up is creational and *accessible to her* because it's connected to a symbol of youth and innocence and protection and creation .so she touches it. The bulb becomes 10,000 candlepower and nearly blinds you, but the *nature* of the light stays the same, as does what it's illuminating. It's just the sudden brilliance of it that's meant to make you ask "Who did that?"

V: I'm at the stage where I'm talking on the phone. You're at the stage where it's ringing. Attention-getting noise.

O: I think I see .but .

O: what does She want of me .? What .is .going to happen .? (lacking words here)

V: I don't know. I'll talk to my Master more about it if I see her tomorrow. *hugs* I wish I knew, but I'm such a neophyte myself. If I were guessing, I'd say that because you aren't feeling suddenly compelled to do something the way I felt suddenly compelled to write fic in a pairing I normally can't even stand to read, it may just be her way of saying *yes, Abbey, I'm here.*

V: Her response to all those candles and prayers. Comfort.

O: *Comfort .*

V: Or it may be that she's trying to strengthen you, either from your loss or to prepare you to bear.

V: I honestly don't know.

O: I'm afraid.

V: *hugs*

V: What's the first thing that Gods in all religions say when they first reveal themselves to mortals?

O: Fear not

V: Yep. Which implies that it's pretty fucking shitworthy.

O: I have studied so much and yet I know so little .**V**: Then by admitting that, you are wiser than countless scholars.

O: I'm just .I'm so awed by all of this .

O: I can say that this whole thing, these last few days .its like my mind has been *completely and utterly fucking blown*

V: You know, the concept of inspired metaphorical writing in the context of the author's own reality is NOT new. HOW many sacred texts were written just that way? With the Divine empowering the author's pen somehow to write, but the author using the words and metaphors and characters of their own culture? Rami, Moses, Buddah .**V**: It's not new.

V: It's just really really kind of hysterical that it's *hobbits*.

O: *gentle laugh*

V: *Hey, Calliope, look at this .hehehehe .I'm getting to manifest as porn featuring three-foot-tall men with furry feet and pointy ears! And I thought it was fun inspiring the Tantric Sutras!*

O: *ggl* Hobbit Smut of The Gods

V: They've done crazier things.

O: Indeed.

V: Indeed, if this weren't so strongly of Mars for me and the Mother for you, I'd say it had Loki's fingers all over it.

O: *amused* Indeed. Just paint my face green and call me Jimmy.

V: Doesn't mean it's not Him. He's notorious for giving the others Good Ideas.

O: True .He's such an interesting character .

V: I'll have to ask Him about it this morning.

O: I will be intereted .am already longing to see what comes of this your conversations .with Him .with your Master .

V: OH! *thunk*

O: what?

V: I gave her my tape of LOTR on VHS, which has before it several awards shows, courtesy of dear Wolfie. I am going through my email, and there's one from her.

O: Oh!

V: *I'll get to the movie itself later this weekend, darling, as I fear that three hours is a bit much from my schedule at the moment, but I have to ask who the tall boy with the dark curls is. I have a feeling that he is one of My People, and if I can read this through your less than stellar video footage, I would think perhaps his most recent life, as*

285

well. I am curious to know what would put a spirit in hiding for so long.

O: O.O

V: She, for the record, was, in her first manifestation, a star-spirit or High Elf.

O: Oh wow .just .awe .amazement .

V: The footage she's talking about is the SGAs. Orli is only in the background of a few shots. He never even presents or talks on the red carpet.

O: *blink*

V: You're not crazy, and by the looks of the last 48 hours, neither, perhaps, is Dom.

O: Its the culture what gives me the idea I'm crazy. We're just not *equipped* for this .

V: If it won't squeeze between the covers of the Bible or a department store catelogue, we don't accept it.

O: Exactly. But *my heart knows*

V: *I will give you my first impressions of the others for now, but remember, love, video tape is not the best means of this. I really should be meeting your boys if I am to be any more than accurate in the broadest strokes. Mr. McKellen seems to bear the spirit of Zeus, wise and a bit naughty. Mr. Wood needs nothing more than video tape, in truth. I could have done it from a photograph. His spirit is a pure Wood Elf stronger and truer than any I have seen in many an age. What he's doing here, I do not know. He does not belong. The stout fellow is of Baldir and the Great Mother, and Mr. Wood's two companions both carry streaks of Faerie wider than they are tall, that apparently not being much to say.*

O: woah .

V: When I saw what she identified Elijah as, I gasped. Wood is not his family name very far back. His grandfather changed it.

O: *amazed*

V: It was something unpronouncable and French, apparently. Lij being French/Irish in bloodline. But of all things, to change it to *Wood*

V: Are you familiar much with Baldir?

O: It raises a blip on the radar .I know I'm *familiar* .

V: Norse. God of farmers. Gentle, beloved, quiet, peace-loving. Placed his hand in the jaws of the wolf Fendi to save Asgard.

V: My Master claims Sean bears the double energies of Baldir and the Great Mother.

O: And the only response my mouth forms is "holy sweet mother of GOD!"

V: Like we haven't seen this coming?

V: Remember their *names?*

O: But still!!!!!! Its jus…its so…I mean…I'm gibbering here. Totally gibbering

V: Chosen One, Giver, Young Lord, Of the Tree, Kingly, Wisdom of God, Devoted Warrior, Beautiful Youth

V: Elijah, Sean, Dominic, Shaen, Viggo, Ian, William, Orlando.

O: I'm shaking. Hard.

V: It's just a movie. Like. Fucking. Hell.

V: There are energies being tapped here that I can't even begin to comprehend, nor to fathom *why.*

O: *tremuloulsy* If this is just a movie just a book .just .then I'm the Queen of Spain.

V: Something is happening here that is bigger than the two of us or the nine of them, and it's scaring the living daylights out of me.

O: Me too. I'm so frightened .*the power*

V: It's like the first time as a child that you stand outside and watch a thunderstorm.

O: aye .I even just explained a bit to Strider, who does not and *can* not understand and even he seemed .awed a bit.

V: I guarantee you that the first thing I'm doing when I meditate this morning is back Mars against a wall and demand to know what the fuck is going on, why do it through a movie, and why this movie? (before you start giggling, realize that my spiritual form is very male and bears more resemblance to a young, dark-haired Sean

287

Bean than to Elijah Wood .very hard-bitten and weath-ered before his years)

O: I wish I could meditate. I've had such trouble with it—the clutter, the noise in here .

V: I don't meditate the way that most people do. You have to find your own meditational style .what centers you perfectly. For some people, you meditate with stillness. For others, it's something like pottery or basket making. For others, it's walking in woodlands or swimming. For me, it's fight drills and workouts until I'm blind with pain and exhaustion.

V: You have to woogle around until you find what's right for you, and which Energy you align most strongly with.

V: Sometimes it finds you, sometimes you find it.

V: Hell, I know one lass tied into Venus who meditates with *sex.*

O: I know. I've tried .its active meditation. The closest I can come so far is riding the bus.

O: Staring .the scenery blends .

O: I don't think so much .

O: but its never *quiet* in here.

V: You need a Master, a Guide, a Shaman, an Elder .just like you said.

V: Look in the papers, ask around. Find the nearest Coven or Circle. They can put you in touch with people who at least speak the right language.

O: Despereately. And I know that.

O: Perhaps .

O: I am aware of what I need .there's what's said to be a truly wonderful spirutal center not far .I must call them .and bring a printout of this chat, I reckon .

V: Most of the pantheists and pagans at least know of each other. We're far less insular than Christians. New Druids network with Egyptologist network with Reincarnationalists network with Pantheists network with Polytheists network with Aboriginal Religions

V: Hehehehe

V: I think it's very possible that you're strong with the

Great Mother, because that's the perfect opposite of the Warrior, and I'm so strong with Him. Spirits tend to seek balance.

V: Adrian is strong with Her.

O: Yin and Yang. Male and Female. It is true .

O: One reason I can't quite embrace al the Dianic traditions, because they totally eschew the Father .I may tend to reject the Father because of my own sorely lacking father, but I know He is there and is as much a part of this as She is.

V: Aye. *Balance* is the core of everything.

V: And, of course, with my masculine energy as high as it is, I don't usually do well in the Dianic traditions anyway ;-)

O: Interesting to me .*L* I don't know what or where I am anymore though. But I've always known that *mother* was part of why I was here.

V: And I've always known I was here to fight.

O: *why us .?*

V: You were probably playing mother with your dolls at the same age I was identifying the taste of black powder in a reenactor's mouth.

V: None who live in such times .

O: *My* mother said that by the age of three she could identify that I was a born mother.

O: And not because of dolls.

O: She can't put a finger to it, even now. Just how I was, *who* I was.

V: I tried twice to kill my infant sister.

V: Put makeshift landmines in the front yard. Was fascinated by war movies.

V: But I'm not at all psychotic or violent as a person. Just martial.

O: Wow.

V: When I tried to kill her, I was too young to understand the concept of death myself. I just knew how instinctively my heart wanted to handle the interloper.

O: Understood, that .

V: You'd have wanted to nurture her.

V: Why us? Because we balance.

O: I don't know. I had a lot of problems when my brother was born.

O: The rejection. THe pain.

O: It still is agony. *he was chosen and I was not*

O: (by my father)

V: For that I feel very sorry for you. At least my family was very eglitarian about my sister when she was born. They even showered *more* love on me so I wouldn't feel left out. I just was a stubborn little bitch who didn't want *anyone* else in *my* family.

O: *gentle laugh*

V: There was no real split in my family until I came of age to begin rejecting family morals and philosophies and Caroline was still in lock-step. *Now* there's a difference, even if my parents try for there not to be, simply because I've broken their hearts and she goes faithfully to youth group twice a week.

O: *nodding* I understand that.

V: Odd. The nurturing home fosters the warrior, and the warring home fosters the nurturer. Yin Yang.

O: *blink* Hadn't thought of that .

V: And look at our partners .again, Yin Yang. Your Strider is very martial, masculine .sword collection, computer toys, bang-bang games. You're attracted to Sean as a soulmate, a like. I'm attracted to Sean as I am to Adrian, who is borderline effeminate, physically androgynous, and deeply caring and nurturing.

O: *more thoughtful nodding*

O: But there is no Pair-Bond attraction with Sean

O: he isn't a Yin to my Yang

V: For you, you mean?

O: I see the same .the kindred .and I have a longing to have that LIKE beside me. Maybe .

O: maybe is longing for understanding .

O: or to be understood.

V: Aye, but there is a pair-bond attraction for me, which I've wrestled with. I couldn't understand why I was falling

290

for someone so utterly masculine in look, until I realized his was a feminine heart.

V: He is so like Adrian in heart that it scares me sometimes.

O: *nodding*

V: And for you, that masculine look is enough to give you some eye-lust pair-bond attraction, but your heart wants to just sit by the fire and be friends with his.

O: It does.

O: I can be attracted superficailly to Sean. But its not *that* kind of feeling, truly it isn't. I want to be his friend, to have coffee together. To sit by the fire and smoke a pipe and *talk* And you've named it so welll now

V: And I've just realized that I have been unspeakably presumptuous all night. Please forgive me for this. Just had a reality check: VB, you're 19. You've never met this woman. You're a neophyte in your own religion. What right do you have to be picking apart her psyche?

O: *shakes head* VB, I've never had this experience before, and its incredible. *and right.*

V: Your first touch of the Divine is only, in my limited experience, comperable to one thing: your first orgasm.

O: *dryly* No frame of reference, I don't remember it.

V: :-)

V: I need to at least put a load of laundry in if we're going to keep talking. brb

O: *blush*

V: Update: load *to* laundry room accomplished. Now must remove load from dryer, transfer washer contents to dryer, fill washer.

O: *L*

V: Accomplished!

O: Huzzah!

V: I now have done .um .let's not look at the To Do List Of Doom, okay?

V: After all, I still have, what, twenty hours?

O: *gentle laugh* and I've not uploaded my shelled fic, nor shelled any more of it

V: But hopefully Orange feels less stressed and overwhelmed and insane?

291

O: Somewhat, yes.

O: THis has been A Big Few Days

O: And my poor wee mortal brain is strained something awful.

V: *hugs and wishes could do it in person*

O: Someday.

O: I will be afraid, though. After all we've been through .those first few minutes hours maybe .

V: Will be amazing.

O:Terryfying. awkward. incredible

O: I do feel less insane now

O: although I feel so *awake* that I cannot ponder sleep. Tomorrow will hurt

V: We wonders .

V: Does Strider think we are crazy? Adrian has his worries sometimes.

O: He worries. But he trusts .and he loves .and he accepts .but he worries.

V: Then again, so do WE, and we're INSIDE it.

O: Yes

V: Hmmm .washer has stopped. Should transfer to dryer and put another load in.

O: *L* what is it with Ob and the SHameful Site Neglect?

V: I just realized something that has officially Freaked Out my inner artist.

O: what's that?

V: Would you say that it would be an understatement to claim that Sean and Lij have a different look about them? That they do not resemble each other? That one could not be mistaken for the other from a hundred paces at midnight with no moon? That similarity is confined to gender, height, and race?

O: yes .

V: That's what I thought. Now look at that last icon. I swear on all that's Holy that I did nothing to it but put one half-pic beside the other. All their features line up so evenly that it looks at first glance like one person.

V: WTF?

O: It really is trippy.

V: Have decided that this is simply open season Brainfuck time for VB.

O: think we'd be used to it.

V: Yeah, but when the Really Obvious Things (like *Sean and Lij look nothing alike*) start coming apart at the seams, I go into bibble mode.

V: Challenge my brain, my spirit, I deal. Challenge my eyeballs, the bibblage begins.

O: *ggl*

V: *looking at other pics side-by-side. Jesus H. Christ. It's optical illusion. It's optical fucking illusion. Elijah's eyes are the same bloody size as Sean's, they're just set differently with the upper and lower eyelid more prominant, and being blue and dark-lashed in such a pale face, they stand out far more than golden lashes and hazle eyes in tanned skin.

V: Their mouths are the same size too, only Lij's jaw is more square and his chin shorter, which gives it that cherub look, and their noses are the same length, only Sean's is rounded and Lij's sharp.

O: *wow*

V: Their foreheads are the same height, their ears even the same size and set the same.

V: *cannot get over Mr. Elijah internationally-famous-for-huge-eyes Wood actually having perfectly normal sized peepers that just happen to be unusually set.*

O: Interesting. *L*

V: "And the world turned upside down."

V: The song the British played at the end of the last battle of the American War.

V: You know, I'm feeling daring. I think I might try something .it's only worked once before, but I've only TRIED it once before.

O: what is that?

V: It's sort of .a psychic phone call. The Divine have to agree, but the last time I tried it, I had felt a very strong connection to a total stranger I saw at the gym and asked to sort of be 'put through' and found out that he was a strong Fire elemental connected to the Warrior spirit.

O: oh!

V: I'm entertaining this mad idea about trying to 'reach out and touch' one of the boys.

O: Ooooh~

V: I'd probably go for Orli or Lij. If Orli has a strong presence of High Elf, I've felt that before with my Master, so would know if I touched him.

O: *nodding*

V: However, Lij is a powerful Earth elemental and a Wood Elf, which is strongly tied into the Warrior spirit, so I might well be able to grab him more strongly than Orli. Also, he strikes me as someone who's more in touch with *himself* than Orli, which would make it much easier. And I'm not exactly a Master, so easy is good!

O: Easy is *very* good .

V: Not a chance in hell with Sean or Ian, don't *know* about Sean B or Viggo, and Billy or Dom would be hard as anything .Faerie spirits are *hard* to pin down.

V: We're not talking tonight or even this week, of course.

V: My Master would probably actually want to wait until they were filming in NZ again. Surround them with all that creational energy in such a natural and wild place, get them deep into their characters and in touch with that primal, emotional part of themselves again, get them so tired barriers come down .

O: Oooh .just so intrigued

V: It wouldn't be mind reading or anything, I'll tell you that right now, nor would it be a psychic conversation or IM. It's like .I might feel the glue of the hobbit feet between his toes, taste clove smoke on my tongue, see a makeup brush flicker at the edge of my eyes, smell drycleaning and ash and Sean .

O: but of course it wouldn't be a dialouge, that's not how it works.

V: It's a spattering of sensation, of sense-images like raindrops, and a general sense of *how* a mind works or the *shape* of a spirit. If I reached out to my own mind, I'd get a shape of ruthless precision, card-catalogue memory, deep self-loathing, militism, and explosive creativity tied strongly to visuals.

V: But I wouldn't know that my name was Amy, that I was born in Sheffield, or that I'm a LOTR slash fan.

O: Probably better that way.

V: Now my Master, she can tell the *words* of my thoughts sometimes.

V: I've had her look up during a frustrating session and just calmly say "Of course I can speak Latin, yes, I'm a bitch, now get back to work and stop thinking about that story."

O: *gently laughing*

V: But my Master is eighty-seven and has been at this since she was a child of six.

V: I'm nineteen and have been at this about fourteen months.

O: Probably good to keep expectations low then .

V: Exactly. I'm hoping, given distance and the fact that I've never seen him or felt his aura in person, to *maybe* get a sense-droplet or two.

V: Of course, the most familiar of those would be the strongest, so it could well be Sean-related ;-)

O: I will continue to be intrigued .

O: Veebs are you at all angry that BoE has gone two days with no updates?

V: ANGRY?

V: You've got to be bloody kidding.

V: I know what you've been going through.

V: Not to mention that daily updates were beyond my expectations anyway.

V: I've been amazed you've been able to do that at all.

V: I can't believe you find something new every day.

V: I was honestly expecting once a week or so.

O: *L*

V: You're currently *literally* dealing with your very existence in the universe.

O: I can't live down to those expectations, love

295

V: What kind of absolute monomanical cunt would get on your case for ignoring a website for forty-eight hours in favour of your *soul?*

O: Well, all right, I admit that when you put it *that* way .

V: Not this absolute monomanical cunt, I tell you!

O: it does take on a certain .Absurdity?

O: But BoE *matters* to me.

V: Matters to me too.

V: Abbey matters more.

O: wow

V: You matter more than Sean, Sam, and BoE put together, love.

O: how .how does one even respond to praise like that .*love* like that? How is it that I am blessed with *so much* .?

V: Because you are a good heart.

O: thank you

V: And you don't need to respond. Just continue to be.

V: You *are* a Sam-heart. Remember the way he reacted to the thought that he could be one of the most important parts of the story?

O: of course . I remember every word of that dear lad's story.

V: You seem honestly amazed by praise. I, to put it quite bluntly, am politely humble about it to avoid being a complete jerk, but I bask in it and adore it and do what I can to get more of it .posting to lists I otherwise don't read, for example. Am not Sam heart. Am many things, but Sam heart isn't one of them. I lack the humility.

V: Not to mention the nurturing.

V: <— is not caretaker type.

O: Don't think for a moment I don't bask in it and *crave* it.

V: Ficback, of course, but I mean *you* feedback.

O: As do I.

V: *Abbey* feedback, not *Abbyfic* feedback. You seem more uncomfortable with that.

O: I am uncomfortable with it. I crave it and hunger for it, because there is a yawning need for it. But I don't know what to do with it once it is here.

V: That's not VB's problem ;-)

V: VB has Ego Issues.

V: That she is aware of and working on .

V: But not getting far on.

O: *L*

V: My Master calls it "Fighter Pilot Syndrome."

V: If you don't think you're the biggest baddest motherfucker out there

O: Ah. *light goes on*

V: What was dark?

O: the idea of Fighter Pilot Syndrome—I had to think on it and read that before I could quite follow. I follow now.

V: Well, I'm glad to know I've done *something* constructive :-)

O: *something* indeed .*dazed smile*

V: Am still thinking I should go to bed for a few hours, but want to make sure first that all is, if not well, at least stable with you. Is there *anything* more I could do?

O: Oh darling .Most dearest and then still dearer of Amys .I'm all right. It shall be a long road to walk, of that there is no doubt. But I no longer fear I walk it in spinning madness, nor do I fear I walk it alone and afraid .

V: *hugs*

V: I'm so glad to hear that.

v *tight hugs back*

V: See you later?

V: I *will* of course, say a proper good-bye before I leave for the con.

O: Always. There and back again, and still shall you see me again.

V: Lovely.

V: Night

****

This next chat took place between four people on April 9, 2002. Abbey is represented again by the letter "O." Amy did not participate. I have called the other participants "Patty (P)," "Linus (L)," and

"Charles (C)." Comments from Abbey and Patty follow the chat transcript.

P: Frodo likes shelving books. No surprise there.

O: So I noticed. And music.

P: Yes, fascinated him to no end, our notation!

O: THe musical notes themselves?

P: You know you're possessed when you sit for fifteen minutes studying a song cycle you know by heart anyway.

O: Posessed. A loaded word.

P: Our way of notating—the staves, dynamic markings in Italian .that's unfamiliar to him.

O: Yeah, well, I use it in the only sense I can—that he's there in me.

O: I understand. Far too well.

P: *hugs*

O: THough I was intrigued by the "story" that Pip gave me earlier

P: Dear, now I'm worried.

O: Why?

P: That you aren't .handling this well.

O: explique, sil-vous plait?

P: The fear.

P: That it's taking a toll on you.

O: Its new. I"ve had .others .before. But not like this.

P: You two need to share your space, so to speak.

O: And all the words I have to describe it are judgemental—on Pippin?

P: He's a curious young Took. No other way to put it.

O: yes .?

P: Well, he might scare you with his eagerness.

P: He does scare you with his eagerness.

O: but what does he want?

O: I've a degree in psych. I was raised by a nurse, in a completely non-spirtual, non-religous house. I have no foundation for this

O: I'm completely unmoored.

O: I mean, I thought I was skirting sanity before this happened.

P: *hugs tight* And I have no way of exactly teaching—all I know is feeling it.

O: When .when I let go of the fear .when I let it happen .its .its right

O: its only when my damned brain chimes in that I begin to doubt.

P: *rocks you* I've been—I've been dealing with ghosts, Abby, ever since I could crawl. So, this kind of visitation, when they began, was nothing in comparison. Second nature. You've just now heard something from me that I dare not speak. To most people.

P: I won't take the ghost survey because I take it so seriously.

O: though he's quite clear on what he needs.

O: Merry.

O:: He's called his name, over and over, and he seems to think I should have them both in me at once.

O: Merry shouldn't be separated from him, he says, and I know it as well as anyone.

O: I tried dryly pointing out that with the two of them going at it in my brain all day I'd never get anything done. HE was not amused.

P: *nods, that would do it*

O: ?

P: Telling him that his Merry would be a hinderance in the same space.

O: Wouldn't he be? Its already so crowded in here, and I feel like I'm losing my mind.

P: For you, yes. Pip doesn't understand that he himself is almost too much to handle, for someone inexperienced.

O: And I've never had more than a flash of Merry. I'm not trying to push him away, but he's not come to me either.

O: You'd think he'd realize it.

O: look what happened to Merry when he chose someone truly truly inexperienced?

O: at least I'm open to it.

O: plus I have a constant, nagging fear that I'm making all this up.

P: *hugs* If you're making it up, then I am, and I frankly have trouble doubting what's in my own mind. It doesn't occur to me to doubt. But then, there's a near-full 20 years talking.

O: True .

O: I always doubt. I always have. I've always feared that everything is just "me making it up".

O: I have trouble owning a lot of my own experiences because my mind says "I made them up"

O: My brother being with me in high school (he died before I was born). Made it up?

O: Being raped almost every night for a year and a half. Made it up?

O: Sharing a body with a hobbit. Made it up?

O: I don't even know.

O: I'm losing all my defenses.

P: I, frankly, don't think I have any left, and haven't for a long time.

P: I'm a walking funnel of susceptibility.

O: *gentle smile* I'm rather glad. Its .good .to see someone else .doing this .being ok .

O: At lunch .

O: I went to the office supply room alone. Shut myself up in a little corner.

O: Curled up. Silence. Counted my breaths.

O: He took over for a while. He was going through me, like one would a drawer, looking at things, rifling. It was terrifying .but when I let him .my heart stopped racing and I stopped being so frightened.

P: How long did that take?

O: half an hour?

P: *slow nod* Surprised he didn't keep you another half.

O: He tried. Took about 15 minutes to eat (I was very hungry, and a Took wouldn't skip a meal anyway)

O: he was fascinated by the banana.

O: Then someone came in to shred something and startled me back to "reality" for the remainder of lunch.

P: *giggles*

O: <—skittish as hell under the best of circumstances

P: Didn't think of that. Frodo has not been wondering at my usual breakfast bananas.

O: It was the first time I felt him truly observing the world I live in.

P: He seems less apt to comment on food as on the books and papers my hands and eyes are buried in.

P: Like, I've got cherry coke right now. Big deal. Dr. Pepper-like stuff, cold on her hands, moving on.

P: You know what? *chortling wildly*

O: what?

P: Frodo loves the carbonation.

O: he does?

O: Indeed .but beer is carbonated. Perhaps its a bit familiar?

P: True, true. I wouldn't have thought of that, since I don't drink beer!

O: Nor do I, but he does

O: And I've a distinct feeling he'd like me to down a glass.

P: *cackles* I didn't tell you about the smoke rings conversation that happened at our study group last night!

O: Oh? *intrigued*

P: Nancy was watching Ben smoke his cigar outside, and she just kind of idly wondered aloud, I wonder how you blow smoke rings!

P: And I'm sitting there, nonsmoker, and very thoughtfully I'm making this movement with my larynx, contemplating it, and something in the back of my head says, hmmmm, does that answer you?[10]

---

[10] Although I am not Board Certified in psychiatry, I am comfortable stating that I have some experience interviewing psychotic people with diagnosis of schizophrenia, mania, and severe depression, and never once has a patient told me, "I heard

O: *blink*

O: *wow*

P: Never touched a cigarette or kin thereof, never plan on it *vehement*

O: *soft smile*

P: Pippin, my cousin is not negligent of his Old Toby, either.

O: No, that he's not. Twice I've had a craving for smoke, and I know its not mine.

P: *smiles*

O: but she won't. She flat refuses that. And the beer. No fun at all, what?

P: Mine has no desire. I shan't push it. You'd be wise to do the same, Master Took.

O: I have to push for anything at all. Except this. The words come easy.

P: She's inexperienced and frightened. Surely you've never been thus yourself, Peregrin? *pointed look*

O: *a bit guiltily* I'm not terribly experienced myself, you know. In this as in all things I seem to be following the lead of others.

P: Then take caution, as she is taking caution.

O: I've never been the most cautious sort, you know.

P: That's no excuse, in this situation. Please trust both of us.

O: I'm sorry .

O: and on a completely unrelated note, facial hair is facinating.

P: *claps hand over mouth, doubles over, laughs enough for two*

O: *Looking a bit miffed* I do not need a Took making commentary on my husband and me kissing.

O: Even if that beard scratches .

---

a voice IN MY HEAD." Psychotics hear what sounds like actual, external voices, and they can become quite frustrated that no one else will admit to hearing them.

P: I figured as much.

P: —That said to Abby, not you.

O: very distracting.

O: You know .its actually Abbey, not Abby.

O: And I don't care if he is disturbingly hairy, just shut your fool mouth! *embarassed laugh*

O: Hobbits. *sighs in disgust*

P: *full laugh*

P: *leans on your shoulder*

O: *warm embrace*

P: *content sigh*

O: Don't be getting too comfy, lass.

O: didn't you yourself say there was mischief about?

P: *eyebrows up* Whyever not, Master Took?

O: The moment I let my guard drop .

O: perhaps you should stop putting it up to begin with.

P: That's still a mite hard for her, Pip.

O: He's every bit as stubborn as I am, I think

P: *chin tilts, ponders* Mischief, Pip? And why shouldn't I be comfortable here?

O: Oh, now he won't speak up, will he. But I know. He wants to go find Merry, of course. Though I think he'd be contented with another conversation with Frodo. Stubborn lad. No, I don't get to just relax and read, eh?

P: *prods* Pippin.

O: Yes ma'am.

P: You took affront rather quickly. I wish to know why.

O: I think you may be reading more into this than I had intended. It was rather a tease, you see .

O: Silence again from the Took. Honestly, this hobbit **O:** But we don't know where Merry is. Will you be satisfied any other way, Took-lad?

O: (look at this! I speak to him directly!)

P: (you must)

O: Do you have any idea where he is?

P: No, Pippin.

O: *a whimper*

O: why has he left me again?

P: Peregrin Took.

P: *sharp breath*

P: Stop thinking I've left you high and dry. No Brandybuck ever!

O: *weary look*

O: [he showed up?]

O: [lord, that took always has his way, doesn't he.]

P: *rubs temples slowy this isneffort*

P: Merry, take care.

P: Frodo, nose out, would you?

O: what do you want of me?

P: I want you to stop doubting my love in these present conditions. Pip, it doesn't change!

O: I don't doubt it. I crave it. there's a difference .perhaps I do doubt it by times.

P: *grabs the Took* You little tart, come here.

O: I won't, not if she is unwilling.

P: Says who she's unwilling? Peregrin Took, says who she is here?

O: this one does. She clings desperately.

O: its is all I can do to keep her from pushing me aside

P: Did the absent one[11] fight me when I needed to come to you, when I finally couldn't take it, Pip? Don't fight her when she needs what she needs.

O: she is confused and afraid. She doesn't want to fight me, but she doesn't know what else to do.

P: I'm in her space when it's damned well full enough, you fool of a Took *crushing embrace* Just so I can touch you .!

O: *clinging* but where do you keep going? every time I find you .something happens. and I'm lonely.

P: Brandybucks are drifters. However: there's a lass an ocean away from here who's dead fond of me *rakish grin*

---

[11] I think they are refering to Amy and her heroic willingness to channel Merry.

P: *cuddles Pip close* Aye, but no .don't you fret at my fooling, love.

O: If a lass turns your eyes from me .ah, I am being cruel, saying cruel things out of my own confusion. I am just as afraid as she is.

O: do you know what its like to doubt your existence? She is sometimes so convinced that I'm not real, she almost convinces me.

O: just now she went into the other room and stared into her own eyes, and I don't know what she was looking for.

O: me, madness, I don't know.

O: Just hold me. It may be long before I find you again.

P: Frodo's lass looks in mirrors as if in a trance, you know. Strange habit, but a sort of ritual. As if it lets her look into his eyes.

P: So perhaps she was seeking you *soft kiss in softer curls*

O: she was. She tried to speak to me and I couldnt' answer. I can't assure her. Why .*sighs*

P: When the channel's clear, Frodo said—so is our way clearer. But yours is not so clear, obviously. Makes it harder on you as well *works waistcoat buttons free without preamble*

O: but .its rather like being watched, you know. Its .odd .but .

P: She doesn't draw you as I see you *ponders, slips the garment away*

O: *tenative hand raised to run through curls* This isn't what I expected .

P: Lass far away. Such an ocean lies between, Frodo says.

O: I wanted this, of course, but it seems so rushed .and she sits here and doubts, and .

P: *nuzzles gently* I just miss your warmth, Pip. But whatever you desire, 'tis yours.

O: you. always you, from the moment I knew what desire was

P: *holds hands up, eyes plaintive* Then you guide me. You show me what you please.

P: It's dreadfully hard being shuttled from mind to mind, Pip .

O: It must be. Its hard enough staying here.

O: but I can't leave either.

O: *trembling fingers stroke along jawline*

P: *bites lip, strained wild eyes* If I came to you—

P: Madness, Meriadoc.

O: If you came to me I should be complete, always.

P: You're paining this body. Pippin, forgive me—Merry. This is harsh business.

O: and yet she fights it. She likes the idea, but she fights that too. Will she ever stop fighting me?

P: Frodo, I said—

P: I said, you are paining this body.

O: Don't hurt her, she won't let you back!

O: and I will have lost you again!

P: If you can't feel it, concentrate on your empty, addled skull!

P: ——frodo

P: *head in hands* Pip .I've made a mess again, haven't I?

O: Or I have.

O: *embraces, desperately*

O: don't harm her.

O: If she comes through unharmed

P: No, Pippin. Just so happens we've a fool hobbit in an untried Person's body. That's all. It's a hard combination, I guess.

O: will she learn?

O: she has no discipline. Her mind is fickle as a flower.

P: She'll learn if you're willing to, I think.

O: She longs for my presence, even as she doubts it.

P: You're a fine one to talk, Pip.

O: I think she wants—

O: *shy smile*

O: she wants to learn, I think.

O: even if the rain is enough to break her focus.

O: she is crying. I am crying. Merry .Frodo .I don't know what to do.

P: —She holds it out. So hold yourself out, if you have to hold back, sometimes! Don't hurt her the way this one's hurt! But .I must tell you .don't let her reject you, either.

P: Frodo—?

P: —Don't ask, Meriadoc. Please, never ask. Never ask why it hurts more than it ought. I said it once .

O: She wants to believe so much, I think. I want her too. But not if it will break her .

P: Too full.

P: *jaw askance* Frodo—do you—mean?

P: —Let her keep her secrets.

P: —She keeps a good many for me.

O: *head whips between the two*

O: .I

O: .

P: Frodo .do you—do you mean—

P: —How else would I be so happy here? Untorn?

O: *light dawns*[12]

O: and yet he never speaks!

O: *clings to Merry for a moment, touches the familiar face fondly*

P: —I'm wanted. You've the space a bit longer; you're a thorn somehow, but you have it. She doesn't hate you. She simply—doesn't recognize you. Not the way she recognizes .not the way she .*falls quiet, staring off*

P: —You have leave of her, but you haven't residence.

P: —And Pippin, you've residence where you are, you most certainly do. But be gentle with it, I implore you.

---

[12] I believe this is illuminating the "fact" that Abbey has unknowingly carrying or channeling Samwise Gamgee all this time (much to Frodo's delight),which is why she's had such trouble adding Pippin to her repertoire.

O: and at last I understand.

O: a lesson in patience .not one I'm ever fond of learning. but Merry .oh, Merry, I shall miss you so, and not knowing how long .

P: —What else did you think, dear Took?

O: I know I must let you go

O: I know I must face this alone. but .but *sobs* but I cannot bear it

P: Pip, I'm not gone yet!

O: but you will go we both know that

O: and if Frodo has his way, sooner rather than later.

O: And i don't want you to hurt that one further!

P: *shaken laugh* I wonder if indeed it really's capable of being hurt!

P: —She has a name, a heart, a mind, and you shoot daggers through it. Take care.

P: —Her head hurts.

O: Then come to me.

P: *rocks Pippin, gasps* You mean—

O: she doesn't believe I'm real anyway

P: Can she take it, Pip? Can she really take it?

O: what is two figments of imagination?

O: She can scarce take me, she dismisses me.

O: if you come .perhaps we will see.

P: —Abbey.

O: *shakes self* I get to speak too?

O: I don't even know who's talking to who half the time, though you all seem to have it sorted out.

P: —Of course. So is Merry here. So is Pippin there.

O: I am talking to .Frodo, now?

P: —Frodo. This is Frodo.

O: I've almost never cried over a .chat before. But the tears on my cheeks are real, and I hissed at my husband when he broke my focus for a moment.

O: I want him to come. I want Pippin's ache to end. But I am afraid.

P: *cowers* I'm afraid. Bloody afraid, sorry! So I crack about things!

P: —Don't crack about this.

O: I want this endless longing to stop. I want his voice to stop crying his name.

P: —If you want him to come, melisse, then he will come. But you must first give consent. And before that, you must stop doubting his validity.

O: This whole time, even as he speaks I stare at the floor and my mind screams that he's not real, that its a game.

O: But I can't believe that either.

P: —Yin and yang, you call the concept. I read it. She has a balance. You have one half of a balance. Do you understand? Merry will help rather than hinder, but you can't fear the act of taking him in itself.

O: But I can't stop thinking of what Victoria's Master said.

O: My heart understands. But my head refuses to.

P: —That's the way it will be, till you take a balance, Abbey.

O: your heart understands, that is a part of it

P: The day Pip speaks wisdom's the day .

P: —You leave this place, Meriadoc. The day you leave it indeed.

O: *deep breath*

O: then let him come.

O: Come to me

O: Come to him

O: bring balance. make the madness stop.

P: *looks at Abbey* Here—well. Goes nothing.

P: —Pain's swelling. Quickly.

O: my heart is racing

O: and all is silent

P: Abbey, it's lighter here. What have you, now? In you?

O: I .I don't know. Worry over her pain comes to mind first.

O: and why can't I hear him? them? Now?

P: Well, you have both halves now. A wildness and a tempered but steely will.

O: he is here?

O: I know .the longing seems gone .

P: They're most likely ravaging each other in a quiet place,

309

the likes of which even Patty cannot reach in herself when I am there .not alone .

O: *soft chuckle* I'm not sure how I feel about that.

O: He must be here .I can't really feel much of either of them, but .

O: the happiness .

O: my heart .

P: I'm telling you: they're preoccupied.

P: A fantasy shut off for you, at the moment.

P: Too much shock.

O: *confused*

O: *embarrassed laugh*

O: wait, if you're saying

P: You're too shocked to see them. And they're very purposely being private.

O: They deserve their privacy.

O: And it will be different now, I reckon?

O: Perhaps I can walk down the street now without a voice in my head whispering Merry, Merry with every step.

P: That's how it will be.

P: Of course, they interact with each other in mass quantities as well. Sometimes they dictate what I see. Sometimes I do some breaking and entering *eyes shift, devilish and then pained again* Urgh. Merry.

O: Oh, you poor darling *opens arms*

P: *falls in them, eyes close———what?!* *gets abrupt IM from charles, gasps*

O: What happened?

C: ::clings::[13]

C: Can you feel that?

P: Yes.

P: My head is pounding.

P: My palms are sweating.

---

[13] Patty began copying and pasting Charles' messages into this chat with Abbey. I have edited the transcript so Charles' comments appear to be posted directly.

C: ::breathlessly, heart racing:: I don't know . what's going on
P: *clings* Oh, my god, Charles .
O: Now what *worried*
C: I think I'm hyperventilating . this just . I have no idea.
C: It just started all of a sudden
C: Contact.
P: Just who are you, in there?
C: I do understand .
P: [Frodo, my god, that's nerve!]
C: .but not like that.
P: *sighs* Okay. And I have trouble making this point.
C: For a while . there was someone
P: Contact—what'd you mean by that?
C: I felt it, suddenly. For certain.
C: Your trace.
P: And what did that trace feel of. Who did it feel of?
O: *holds you and listens*
C: It felt of you. But it hasn't . not for the past few minutes.
C: And it doesn't now.
C: There you are again.
P: *slow nod* You're onto something. Does it have a voice?
C: I've never . heard. Not even from you. I'll try .
C: Thick. Viscous.
P: Here I am. If you speak another tongue, I may just understand you, Curulambe.
P: fuck, here we go]
O: *holds you tightly and waits*
C: Sono kai ne . antarema na annishem.
C: Estelarne fa anteglies.[14]

---

[14] I asked David Salo, linguistic consultant for the LOTR films, to review these and other "channeled" statements. He explained, "I can confirm that the speakers are neither speaking Black Speech, Westron, Quenya, nor any other language created (or even recorded!) by J.R. R. Tolkien. For instance, the sound 'sh' simply does not exist in Quenya or Sindarin."

311

P: All foreign to me. I'm sorry. I don't know this world now.

C: I don't know it either.

C: That wasn't me.::swallows hard::

P: *searches* Let's stick to a common denominator tongue, shall we, he-who-inhabits-Curulambe?

O: *wide eyes and rubs your shoulders*

C: Heaviness to the left.

C: Reaching through a field of blood.

P: A FIELD OF BLOOD, you say .*closes eyes in pain, memory, searches—*

P: [abbey, who is that, who is that! someone who fought!]

C: It's you. All of you. The pool will never be filled.

P: *lurches* Eru .!

O: I don't know, I don't ahve an answer

P: [frodo run frodo————]

C: ::bites his lip, shaking:: I don't know . I don't know

P: *shakes too, flees*

O: *trembles*

P: *clings, gasping tears*

O: What happened? Oh, Patty darling, mellon, what happened?

P: That was—that was darkness.

C: And so things can reach here, too, and scorn me, and bite, and tear again?!

C: ::wipes his eyes repeatedly, tucking his knees into his armpits:: There you are again .

P: *wounded blink*

P: *locks down, locks them down safe, speak no more tonight, Frodo dear, find sleep with your Sam, speak no more and let me, let me!*

C: Selarno ef antarie.

C: What is this?

P: Charles . translate that .it's only me now *whimpers*

P: It sounds like Elvish!

C: it's as foreign to me as it is to you

P: And the one who would understand it has withdrawn, so deep in me!

P: [because I have put him there for the night oh no that dark coming through you will not touch!]

P: Abbey. C doesn't know what's rampant in him.

O: Patty, I'm confused, and I'm afraid. No, afraid doesn't cover it.

P: *head hurts horribly* So am I. Damn Charles and his impulsive IMs and his trying to control what he has and can't, letting things come through him any old way without knowing what they are .

P: *hugs tight* This is between me and him now. But it scared Frodo to death .

O: what happened? what happened?

O: the fears this morning, they are coming back full force and I am shaking

P: When Frodo tried talking to it. Charles' demon may be something of Mordor stock, or may not be. May only echo it. I'm dealing with Charles now.

O: Are you in danger? Am I?

C: Fair of face but not of mind.

P: *hears faintish familiar whisper, purses lips*

P: Don't know yet. Let me dig .

C: ::reaches for something::

C: ::strained:: There is . a black pool. Stagnant on the ceiling.

C: A place where law does not comply.

P: No. Wild blacklands never have laws, do they?

C: Hanging from the floor with nails in his feet.

P: *tilts head, shakes* Torture. Torture, isn't it?

C: A cave . blood and water.

P: Oh, Lord, Abbey

P: What might have been. What might have been~!

P: *jaw hangs, takes this glimpse and is horrified, wonders at it*

C: A cave . blood and water.

C: Questions in the dark .

P: Aiiiiiiiiiiiiii!

P: Oh, Eru, this wasn't meant to be known. No. Guesses are for burning, once a rescue's made. They got out. They

313

got fucking out.

O: No. no. no. no.

O: oh god.

C: .my tongue cleaves.

C: A twisted benefaction.

P: *flicks her own in a soft hiss*

P: I know what I've seen.

C: I . don't.

P: I hope you never do, Charles.

C: .lasciat' ogni speranza, voi ch' entrate[15] . rivers flowing upward from his wrists.

C: The pool is in the wrong place, and it will never be filled.

C: The blood tower.

P: STOP!

O: my gods, I'm in a daze, what is going on? what is he seeing?

C: ::chokes::

C: It keeps coming. Solidifying.

P: It never happened and it will never happen and must never happen and .

P: A horrible alternate fate. More pain than was given, though as if stab and stumble and whip and sting were not enough .

O: Alternate fate?

P: Blood tower. Do the math. Or if you don't, you'll be much more peaceful of mind than I am now.

O: *weak joke* am feeling dense as a radish, I'm trying so hard to see but the fear the fear the fear no you can't take him, not when we've found each other, please, help .tell me .

---

[15] Per David Salo, "the Italian words are quoted from Dante's <u>Inferno</u>, Canto iii, line 9: 'Let go of every hope, you who enter,' often rendered as 'Abandon all hope, ye who enter here.'"

C: Thou wert the faceless one of Lórien.
P: *jaw drops*
O: NO
C: Thou hast within thyself all methods fell.
C: Thine eyes are black, as black shall never be.[16]
P: Oh, Abbey. He's gone, he's gone, he's saying these things. Cirith Ungol never became the blood tower, save it were Orc blood. But he saw another blood taint it, blood nigh unto a death. Now, Lorien——*strains, watches him horrified and incredulous*
C: Thy tongue pronounceth all that hath no voice.
P: *weak* I I only understand half his nonsense myself, and I dare not let Frodo out!
P: *holds onto you*
O: *clings despereately*
P: *closes her eyes, commands: name me, then*
O: I trust, but I am so afraid I cannot swallow
C: ::is left quivering:: I . do not . know .
P: Fuck *hugs tight, sniffles*
O: *sobs and clings*
P: He .*shifts uncomfortably* I don't like that vision of the Cirith. This vision he's conveying of Lorien is somehow far worse—thine eyes are black .thy tongue pronounceth all that hath no voice——
P: All shall love me and despair!—this, too, is a terrible alternate.
C: Tarimishé.
C: Lasto beth tin.
P: *tears up* Oh .
O: I dont' know that I understand, except that I am afraid
P: *whispers* I am, too.
O: Come back to the light .?

---

[16] Iambic pentameter! Very Classy. Neither David nor I could identify the source of this material; it is possibly original. If so, my hat is off to Charles the best iambic pentameter I can come up with on the fly is "the RAIN in SPAIN falls MAINly ON the PLAIN."

P: He's communicating horrors that something wants me to see.

O: And you show it to me .am I too meant to see?

P: *tears up* Oh .

C: Thy voice pronounceth what men cannot know.

C: I cannot look upon thee but I know the length that thou hast come to, for thine eyes.

P: He's talking about—he senses .he knows—Frodo in me—but he can't place a name, he can't—*struggles*

O: Don't say his name! don't! don't think it!

O: *sobs*

P: What .is Tarimishe?

C: ::is left again, blind:: I don't .

P: I mustn't call on [Frodo]. Even if I don't understand this horrible Quenya.

P: Something horrible's calling through you. Calling for the voice that's in me. Do you understand?

C: ::nods::

P: It didn't claim the prey it desperately wanted.

P: And I will not yield up that prey.

C: .I see it.

C: I look into the mirror; there thou art.

P: *shivers, recoils* No, you do not. Because I will not give it. You can't have it

C: The tower and the pool are not for thee.

P: No, they are not. They are for the victim in me. The victim that was not a victim, by the grace of another's love and bravery. You shan't pass here, Nameless One—you--shan't.

P: Fuck, fuck, FUCK! LEAVE IT TO BLOODY FUCKING CHARLES TO CHANNEL A RINGWRAITH![17]

C: He is thine.

---

[17] A literate wraith, nonetheless, who extensively quotes Dante and Shakespeare. Apparently the Minas Morgul Municipal Library is well-stocked in Western Literature.

C: And thou shalt know me well, for I am his.

P: Holy fuck.

O: Nooooo!

P: A Ringwraith or WORSE.

C: Thy voice upon the rocks at greying dawn.

P: *sneers* Never.

P: *eyes wide, blinded in the sun, suddenly*

P: You wretch. Wasn't killing you once enough? *blinks* For shame! Don't you know better than to cross this maid?

P: Oh, oh my, Abbey——

P: MERRY!

O: No

O: no

O: no

C: More the fool thou, for I have had my time.

P: *hisses in pain, eyes bleeding tears just like yours*

P: Witch King, Abbey. Witch King.

C: Always hast thou thought only of thy shell.

P: You'll take the edge of a sword of another sort, this time 'round, mark my words.

O: No, no, you cannot have him! you cannot have him!

C: But steel cannot cast down what steel raised not.

P: No, steel raised thee not! Gold did, gold and flame!

N: *ragged breaths, eyes close, clings*

P: Oh and I am Eowyn after all

P: *opens eyes slowly, strokes your hair numbly* The bastard argues a lot, doesn't he?

O: *wordless sobbing*

C: Yes, flame! Dost thou think fire can last me long?

C: My time is spent. My gold I have passed on.

P: No. Because Steel struck you once. Steel from two sides. And now with your gold gone, what then? You're a shadow. Pass in peace.

P: *eyes on the floor* Abbey .how many does this make, now? Eowyn Frodo Sam Merry what, my traffic's worse than AOL at rush hour .

O: I cannot leave his side, I cannot let him pass into shadow, not without me by his side, not a second time

O: He cannot take him!

C: ::sneers:: And so I would - but now my way is barred.

P: *raises chin high, firm* Name that which bars you,—wretch. Wraith.

P: [a name for a name pray with me abbey pray the cancellation is done, is made, and will in doing so unmake]

C: I name it by the name Tarimishé.

P: O flatter me, King. What does this mean, this Tarimishé?

P: [if he tells me what it means, he undoes himself he surrenders.]

C: My power is spent - on sufferance I depend.

C: Now, I find none. To what, then, shall I turn?

C: For I must pass, or stay - and feed, and feed.

P: Aye, on me and mine! You must tell me this. Tarimishé. And you will know peace.

P: Tasartari—wait! Tari means queen .

P: *thinks madly*

P: mishé. Abbey .we need to find this .mishé.[18]

C: Dost not thou know what this shell calleth thee?

P: You call me a queen!

P: *eyes on fire, understanding, understanding!*

P: You .call me queen of—of—

P: Abbey, find a Quenya dictionary online, quick .a translator, something. Our live action translator is REALLY possessed, in your sense of it.

O: Am sharing with Linus, out of terror

F: mishé . . . it is death

---

[18] Per David Salo: "*Tári* does indeed mean 'queen,' but *tarimishé* means nothing in any Elvish language. The sound *sh* simply does not exist in Quenya or Sindarin." The famous Ring Inscription begins with *ash nazg*, which might lead a greenhorn to believe that the *sh* sound is fair game, but David clarified this. "The Black Speech and Quenya use the same symbols, but have different values for the letters. On the One Ring, the letter which represents *sh* stands (in Quenya) for the sound *h* in words like *Telumehtar*, just as in English the letter Z stands for the sound of *z* in 'zoo,' but in German it has the sound *ts*."

318

O: Looking in dictionary
C: I call you queen of lands beyond the dust.
P: And that I am, O King.
C: I call you both the Lady of the Air.
C: I call thee ancient foe, victorious.
P: That I was.
C: I call her but thy pawn, in this last game.
P: But—you also call me Queen of Death.
P: The queen of your undoing. Is that not so?
C: I call thee no such thing, my worthy foe.
C: That title wouldst thou claim; it is not thine.
P: Then whose death, prithee—mishé?
P: *bows low, imploring*
P: *blinks at the ceiling* Eowyn, Eowyn, I've found you a name you never knew you had .*tears, tears, tears*
P: *clings tight* Abbey, stay on. The end's nearing. Please trust me.
P: I told you I'd dig this out .to the very end.
P: I have done that.
P: It's nigh.
O: I trust, I trust, and I will not leave, nor shall she, and my sword is unsheathed and ready
C: Thou art of Death the handmaiden, but still a Queen in thine own eyes. Is it not so?
P: It is so, and in doing so, I smite the once and for the last—O begone, Winged Terror, abate the now and may I rule my realm of Air in peace!
C: ::collapses, shaking and sobbing::
P: *gasps* Oh .oh
O: Oh
P: *wails* Oh Abbey what have I done to him to all of you!
O: *clings*
L: Brilliant blue.
L: Blinding.
P: I'm sorry, my dearest, dearest .
P: Yes, Linus, blinding. My eyes and his—wide open. And this, too, has passed into shadow, and for good.
C: ::clutches back, blindly::

319

O: *sobbing*

P: *whispers* Charles, do you know what passed through you?

P: If you do not, I say you may not want to know.

C: I felt . its wings .

P: *slow nod, eyes grave*:

C:.it grabbed me by the poet.

O: The ill omen, the ill omen! Ye gods above, I felt it all day, he felt it all day and we knew, and this is real

P: Aye. By your wonderful poet-soul, my dear.

L: I . . . am not so sure he is entirely gone.

L: Diminished, yes. Past back yes.

C: It was . more than speaking . it was me speaking for it . or something, I don't know.

P: You were speaking for it, yes. It spoke through you. And another met it through me.

C: I know .

C: it was . I was a slave tillerman.

P: Tarimishé. It called her that. Do you remember?

C: That was me .

P: *squints*

C: .it wouldn't use her name.

C: So it had me make one up

P: Aye.

P: It was afraid to speak that which slew it.

P: *eyes wide now, nearly ecstatic* Oh, Abbey.

L: Darker, black, fouler, reeking, stinking, sweltering, grueling, torturous fate, thicker than night in its velvet cowel, and blacker than death it was.

O: and now?

O: Linus?

L: Grey, grey and faded, aching, angry. So angry and small. Red. Defeat but red, and red. Burning hotly, smouldering, smoulder . .

P: Why this wonder? Oh, why this wonder even though I'm slain with such pain inside? This ecstasy?

O: *wordless*

P: These revelations both terrible and true? *breathless,

nearly smiling*
O: True, this really happened
C: It . was . bat-winged.
C: Leather and stone.
C: I felt it go .
P: Charles, did it—did it leave for good?
O: And by Eru, I swear I have a real live sword in my hands. We went into Strider's office and borrowed it
P: Oh, Abbey. You will believe me when I wake and say, I fought the Witch King till two AM. I'm not alone, can't say how grateful.
P: Charles, did it—did it leave for good?
C: I don't know.
C: .it was talking about you, too.
C: Not just about her
P: *grits teeth* I know that.
P: Because I, Patty, guard something—nay, two some-things—that it wants.
O: We fought him. they fought them. Us. Them. You. She. Him.
C: Not in . the whole thinin
C: Just one part
P: Tell me which part, by all means.
C: It wanted me . to make it clear that it was both you . and her.
P: *nods, continue—*
P: Oh, yes. We have the whole bloody cast nearly, don't we?
O: Linus doesn't think it was the witch king, he says it was a wraith.
L: The battle wouldn't let me in. But I was trying wrong, I didn't know what was happening when I tried. I tried to get in, instead of lending strength.
C: I call you queen of lands beyond the dust. I call you both the Lady of the Air. I call thee ancient foe, victorious. I call her but thy pawn, in this last game.
P: *shivers violently*
P: It's the fucking Witch King.

O: I believe you.

P: Then—I am queen of lands beyond the dust? Eowyn and I are both lady of the air? I am ancient foe, victorious? Eowyn is my pawn in this last game? This is what he says. Yes to every one of those.

C: The image . is still there.

C: What it wanted.

P: Tell me the image of what it wanted.

C: The tower, and the pool.

C: A place where the laws of physics do not apply . where one hangs from the floor

C: .stretched towards the pool at the top of the tower.

P: *sarcastic laugh* Whirlpool at the top of the tower, he forgets to add. Dark Wizards and Lords love that trick dearly.

C: ::shivers:: So far . so far

P: The one hanging from the floor. That's desired, too, is it not?

C: .that's . not desired.

C: it already had that.

P: NO!

C: It was . a man.

P: A man?

P: [echo at the back of my mind, abbey, two voices in unison: a Man?

C: Short hair . dark hair.

C: Broad.

P: *tilts head*

C: He wanted it, too.

P: *thinks* Oh my.

O: who .?

P: I'm .gasping to understand—who.

P: *gently* Charles—can you, can it—name that man?

C: I can give him . a name. One that derelict savior suits him .

P: *soft sigh, then thinks* Was that man—always as he was in that vision? Or did he end his life a changed form?

P: Saruman was once not so white and gray

C: I won't do it.
C: You won't take me.
C: Give it back.
C: You took it when you left.
C: Where is my poet?
C: Give me back my poet.
P: *blinks helplessly*
O: *strokes your hair*
P: Charles. You are a poet. I did not take your poet.
C: No I'm not. Not anymore.
C: He didn't want to go with you.
C: You shall not have him.
P: Okay, this has gone fucked quite quickly.
P: Charles channels the bloody witch king and he loses his inner muse in the process *rocks .*
C: ::collapses back into his chair, shivering:: Oh, my God . what .
C: .it wasn't . I'm so sorry
P: Charles has just come back to himself.
O: we have not won the war yet
P: It makes sense, doesn't it?
P: That the hobbits, the good, the brave, should have homes in us—-
P: And the dark, too, finds a place in someone. In Charles, though he be unknowing, unwilling.
O: I shall stand and fight alongside the knight, the Dark Slayer, my love, I will stand and fight at your side, Queen of Air, if I must.
P: *bows* Peregrin.
O: We thought we slew the dark. Perhaps the dark cannot be slain. But we will fight it
O: and I have been at your side, at your back, and do not doubt that
O: I will not let him be taken from me again. And he has returned, and now shall I guard him as he once guarded me
P: Abbey .what do I do .with Frodo and Sam?
P: *trembles*

P: *locks*

P: They shan't be had, oh no they shan't be had—!

O: They will not be taken.

P: *whispers* Never.

O: never.

P: Queen of Air is tired, Charles. She is only human *tentative hug*

C: ::hugs::

C: I'm . I don't know anymore.

P: *shivers* Nor I.

P: Charles 's leaving.

P: I told him to sleep.

L: Charrals. Charrals. The meaning. Its not clear.

L: Before we part, there is—one here—who wishes—to call you Charrals. Does this—word mean aught to you?

O: Its not I that calls him by that name!

L: Merry isn't here, but something is.

O: Is it for good or ill?

L: I don't know. It just is. But it responded when he spoke.

L: Sono kai . . . whatever it was he said.

C: Idiot. Always wouldst thou give time to thy foes.

C: Time is the one thing thou shouldst never have given me. I have my crown.

C: I have my crown, and I have my feast.

P: Feast? Show me this feast, prithee.

C: Fair is foul, and foul is fair. Hover through the fog and filthy Air[19], O adversary. I bid thee farewell, Tarimishé. But I doubt thou wilt.

O: my sword is at the ready and I am with you, lady of Air

P: *terse nod*

P: Let it be either: farewell or fare war.

P: *chokes* Abbey, she's just declared—-

O: we know, and we stand at the ready

P: War. War of What, this time 'round?

P: *rocks two sleeping hobbits so deep in her breast,

---

[19] MacBeth, Act 1, scene 1.

324

seals them in sleep till death or waking part*
C: Fare well. And fair war, for I am sure it shall be.
P: *raises sword* Let it be.
P: *chants* In dreams I shall meet thee/In dreams, heart to heart/Here and forever/Thou or I sever:/Minions, depart!
P: Good night, Charles *pensive look*
P: I will be waiting there.
P: *waits with bated breath*
O: and drawn swords, we wait
P: No, we will not leave each other, none of us: Somewhere, in dreams/we will meet again!
P: Eru speed *swallows numbly*
L: Charrals antamarien tolo du an tuai. Becomanté nonto astine lethul angmai. Anto lethul angti sulo sutari ashire lanke ang contarre gilumanshia . . . nonto cantintine asolocontatire. Sul, sul, angcontiare . . . sul.[20]
L: Sul, sul, sul . . . dekin abul niaght.
O: Now I lay me down to sleep .
P: Linus, my heart, be brave. Abbey. Though I buy it with a great pain: you are going too. Pray the Lady .
P: *whispers* Tye melan, mellyn.

Abbey noted the following in her diary.

> This was a strange event. Patty was suddenly contacted by a friend of hers, Charles, who was channeling something strange. As of now I don't know if it was truly the Witch King; somehow I doubt it. Perhaps he wasn't true channeling anything, but the whole thing seemed to be part

---

[20] Per David once again: "L's pseudo-Quenya has syllabic constraints somewhat similar to those of Tolkien Quenya, but L uses many sounds not found in Quenya at all. I'd be inclined to characterize these productions as similar to the glossolalia found cross-culturally in real or supposed trance-states; though many people can produce similar strings of sounds without any change of mental state."

> of the "awakening" process, perhaps for all of us?
> Patty became quite aware while talking to this
> Charles-Wraith thing that she had Eowyn. There
> was battle with words, though it was not settled
> and the challenge lay out that we would continue
> to fight in the dream world. This was very
> frightening—I chose to sleep with Mike's sword
> by the bed, my hand on the hilt.

Linus and Charles could not be reached prior to this publication, but Patty did come forth to offer comments. She discovered the BoE Yahoo group in early 2002, through fanfiction circles. Patty enjoyed online role-playing, in which groups of people would chat "in character" and create impromptu stories with agreed-upon themes. When OB began to confide in her about the "hobbit channeling," Patty assumed this was typical interactive fiction composition and was happy to play along. She recognized some of VB's "Westron" words as Hungarian, for example, and was intrigued by the construction of a new imaginary language.

Patty believes Charles participated because he hoped there was an actual paranormal connection, but he drifted away when he realized it was all bunk. She felt that Linus, on the other hand, was trying very hard to convince himself something otherworldly was happening. Abbey finally told him she and Amy were channeling the genuine article and he was not; apparently they didn't appreciate this newcomer barging in and stealing their spotlight. In Patty's words, "What I observed was others *wanting* to be a part of it, and Orange playing arbiter as to who could play and who couldn't."

Linus was enraged by Abbey's accusations, to the point that he left LOTR fandom. Patty was appalled to realize not only were Abbey and Amy quite serious about the veracity of this hobbit channeling, but she had helped them further their bizarre beliefs by being part of an environment where it all could flourish.

Patty confronted Abbey about her ludicrous behavior, with the usual result: Abbey immediately cut off all contact with Patty and attempted to turn other mutual friends against her as well.

****

In addition to his discussion of pseudoQuenya in the chat transcript, David Salo also took on the task of debunking the roughly 970 "Westron" words put into a dictionary spreadsheet by Amy and Abbey. David felt he was qualified for this task. "Tolkien wrote more about Westron than has been published, and those documents are now in Milwaukee, Wisconsin, where I have seen them. I have a very good idea of what Westron looks like."

David noted that around 130 of the words were authentic Westron, coined by Tolkien and reported on websites like http://www.uib.no/People/hnohf/westron.htm. If the "channelers" were truly tapping into the same source as Tolkien, they should have also reproduced some of the Westron words from the records in Milwaukee that Tolkien wrote down but never published. Needless to say, they did not.

David did some linguistic snooping to suss out the remaining pseudoWestron. "After Tolkien's own examples of Westron and Adûnaic, the primary source for words, and, I think, overall structure of the word-list was an online Modern English > Old English glossary, http://www.mun.ca/Ansaxdat/vocab/wordlist.html.

"The person or persons who manipulated this text would convert an Old English word to a pseudo-Westron word by the simple expedients of dropping one or more letters from the end of the word, dropping a few letters at the beginning of the word, or changing a couple of letters. The point of this artifice is, I suppose, to cover their tracks and make the source of the vocabulary less obvious[21]. It is to some extent effective, but fails when faced with the original text. Another trick used to disguise the words was to change all examples of *f* to *ph*, and of *c* to *k*.

"In a number of cases, the defining word was taken from the *wrong line*; e.g., the verb "bequeath" was given the pseudo-Westron form "brukan"; in the glossary, "brucan" is just above "bequeathe" [sic], but the correct definition is the word on the line *below*, "læfan".

"In other instances, grammatical indications became part of the pseudo-Westron word; so, for instance, the word "beyond" was glossed as "begeondan (+dat)" meaning that the preposition "begeondan" must be followed by a noun in the dative case; but in pseudo-Westron, "begeondan" and "dat" are squeezed together into "begdat!" Likewise, "neck" is glossed as "hals (m.)" meaning it is a m[asculine] noun; but in pseudo-Westron this becomes "halsm."

---

[21] Amy could hardly have people Googling her "Westron" words and discoverng they came from an old English website!

"Of the words in the pseudo-Westron list, over 300 can be shown to be taken directly from the glossary, and another twenty or so are probable but less provable because too much of the word was changed.

"The prevalence of the words of OE derivation is much higher toward the beginning of the list, sorted alphabetically by Modern English word, than toward the end. I surmise that at the beginning, the inventors intended to supply a pseudo-Westron word for every Modern English gloss in the Old English glossary. However, since the glossary has over two thousand words, this proved to be beyond their powers; as they continued through, their choice of Old English words became far more selective, skipping over large swaths of the glossary.

"At some later period, a selection of Hungarian words (whose source I have not been able to pinpoint) was added; and yet later, an effort was made to coin new words on the basis of the existing vocabulary and a few simple morphological rules. My impression is that these later compositions are largely related to food and sex; there are words for eight different mealtimes, for instance, as well as compounded words for 'masturbate', 'orgasm', 'semen', 'slut', and similar terms.

"It is possible that other languages lie buried in this list. But with what I have found so far, the majority of the pseudo-Westron vocabulary is already accounted for."

****

Finally, as part of his linguistic review, David Salo also had an interesting response to a comment that the Channelers had decided that Mirkwood is in Finland, and the Shire in Hungary.

It sounds — from my linguistic background — like a peculiar misunderstanding of the nature of the Uralic language family (which includes Finnish and Hungarian) and its relationship to Tolkien's linguistic constructions. Of course, Tolkien (though he had some interest in both countries) never made any such geographical connections. Hungary is much more like Rohan than the Shire, and Finland has hardly any mountains! The real-world basis for the valley of Rivendell *is* known, though perhaps not well known; it's the valley of Lauterbrunnen in Switzerland, containing the villages of Lauterbrunnen, Wengen, and Muerren.

It seemed a shame to tell David, after this fascinating explanation, that the "insight" about Mirkwood came when Amy was channeling Legolas in an antique store. Legolas espied a Finnish belt buckle that reminded him of an amulet he used to wear. Abbey and Amy concluded, "Given the distances and terrain, and the fact that Quenya was similar to Finnish in the ways Aduni was similar to Hungarian, we made an educated guess that Mirkwood was located in Finland." This would put Rivendell and the Misty Mountains right in the Gulf of Bothnia.

Perhaps the flood at the ford of Bruinen got a tad out of control.

APPENDIX B

The Sham of the Past

In February, 2002, Amy set up what might have been her first large-scale elaborate Internet scam. The following excerpts are from Bit of Earth's original message board on Yahoo Groups.

2/12/02, "Some Ozzy Bloke:" VB's hubby here with a new and improved (okay, maybe not *improved* picture of what's going on in The World of VB.

The eye has gotten significantly worse. When I pry the lids open to put the little antibiotic drops in that the Doctor gave us, the white and blue parts are just various stages of red and redder, and the tear duct is oozing this thick yellowy goo. She claims that this is "feeling better" and that it doesn't hurt. I claim that said claim is bullshit.

I've been reading her the list mail … The various well-wishes, good karma, and virtual goodies have been received with a lot of gratitude, and I'm supposed to thank you all for being such cool people.

2/14/02, Some Ozzy Bloke: Both VB and I would like to thank everyone who's been sending positive energy, cybernetic hugs, good wishes, etc.

She's in hospital now, for how long we don't know, and they're talking about "saving the vision in that eye" which quite frankly has me scared shitless.

I'll be bringing my laptop to hospital so that she can stay in touch with the outside world. I think that she's probably digging herself into the hobbits and you guys the better not to think of her eye.

I've got to say you all seem to be one hell of a cool group of folks, and that she's lucky to have friends like you, real or cybernetic.

2/14/02, OrangeblossomB: This is quite probably the silliest thing I've ever written, and I include my parody of Teenage Dirtbag in that equation asked Sam if I could borrow his talent for five minutes—he said no, though. Veebs, let this be a token of how terribly we miss you!!!

Veebs sat there on her old desk chair,
And wrote and scribbled and twisted her hair;
For many a year she had sat right here,
Writing every Fandom that come by.
Done by! Gum by!
An apartment, a chair, she dwelt there
And wrote whatever come by.

She fond her home in a heavy tome,
Read and watched till her mouth did foam;
Tolkien's the man and now she had a plan,
To make a mighty E-group.
See-group! Me group!
All about Sam, she'd give him a home
And make a mighty E-group

The group she made and members she bade,
To make piles of messages through which to wade
That Hobbit-lad Sam who was son of Ham,
Would have been happy if he could know it.
Row it! Show it!
Even a website would soon be made,
And he would be happy to know it.

Then she did spy something in her eye,
It got itchy and red and she said "Oh, my;"
Yellow gunk did ooze and so she did choose,
To go and see her doctor.
Procter! Mocktor!
A nasty infection right in her eye,
So she went to see her doctor.

The doctor said, "you're eye's quite red,"
"You best go home and go straight to bed;"
"But I've got to write! O, what a plight,"
Said VB because of her eyeball.
Cryball! Myball!
So home she tread, "Make it dark!" she said,
"The light,it hurts my eyeball".

She had someone there to take good care,
And to write or to read she did not dare,
She was frustrated and sad, and sometimes
quite mad,
And the eyeball, it didn't get better,
Sweater! Met her!
So to the hospital she went there
Cause her eyeball, it didn't get better.

Now she and her dude eat hospital food,
And we hope that the nurses are never rude;
We miss her so, want the germies to go,
So she can get well and come back.
Run Back! Some back!
Without our Veebs this list is screwed,
So hurry, get well and come back!

2/15/02 (name withheld): Urgh, I wouldn't want to live in LA, but I would love to be there next week— Sean will be making an appearance at a local bookstore on the 18th *with* PJ, Fran and Philippa. (!!!) Anyone reading who could make it and take photos? Pleeeeeeeease?

2/15/02 (name withheld): Do we know anyone who is in LA who could get something signed for VB as a get well soon? it would surely make her day if at least Sean signed something and wished her well. unfortunately i'm in London and don't know anyone in LA, but most of you guys on the list are from the US, so i thought it was worth put ting the idea out there.

2/15/02, OrangeblossomB: What a fabulous idea! I so wish I could fly down there myself now. Any SoCal Samfans wanna do this for our lovely Veebs?

2/18/02 (name withheld): They had said no autographs before the talk, but I decided to cheat for VB's sake. Sean turns and smiles at me. I hold out a copy of VB's drawing, "My friend is in the hospital. She drew this and it would mean a lot to her if you would sign it," I told him. "She wants me to sign this? This is gorgeous. <signs it> Tell her that I love it and I hope that she gets better soon."

02/18/02, Ozzy Bloke: About fifteen minutes ago, I finished reading VB her mail. I just finished retaping her eyes, because since then, she's been a weeping, babbling, blithering wreck. I can sincerely say that if she could give you all a very big hug right now, she would. Many, many, many, many thanks to EVERYONE involved in this.

Amy was never hospitalized for an eye infection. "Ozzy Bloke" or Adrian, her alleged fiancé, was neither from Australia nor engaged to her. It seems most likely that these posts were written by Amy herself, although it is uncertain what she originally hoped to accomplish with this masquerade. She received sympathy from many members of the Yahoo group, and she also was mailed a printout of one of her own drawings, signed by Sean Astin.

I included the poem by Abbey to show how hard she tried to attract the attention of Victoria Bitter. It prompted an amusing counter-poem by "filk" musician, FnordChan (to the tune of the Johnny Cash/Evrin Rouse song, "Orange Blossom Special").

(cue harmonica intro)

Hey, look a-yonder comin'
coming down that in-ter-net
Hey, look a-yonder comin'
Comin' down that LJ-net
It's that Orange Blossom Special
and you ain't seen nothing yet

Well, I'm shacking up with VB
And I got dem ol' closet blues
Then I'm worried bout poor 'Lijah
And all of the weight he lose
He's on the Orange Blossom Special
'Til he pay dem New Line dues

"Say, man ain't you dating VB?"
"Well as she's dead,don't reckon I'm ever going back to VB."
"But ain't this 'man' you with really Ms.Bitter?"
"No I swear he got a ding-dong-ding-dong-ding-dong-ding-dong-do."

Hey, talk about a-lyin'
And changes to Jordan Wood's sex
Hey, talk about a-stealin'
And cashing all the TentMoot checks
It's that Orange Blossom Special
The mother of all fan train wrecks.

APPENDIX C

A Knife in the Heart

This is the "suicide letter" Amy Player sent to her parents, just prior to moving to Los Angeles in October, 2003. Although Amy was apparently hoping to sever all ties to her family of origin, this letter produced the opposite effect. It prompted her parents to open a Missing Person investigation with Detective Myers, which brought Myers to my doorstep, opened up the can of worms about "Jordan's" identity, and ultimately resulted in my declaration to "Jordan" that "he" would regret it if I caught "him" in one more lie.

This letter is part of the public record of the Oregon Department of Justice, in the Bit of Earth case file. I present it here as a final example of Amy's astounding capacity to fabricate and manipulate, as well as her utter disregard for the emotions of people who love her.

* * * * * * * *

Dear Mom and Dad,

I'm writing this letter as an apology. For a year now, I've been trying to placate you with pretty fancies in hopes that I could force reality into step with my lies. I wish that the reported successes of the past year were more than ill-borrowed dreams. I'm not the hottest new thing in Rings fandom. I'm not even in Bit of Earth anymore.

The ugly truth is that I'm a failure, in every way that one may be counted as such.

School, though meant to be a doorway , has proven only to be my first failure. Both my innate dishonesty and the laziness I have long concealed beneath the flash and dazzle of false ambition conspired to unravel any chance I may have had to navigate the halls of academe. So many told me of my potential, couched in sweet-sounding "you justs." You just need to....

But I didn't. There was no thrill in study, in writing papers, in going to class. An A earned the same way as everyone's held bland disinterest at best, but an A I had cheated or talked my way into-the more intrigue and intricacy the better-was the headiest brew. Someone once said that politics were beast that eats itself, but I thrived on the excitement of it.

At CNU, I played that game so hard I actually played myself out of it. My intrigues were a major part of why Jeffery got fired, but I soon discovered I could neither cheat nor charm Steven.

So I went to GMU, but my heart wasn't in it. The school was just too big to work with.

By then as well, I had chosen the identity of the tortured counter-culture over the identity of the smart girl. Straight A's don't go nearly as well with black lipstick, vegetarianism, and gay pride marches as leaving "conventional education" in a cloud of lesbian ennui and heavy eyeliner.

Now, I have no longer abandoned school as part of my latest Identity, but out of what ironically may be my both first and last honesty. My potential, like nearly everything else, was a mere sham and shadow.

I learned this also when I found myself with an employer who could not be impressed simply with good salesmanship and a flashy vocabulary. I was fired from Meier and Frank after 3 months. The "job" at WinCo never even got as far as an interview. Rather than a shooting star, I've been no better than a beggar, living perilously balanced between Abbey's charity and my own unsavory "suppliments."

Of course, I have been telling you all along that I've been planning on returning to school and holding down a job, you're probably wondering how much else I've formed of whole cloth. The answer? All of it. Or, at least most of it.

Bit of Earth has been doing that well, but I've been off their staff since November of last year, and had no association at all since July. Far from getting casual birthday calls from Elijah Wood, I haven't been part of talking to any of the celebrities or their people. I never even got to meet Sean after DC, since I was a little busy during Elanor. I've been "busy" a lot lately, and I guess it's just whatever small luck with which I have been graced that I've never been caught by the police for it.

The July thing, my last fling with BOE, was also the beginning of the end as far as their discovery of my true colors. I swore to get them the permits for Hall of Fire, and when I didn't , they nearly went under financially. Fortunately for them, their current staff are actually competant, rather than merely skillfully pretentious.

I dearly wish I could claim my expulsion from the organization I founded was some unjust rebellion, or that my transgression at the Hall of Fire was some simple isolated misstep.

When I first came to Oregon last October, Abbey was battling with the demons of a serious depression, and her husband was blind to the rapid decay of their marriage looming precariously on the horizon. I wanted to be the hero, to ride in on a white

747 bearing all the answers, and I played the role of competancy so well that she soon handed me the reigns of household finance, as Mike tended to be a bit irresponsible.

I wasn't irresponsible, but my priorities were elsewhere to say the least.

At my hands, they lost their new house, erred in their taxes, incurred penalties, lost all their credit, lost her unemployment benefits, their savings, and wound up deeply in debt. I should have been caught then and there, but I managed, in the first of many silver-tongued but temporary escapes, to blame it all on Mike.

They divorced in February.

In sum, I will bluntly if with deepest shame, confess to having stolen $11,000 from the Rices. I didn't mean to sail through it, or honestly, to need it at all, but things in my life have rarely ended as I meant them to.

I know that I had held out hope for Abbey to leave Mike for me, that I desired her, wanted her, but I don't know if I loved her. I don't know if I'm capable of love. If I'm not, I can swear to you that is not for lack of receiving it. Whether I can love or not is not your fault. I've spent my whole life blaming others, but here, in the cold and useless light of hindsight, I see the only hands that have woven this bitter noose were my own.

Love or no, I can feel jealousy, and that I did feel to a despairing degree. When she proved not to love me in any way but the platonic. I bitterly resented first Bob, then Jordan, whom she loved even more deeply, and whose love from her I so envied that it drove me into what was at last my undoing.

At first, I just claimed Jordan's glories as my own to you. Young and wealthy, he came to us from Los Angeles with Rings connections dripping from him and a cell phone choked with agents whom he knew by their first names. He made Bit of Earth a fandom force to be reckoned with within weeks, swept Abbey off her feet, and I hated him for both.

I began to go farther, not just claiming his glory in a few private phone calls, but taking advantage of the androgynous nature of the moniker to steal it for myself. I started using it at work, then eventually even started trying to pass as a boy, and persuading the DMV to put his name in with mine on my ID, which let me get a Sears card in his name.

The BOE staff knew about some of the cross-dressing, but thought it was a lesbian thing. They knew nothing of my usurpment of Jordan's identity, nor of the thrill it gave. I felt surged with borrowed power, the disguise of life afresh. I held his reputation like a warrior wearing an enemy's skin, and the card gave me yet another level of protection and freedom.

I had been claiming that my money came from you, and despite my lack of a productive job, they had been letting me stay because of how often I bought things for BOE, the house, and Abbey in particular. With the card, that façade of wealth remained even in periods too tight to chance embezzlement.

I even tried once to use his name online, that blissful place where identities are as sweetly fluid as free hotmail accounts. But I've dipped too many times in that well, and this February, the water proved poisoned.

Once again, though I had a temporary reprieve, convincing Abbey to leave Live Journal and much of social fandom because "a bad ex was spreading ridiculous rumors about us." It was my luck she believed me and walked out without a second look, and thus never noticed I'd been attempting to cover my ass by posting in her name as well to back up my stories.

In the end, I had to leave the internet entirely, scattering in my wake the now most bitterly ironic rumor of suicide.

My lie to Abbey unfortunately, though utterly false in intent, does have a grain of ugliest truth. I do have many a justly bitter ex. I've scammed my merry way through half a dozen fandoms, taking prey on many a lonely heart with glib emails and a well-tailored nom-du-jour.

Ironically, thanks to two bitter exes, Adrian and Lauren, the others, including many who would love to see me jailed at the least, now know my true name to be Amy, regardless as to whether they knew me as Rebecca, Ciyerra, Victoria, or yet some other. Jordan is the first mask I may have cast from life, but his is far from the first I've worn.

But I've gone too far now. They caught me in the identity theft, found the card in my pocket. From there it careened, and soon they knew of it all, and the disappearances of a few dvds and other pawnables besides. They threw me out, and it was all I could do to beg myself the undeserved indulgence of being driven here. I borrowed money from one of my suppliers on pretence of securing salable stash, and used that to pay them back. They have their money now, and my debt is of no matter, and my debtor no angel undeserving.

Since there was no chance of them taking a free-loading, identity stealing, drug using con artist and thief to LA, I told her to leave me here, that I knew someone online who would take me in until you came for me.

What truly awaited me was my own time to leave that which I have done and sail into the West, though unlike Frodo, I fear I have benefit of neither Elves nor boat.

I have sent those things precious yet unpawned to you in a box. Look for it soon. Have whatever memorial you feel fitting, even if that is to fly West and spit on the grave of an offspring gone so bitterly wrong through no fault of your own.

I fucked up my own life beyond repair, but I've also hurt a lot of others. I don't want to keep draining and taking.

I can't come home. Caroline will be 17 soon, and my loans are burdain enough without adding debt and rehab and quite likely incarceration of a sister to stand between her and school. And Grandma and Om and Bege can be told I had an accident instead of seeing me like this. Tell them all I love them.

Tell Mommy I'll miss our walks, and I hope her sculpture do well.

Tell Daddy he'll save the world someday, and that I love him buns and tuckets.

Tell Caroline I'm sorry for the blonde jokes. She's smart, beautiful, and honest. She'll go where I should have.

Hug all the animals for me.

Tell Christine I'm sorry I couldn't be her bridesmaid.

And the others-honor my last request and tell them nothing. I have brought so much pain to Abbey and BOE, let me at least not hurt them with this, too. They think they've left me behind. Let it stay that way, so that my scandal doesn't plague them or BOE any more. Not hurting them <u>again</u> is the least that I can do for people who were so kind.

Say my goodbyes where I ask, likewise please keep the silence where I beg you.

Let me at least get the ending right

I was always good at endings.

Love

Amy

ORDER FORM

Name _____

Address _____

City / State / Zip _____

Phone _____

Enclosed is my check or money order for
$18.45 ($14.95 for **WHEN A FAN HITS
THE SHIT** and $3.50 for shipping and
handling.)

Orders can be sent to:

Turondo Unlimited
P.O. Box 13975
Salem, OR 97309

or

email: orders@turondo.com

Information available from
www.turondo.com

Additional titles available from
HEISENBERG PRESS:

Identity Fraud: Committed by the by the Government Against the People by Thomas Marvin Maxwell and Ken Gullekson ~ ISBN 0-9653136-2-X
417 Pages ~ Price: $19.95 ~ S&H: $4.00 for 1st book, $1.50 each thereafter ~ web page: http://home.pacbell.net/hp-kg/identityfraud2.htm

The Great American Income Tax Ripoff by Ken Gullekson ~ ISBN 0-9653136-0-3
74 Pages ~ Price: $10.00 (postpaid) ~ web page: http://home.pacbell.net/hp-kg/ripoff1.htm

HEISENBERG PRESS
Post Office Box 1178
Glendale, California

ABOUT THE AUTHOR

Susan Astle and Jeanine Renne.
"What shall we have for *second* breakfast?"

Heh heh heh.